THE MAKING OF FASCISM

Class, State, and Counter-Revolution, Italy 1919–1922

Dahlia S. Elazar

Westport, Connecticut
London

Library of Congress Cataloging-in-Publication Data

Elazar, Dahlia S.
  The making of fascism : class, state, and counter-revolution,
Italy 1919–1922 / Dahlia S. Elazar.
      p.   cm.
  Includes bibliographical references and index.
  ISBN 0–275–95864–7 (alk. paper)
    1. Italy—Politics and government—1915–1922.   2. Fascism—Italy.
  3. Latifundio—Italy.   4. Elite (Social sciences)—Italy.   5. Labor
  movement—Italy.   I. Title.
  JN5450.E4   1998
  320.945′09′041—dc21   97–40884

British Library Cataloguing in Publication Data is available.

Library of Congress Catalog Card Number: 97–40884
ISBN: 0–275–95864–7

First published in 2001

Praeger Publishers, 88 Post Road West,Westport, CT 06881
An imprint of Greenwood Publishing Group, Inc.
www.praeger.com

Printed in the United States of America

The paper used in this book complies with the
Permanent Paper Standard issued by the National
Information Standards Organization (Z39.48–1984).

10 9 8 7 6 5 4 3 2 1

For Anna Rebecca and her Father
With love

Contents

Illustrations

FIGURE

Preface

In his classic *Invitation to Sociology* (1963), Peter Berger describes the various images people have of sociologists and their work. One such image is of sociologists as collectors of statistics that reveal the obvious. "A sociologist," Berger writes, "is a fellow who spends $100,000 to find his way to a house of ill repute" (p. 8). Some historians of modern Italy may argue that in this work I do the same; that I disclose what everybody knows: Where the Fascists violently attacked the Socialists—that is where they won power. Nevertheless, what may be a truism in one discipline is far from self-evident in another. In spite of the vast, accurate and detailed historical documentation of the Fascists' violence in Italy and of its role in their seizure of power, there is little trace of this drama in sociological theories of fascism. Sociologists continue to try and explain the rise of Fascism within the democratic paradigm in terms of an increase of supporters. Fascists, from this perspective, acquired power because free citizens elected them to power. The question that needs to be answered is, therefore, who voted for the Fascists and why.

But if we take the historical evidence on the Fascists' organized violence seriously, it is clear that the question of voters is the wrong question to ask. Where electoral democracy does not exist and the rule of law at best—or the very existence of an electoral campaign that is free of fraud and terror—is ambiguous it makes little sense to analyze political change as simply the function of the will of an (unfree) electorate.

It is therefore perhaps not surprising at all that the first to draw attention to these issues were the contemporary Communist observers of Fascism in Italy and Europe. They saw the bloody struggles taking place and the Socialists' helplessness in the face of these attacks. Indeed, the communist theory of fascism, as John Cammett observes, "has nothing to be ashamed of" in its explanation of the rise of fascism (1967, p. 154). The communists have made what, in retrospect, I think are not only the first but also the most acute and precise interpretations of fascism. Fascism, theyargued, was not reducible to issues of class or social base; not even to the question of the crisis of capitalism. Rather, it emerged and prospered in the course of a concrete external political struggle against the Socialists, which also led to crucial internal struggles within its own ranks.

In a posthumous article in *Radical History Review*, Tim Mason, the historian of National Socialism, lamented the "disappearance of theories, or articulated concepts of fascism from research and writing about the Third Reich..." (1991, p. 89). This book, which is neither a historical study nor about National Socialism, may not be what Mason had in mind. I did, however, take his advice seriously and employ his general dictate regarding the "primacy of politics." By putting "class relations and class-state relations firmly at the center of the stage" (1991, p. 90), I try to show that the communist analysis is correct: The political struggles between the Italian Fascists and Socialists were formative struggles that determined not only the Fascists' political fate but their specific social and political significance. I hope I was able not only to disclose some of the unique features of Italian Fascism, but also to contribute to the conceptualization of fascism in general.

During the years that have passed since I first started thinking about the Fascists, I collected many debts of gratitude on two continents. The Department of Sociology and the University of California at Los Angeles provided generous financial support, the University's Research Library was an extraordinary research facility whose librarians could obtain any source, no matter how obscure. I also benefited from a grant from the Center for German and European Studies, University of California, Berkeley. The Faculty of Social Sciences at Tel Aviv University generously helped in the preparation of the manuscript for publication. I thank Yasmin Alkalay for invaluable computer assistance and Tali Kristal for diligent assistance in compiling the index. Nina Reshef carefully edited the manuscript and transformed it into a book.

Many individuals—teachers, colleagues and friends—contributed to the fruition of this study. At UCLA I benefited from the advice and guidance of Jeffrey Alexander, Emanuel Schegloff and Michael Wallerstein. My friends and colleagues at Tel Aviv University contributed their generous intellectual and moral support: Hanna Ayalon, Yinon Cohen, Yosef Grodzinsky, Yitzhak Haberfeld, Hanna Herzog, Gideon Kunda, Alisa C. Lewin, Zvi Razi, the late Yonathan Shapiro, Yehouda Shenhav and Haya Stier. Finally, I was privileged to have Maurice Zeitlin as my PhD advisor at UCLA. My debt to him for his generous guidance cannot be settled with a few lines. He will always be a precious source of inspiration and friendship.

I would have never started this study without Amit's encouragement, wisdom, love, and patience, and I would have finished it much earlier if not for our daughter, Anna Rebecca, who chose to arrive during the last stages of the preparation of the manuscript for publication. This book is dedicated with love to both.

Chapter 1

The Making of Fascism: An Overview

> It is a grave mistake to believe that Fascism started out in 1920, or from the March on Rome, with a pre-established, predetermined plan for the dictatorial regime...All the historical facts of Fascism's development contradict such a conception...Fascism was not born totalitarian, it became so...What I have wanted to demonstrate...is that Fascism must not be viewed as something which is definitively characterized; that it must be seen in its development, never as something set, never as a scheme or a model.
>
> Palmiro Togliatti (1935)[1]

This book is an inquiry into the causes of the Fascist seizure of state power in Italy and the crucial process of transition of the Fascists from "contenders" for power into "rulers." The central question, premised on what the late historian Tim Mason (following the National Socialists' slogan) terms the "primacy of politics" (1968), is how did the political strategy of the Italian Fascist organization (*Fasci di Combattimento*) determine its seizure first of provincial power and then of national power (1919-1922)? How, in other words, did the Fascists' political conduct bring about, first, their defeat of the Socialists, and second, their subsequent taking of power?

The empirical and theoretical significance of the question about the Fascist takeover derives from a critique of sociological theories of fascism. These theories—from R. P. Dutt's (1934) pioneering study to contemporary analyses by sociologists such as S. M. Lipset (1963) and B. Moore Jr. (1966)—concentrate on a single common theme or central puzzle: What were the social "origins"[2] and "bases" of fascism? What were the historical preconditions of the emergence of fascist "social movements"? Which classes supported them, and why?

Hence, despite their obvious divergence on substantive theoretical levels and units of analysis, prevailing theories of fascism are bound together by a single paradigm. They share the same essential problem in their conception of the phenomenon of fascism—and this in turn generates what Robert K. Merton terms a "pocket of theoretical neglect." None of these theories attends to the very process of the Fascists' ascendance to power, the specific nature of their concrete political struggles for power, nor their actual practices when in power. The explanations of fascism simply stop too early—when fascism has yet to undergo the metamorphoses of its own development into "complete" fascism. By tending to equate (or conflate) the analytical notion of cause with the historical notion of emergence or origins, this paradigm necessarily assumes that once fascism "emerged," whatever followed that emergence was already predetermined. Thus, once the fascists seized power, they became, by necessity, hostages to the circumstances, relationships, and social bases that had brought them to power. In short, these theories, and the empirical analyses guided by them, are commonly silent about the role of the Fascists themselves in forming their own political organization, in determining both the taking and the practice of political power, and thus the making of Fascism itself.

Theoretically, the prevailing focus on Italian Fascism's origins rests on an implicit conceptual equation between two distinct social and historical processes: the initial emergence of Fascism and its eventual triumph, that is, its successful taking of and consequent practice in power. The Fascists' struggle for power and their seizure of provincial and central state's institutions are taken for granted as, somehow, an immanent necessity once Fascism, and Fascist organizations, emerged historically. Inherent in this conflation is an implicit conception of Fascism as a pregiven, monolithic, and static phenomenon: It is assumed that Fascist organizations had a unified program, and that their members and leaders shared a singular identity from the moment they appeared until they seized power.

This paradigmatic theoretical neglect leads, ironically, to the depiction of the *fasci di combattimento* and the Fascist regime as an epiphenomenon—whether as the product of the crisis of capitalism, the expression of lower-middle class "extremism," or the culmination of an earlier "revolution from above."

This conceptual conflation has led to empirical neglect. By focusing on the sequence *preceding* the initial historical appearance of fascist organizations, what follows this appearance has simply been ignored. Virtually all the theories examined here are based on empirical observations that stop at the period immediately following World War I. This necessarily leads to the neglect of the period of the Fascists' ascendance, and overlooks entirely several decisive determinants of Italian Fascism, namely, its political strategy, form of organization, mode of operation and, most importantly, political alliances.

I will try to address both the theoretical and empirical "silences" in this paradigm. To analyze the making of Fascism (rather than asking why it emerged, who supported it and what produced this support), we must discover how the Fascists in fact took national power. This, in turn, requires asking what political strategy and practices they employed; against whom; and in alliance with whom. What were the consequences? How, in short, was Fascism created in the process of its political struggles? Underlying this question is the proposition that political struggles can themselves be history-making events. The general theoretical issue here is, in short, the "relative autonomy of politics," or "the possible *independent effects of political phenomena in the shaping and transformation of basic social relations*...within the objective limits imposed and the objective alternatives made possible by the existing circumstances" (Stepan-Norris and Zeitlin 1989, p. 503, emphasis in original). This, it should be emphasized, does not imply a theory of "voluntarism"—let alone indeterminacy—in which any organization can make facts and transform circumstances. Rather, the specificity of the political strategies employed by these organizations, their actual modus operandi, and the political alliances established in the process shaped both the form and content of the political struggle they waged against their opponents. Eventually, they determined the odds of winning or losing this struggle.

This theoretical premise is closely linked with the method of inquiry. The transformation of Italy's liberal state into a fascist state was not determined by the social and political processes that had led to the Fascist organization's emergence. The real determinants of Fascism can be deciphered and explained only through an analysis of the specific process by which the Fascists, as an organization, fought for power. The unit of analysis, therefore, is not the "voting individual" or the relatively loose association of such individuals into a "social movement." Rather, the appropriate units are active political organizations and parties, with their distinct structural contours, and their individual forms of struggle against each other. These are the features that not only create their own specific identities and determine their political significance, they also transform the political terrain on which their struggles take place. This logic of inquiry requires us to examine the unfulfilled historical possibility that Fascism could have become something else, that is, to ask what were the specific moments of Fascism's creation, and why.

Therefore, focusing on the contingencies of the Fascists' strategy implies a counterfactual question, what Max Weber calls an analysis of other "objective historical possibilities." By necessity, to ask how the Fascists seized state power is to ask what were the historical alternatives to this outcome. Could the Fascist taking of power have concluded in a different manner than it did? If so, what prevented the realization of such possibilities? I attempt to understand the phenomenon of Fascism by focusing on what it became, not on its origins, and on the process of its becoming one type of organization and not another. How, then, did the Fascists' specific struggle for power, their organization's structure, leadership, and policies, affect their takeover of the Liberal state?

Analyzing the specific developments and determinants of the Fascists' strategy reveals an essential paradox in Italian Fascism: The Fascist organization, per se, had to be transformed, if not completely destroyed, in order to save itself as a political force. This book, then, also seeks to explain how their struggle for state power affected the nature of their own organization. The Fascists' seizure of state power took the form of a dual (external and internal) political struggle. Through this dual struggle, Fascism was constantly creating itself. The Fascists' assault, first, against the Socialist Party (PSI, the *Partito Socialista Italiano*) and the workers organizations, and then against the Liberal government, led to serious friction within the Fascist organization itself. These internal conflicts were, perhaps, the prime reason for the establishment of the Fascist Party (PNF, the *Partito Nazionale Fascista*), the constitution of its program, and the relationship between the Party and the state.[3] The Fascist organization that seized national power after twenty months of violent political struggle was not the same organization, with the same members, structure, ideology, or political objectives, that had initiated and carried out this struggle.

The Fascists seized state power, not through an electoral campaign over the hearts and minds of Italy's electorate but through a violent campaign against the Socialists' provincial strongholds. Nor was the Fascist organization a product of Italy's "historical origins." On the contrary: To consolidate its rule, the Fascist Action Squads (*squadristi*), the militant avant garde cadres of the emergent Fascist organization, had to be subjugated by Benito Mussolini, who had established the Fascist Party essentially for this very purpose.[4] This is the irony of the relationship between Mussolini and his political power base (which the prevailing theories commonly neglect): It was precisely this element of militant radicalism, decisive in the Fascists' seizure of power, that Mussolini had to submerge to preserve Fascist rule.

The following analysis is divided into three parts: The first examines the pre-Fascist agrarian and political relationships among the landlords, the peasants, and the Liberal state, and the threat to the political hegemony of the landlords posed by the Socialist ascendance. The second analyzes the reaction of the landlords, soon supported by the Fascists, against the threat of the Socialists' post-World War I rise to power. Crucial in this struggle was the Fascists' militarization of the political struggle through the employment of an extraparliamentary, paramilitary political strategy. In practice, this strategy was deployed almost exclusively against Socialist Workers Movement institutions. Just as important were their "offensive" alliances with the propertied class and their "defensive" alliances with state officials, both provincial and national. Here I examine the determinants of the Fascists' tactic of violence, the organization and mode of operation of the Action Squads that executed those tactics and, most importantly, the Fascists' allies. The final part examines the political consequences of the Fascists' political strategy. What made it a successful strategy? How did the squads' explicitly anti-Socialist tactic of violence affect their taking of provincial political power? Who were the Fascists' immediate political allies, and what was the role of these allies in the Fascists' seizure of power?

Here the social relationships examined are expanded to include those between the Fascist organization (and its own transformation into a party) and the Liberal state. My main concern in this section is with the collusion of state authorities with Fascist violence, and the effects of the collaboration between the propertied class and the state on the Fascists' seizure of provincial and national power. I also examine the effect of the Fascists' anti-Socialist struggle on the internal relationships evolving within the newly established Fascist Party.

THE FASCISTS' STRUGGLE FOR POWER

The Fascists began organizing the Action Squads in 1920, during the severe social and political crisis that followed the conclusion of World War I. Mussolini and the Fascist leadership, which had suffered a humiliating defeat in the general elections of 1919, set out to make Fascism a military force. This was evident in the leadership's deliberate efforts to recruit ex-servicemen and officers, the organization of these recruits into small combat units (the Action Squads), and the mode of operation ("punitive expeditions" in Clausewitz's terms) employed by these Squads.

Economically, the crisis of 1919-1920 was grave: Severe food and coal shortages, increasing rates of unemployment, new taxes, and soaring rates of inflation led to a wave of food riots and to an unprecedented number of industrial and agricultural strikes throughout the country. From 1918 on, both the number of strikes and the number of workers striking, in industry as well as in agriculture, increased dramatically. The climax of the organized strikes was the occupation of the factories in September 1920, two months before the first postwar local elections. The factory occupation movement spread from Turin to the rest of the country and lasted for three weeks, involving, at its height, half a million workers.

Growing militancy and radicalization of the Socialists accompanied the crisis. Italy's Socialist Party adopted a radical program. Its call for collectivization of land and for participation of industrial workers in factory management seemed, as the Party's leadership itself repeatedly claimed, to be a prelude to a "second Bolshevik revolution" in Italy. The PSI's success in the postwar elections appeared to verify its "revolutionary threat." In the elections of 1919, the Socialists became Italy's largest opposition party, and in the local elections held the following year, they won electoral majorities in twenty-five of the country's sixty-nine provincial councils. The Socialists' greatest victories were in the northern and central regions, where capitalist relations of production prevailed and where masses of wage workers, agricultural and industrial alike, had been engaged in struggles against employers since the turn of the century. These electoral successes, coupled with union militancy, signified the rapid rise of a workers movement led by a political party whose rhetoric called for the use of political violence against the establishment and in favor of the "proletarian dictatorship."

This was an unprecedented challenge to the political system underlying Italy's liberal state. Since unification in 1870, the state had been based on the system of *trasformismo*, the creation of national parliamentary coalitions through clientele relations with local oligarchies. It maintained, protected, and reinforced the domination of the nation's propertied families over the peasants and workers. Men of property possessed exclusive access to state power, and the allegiance between central state officials and the interests of property was taken for granted. The political hegemony of the propertied class remained uncontested until the electoral reforms of 1911 and 1918, when property restrictions on (male) suffrage were removed and new mass parties emerged. After the war, the advent of the Socialists elevated them to office in many communal councils and provincial governments, and often stripped the propertied class of its accustomed direct hold on these institutions.

Postwar Liberal governments attempted to contain the social upheaval by shifting their policies to capture the support of the newly enfranchised electorate of workers and peasants. But the social reforms enacted by these postwar governments led, in turn, to a crisis among Italy's propertied class and major employers. Responding to what they saw as the abdication of their own political leadership and facing an unprecedented wave of workers insurgency, employers' associations abandoned their customary political methods and began an internal organization drive aimed against the workers movement. Leaders of the employers' organizations blamed the state for "conniving with the Bolsheviks." They were convinced, as the president of the National Agrarian Association declaimed, that "the government was in no way able to guarantee us the respect for property or persons...Respect for authority and for the law...is now totally lacking" (cited in Corner 1975, p. 108, n. 2).

The reaction of the propertied class to the Socialists' postwar ascendance, especially the direct power acquired in many provincial and communal governments, was crucial in the development of the Fascists' political strategy. In the fall of 1920, the landowners of the northern regions turned to the Fascist Squads and requested that they act on their behalf against the Socialist organizers. This was the beginning of a strong, personal, and violent alliance between the regional landowners' associations and the Fascist Squads. While the industrialists supported the Fascists mainly through financial contributions, the landowners' associations in the north embraced Fascism *tout court*. Their unqualified and systematic support of the Fascists eventually led to an official convergence between their associations and local chapters of the Fascist organization. In addition to massive financial assistance, northern landowners actively supported and were directly involved in organizing the Fascists' local chapters or *nuclei* (*fasci*); moreover, they participated and often led the Squads' "punitive expeditions" into Socialist provinces. The Fascists' paramilitary capacity, together with the financial patronage of the landowners, combined to create a unique political strategy and to determine the pattern of its deployment.

The Fascists' violent attacks on Socialist strongholds began immediately after the local elections of 1920, and lasted for twenty-two months, until Mussolini's appointment as Prime Minister in the fall of 1922. The Squads' campaign of "punitive expeditions" throughout Italy's provinces almost invariably resulted in the complete destruction of the workers organizations. The Fascists marched through townships and villages; they intimidated and assaulted striking workers, transported and protected strikebreakers, and burned union halls and Socialist headquarters, which were replaced by the new Fascist unions, the National Syndicates. They attacked local labor leaders, Socialist mayors, trade union organizers, and other working class activists, and forced them to resign, sent them into exile, or killed them. The terrorized population was then forced to join the National Syndicates, and to comply with the rule of the Squads' commanders, who became provincial strongmen. By May 1921, only six months after these expeditions had been initiated, more than two hundred workers had been killed and over a thousand wounded. Over two thousand workers had been arrested. By the fall of 1922, the Fascists had installed their own regimes in all of Italy's sixty-nine provinces.

The Fascist strategy based on this dual mobilization—the formation of the Action Squads and their alliance with the propertied class—was first and foremost an anti-Socialist reaction. This alliance dictated that the Fascists would almost exclusively attack the Socialist provincial strongholds that posed the greatest threat to propertied interests. The provinces under the control of the Liberal Party and its propertied constituency remained virtually untouched by the Fascists. Indeed, the Fascists' tactic of violence was, as one of its leaders described it, "the systematic work of destruction of everything Bolshevik," that is, the elimination of the most stringent Socialist strongholds in the country.

The Socialists were at their strongest, both organizationally and electorally, in the north and center of the country; they were barely present in the south. Each of these regions displayed substantially different basic class relations, especially those prevailing on the land: in the north, capitalist employment of wage labor on a large scale in the countryside and in the towns; in the center, a mix of sharecropping and wage labor; and in the south, seigniorial tenantry. There is, then, a close association between the region, the incidence of Fascist violence, and the number of provinces taken over by the Fascists.

Once the Squads achieved their immediate aim—the destruction of the Socialist organizational structure and the murder of many of its leaders and cadres—the question of how their violence affected the Fascists' actual takeover of provincial political power needs to be examined. There is an essential difference between the effects of violence as a target-specific tactic of destruction, intimidation, and terror, and its strategic value as a means of achieving political control. In contrast to the destruction of the workers' organizations, which affected the Socialist leadership and its working-class constituency almost exclusively, the Fascists' takeover of provincial power affected the political and economic life of the province as a whole, including the position of the propertied class.

Therefore, an understanding of the determinants of the Fascist deployment of violence tells us little about its political consequences. To turn the Socialists' defeat in a one-sided civil war into Fascist political power, the Fascists, again, decisively, needed not only the continued support of the propertied class, but the collusion of local and central state authorities, too.

The Fascist takeover of provincial power occurred in three phases: (1) the destruction of workers organizations; (2) the establishment of Fascist economic organizations, the National Syndicates, and the use of force when recruiting workers (they thereby attempted to restore traditional labor relations in the provinces; the Syndicates, like the Squads' deployment of violence, were sponsored by—and thus dependent on—the collaboration of local employers' organizations); and (3) the Fascists' takeover of provincial political institutions. The final phase was determined both by the collusion of Liberal state authorities and by the support of the dominant class. Nationally, the collusion of the Liberal government culminated in Prime Minister Giovanni Giolitti's May 1921 invitation to the Fascists to join the ruling coalition. The Fascists thus became partners in the electoral National Bloc led by the Liberal Party. The incorporation of the Fascists into the "parties of order," and the national patronage and legitimacy that came with it, won their organization (which was still not formally a party) thirty-five deputies in the May 1921 elections to the Parliament. Figure 1.1 schematically represents the process while Table 1.1 shows the relationship between violence and the Fascist takeovers.

The Fascists' seizure of provincial power was led by the *ras*,[5] the leaders of the Squads' "punitive expeditions." Finally, in twenty-six of the country's sixty-nine provinces, the *ras* took power and set up their own "local tyrannies." These provincial takeovers occurred in the span of mere eighteen months, from the first wave of takeovers in May 1921 through October 1922, when the Fascists moved their extraparliamentary, paramilitary political struggle to the national level. Faced with Mussolini's threat of a *coup de main*, the so-called "March on Rome," King Emmanuel III invited him to become premier.

The collusion of the state authorities was determined by the Fascists' "offensive alliances" with the propertied class, and the latter's continuing political hegemony. In spite of the political transformations that followed World War I, the Socialists' electoral power in the provinces was limited, and the propertied class retained its power in the liberal state's executive branch and bureaucracy, as well as continued to control government policies in the provinces. This was a consequence of the Socialists' political strategy and of the persistence of *trasformismo*, especially Giovanni Giolitti's reliance on the traditional method of clientelism. By refusing to join Giolitti's "bourgeois" government, the Socialist Party limited the arena of its legal national political struggle to parliamentary opposition while it concentrated on building its organization and agitation in the northern provinces.

Figure 1.1
Analytical Model of the Fascists' Seizure of Power in Italy's Provinces (1920-1922)

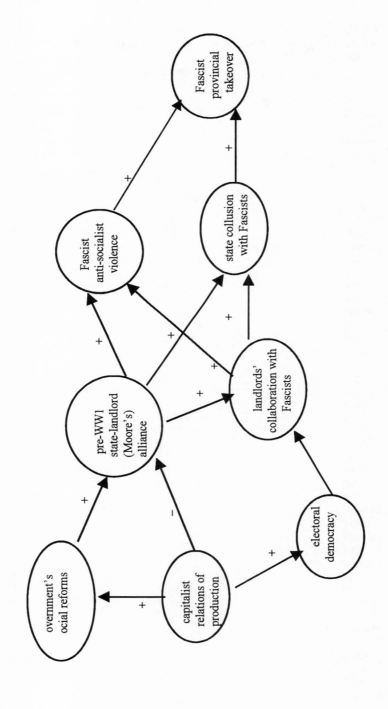

Table 1.1
Incidents of Violence and Fascist Takeovers in Italy's Provinces,
by Region

Region	Violent Incidents	Fascist Takeovers
North		
Alessandria	21	X*
Belluno	2	
Bergamo	1	
Bologna	73	X
Brescia	6	
Como	10	
Cremona	13	X
Cuneo	3	
Ferrara	49	X
Forli	4	
Genoa	14	X
Mantova	42	X
Milan	18	X
Modena	93	X
Novara	21	X
Padova	39	
Parma	18	
Pavia	49	
Piacenza	29	X
Porto Maurizio	1	
Ravenna	10	X
Reggio Emilia	41	X
Rovigo	79	X
Sandino	0	
Treviso	5	
Turin	13	
Udine	10	
Venice	22	
Verona	29	
Vicenza	15	
Center		
Ancona	6	
Arezzo	—	X
Ascoli Piceno	7	
Florence	8	X
Grosseto	2	X
Livorno	13	X
Lucca	12	X
Macerata	3	
Messa Carrara	3	X
Perugia	74	X
Pesaro Urbino	7	X
Pisa	44	X
Rome	15	
Siena	15	X

Region	Violent Incidents	Fascist Takeovers
South		
Aquila, Abbruzzi	7	
Avellino	1	
Barri Apulia	30	X
Benevento	0	
Cagliari	4	
Caltanissetta	1	
Campobasso	—	
Caserta	8	
Catania	2	
Catanzaro	4	
Chieti	7	
Cosenza	1	
Foggia	15	X
Girgenti	6	
Lecce	14	
Messina	1	
Napoli	5	
Palermo	0	
Potenza	4	
Reggio Calabria	2	
Salermo	0	
Sessari	1	
Siracuse	14	
Teramo	7	
Trapani	0	

*X=The province was taken over by the Fascists.

Sources: De Felice, R. *Mussolini il fascista Vol. II*, 1966, pp. 167; Lyttleton, A. *The Seizure of Power, Fascism in Italy, 1919-1929*, 1987, pp. 444-45.

Thus, the Socialists failed to use their substantial representation in Parliament to gain access to the state's executive powers. In addition, local state authorities, which remained staffed by the propertied class and loyal to its interests, were hostile to the Socialists—that hostility antedated, by decades, the emergence of the Fascist organization. So, once an alliance was forged between the propertied class and the Fascists, the authorities' hostility to the Socialists was easily turned into full-blown collaboration with the Squads.

The authorities' collaboration with the Fascists was crucial in the latter's seizure of power. Italy's government, led by the Liberal Party, assisted the Fascists first passively, by its absence from the scene of struggle, and later actively, by taking the Fascists into its governing parliamentary coalition. Thus, the Liberal government legitimized both the Squads' extraparliamentary strategy and the political achievements the Fascist organization gained from it.

However, the Liberal government not only generally failed to defend the legally constituted Socialist governments under Fascist siege, they even aided and abetted the Fascists. Ministerial decrees proclaimed the dissolution of provincial Socialist governments and discharged prefects who opposed the Fascists for being alleged "accomplices of the Bolsheviks." The Liberal government replaced these prefects and provincial governments with commissioners favorable both to the Fascists and to the employers' organizations.

But, as mentioned earlier, the Fascists' paramilitary strategy, especially the Squads' use of violence, affected not only their own political fortunes but also the nature of their organization itself. An analysis of the specific character and development of this strategy allows us to reconstruct a decisive phase of the process in which Fascism itself was invented. From its inception in early 1919, the Fascist organization experienced several internal conflicts that led to significant changes in the composition of its membership, its leadership, and its program. The factions within the organization created during and by the struggle for power developed their own distinct social bases of support, independent financial and political alliances and, in consequence, distinct and even conflicting political objectives. A new Fascist cadre emerged, composed of the leaders of the Squads' expeditions and the new provincial strongmen. As Angelo Tasca puts it: "Men who have killed together, burned houses, terrorized whole country-sides could not stop or separate. To commit crimes at top speed became a law...The bond uniting the aggressors was not their own blood, which was seldom spilled, but the blood of their victims" ([1938] 1966, pp. 180-81).

Bound together by this "unifying effect of violence," as Tasca calls it, the intransigent faction was both a prime mover behind the Fascists' political strategy and its major beneficiary within the Fascist organization. The violence of the *squadristi*, one of the main components in the Fascists' political strategy, enhanced their influence on the organization's leadership and program. But this "spirit of violence" did not go uncontested, nor did the influence of the propertied class on Fascist provincial leaders and, through them, on the

Fascists' organization. Two specific and at times even dramatic internal debates in the Fascist organization—the first, the Pact of Pacification with the Socialists, and the second, the transformation of the Fascist organization into a party—exemplify the rupture in the organization. In these debates, the Fascists were split between "intransigent" Squads and "moderates", or "revisionists." The "intransigents" objected to the Pact and demanded the takeover of the state by the Party. The revisionists, represented by the intellectual and urban elements, demanded that the Party be subordinated to the authority of the state to permit collaboration with the existing state bureaucracy and elements of the old ruling classes that were now supportive of the Fascists. Eventually, the revolutionary Syndicalists and ex-Socialists, who were among the founders of the original Milan *fascio* in 1919, opposed this turn to the Right and soon left the organization.

Thus, the Fascists who eventually seized national power after twenty months of violent political struggle were not the same men who had initiated this struggle. How, then, did these internals struggles and factions affect the nature of the Fascist organization? What issues divided them? What determined the intransigents' ascendancy within the Fascist Party and their unique relations with Mussolini?

The prevailing theoretical assumption that the Fascist takeover is but a linear continuation of the movement's emergence overlooks this internal ideological and social differentiation among the Fascists themselves. The destruction of "provincial Fascism," that is, of the Fascist "mini-states" that had been established in northern Italy during the first years of the organization's struggle for power, was a crucial condition for the establishment of the national Fascist state. These strongholds constituted a major political force in Italy's numerous provincial and local governments, and subsequently served as springboards for the Fascist seizure of state power. At a certain stage, however, they became an impediment to the consolidation of the Fascist Party and its regime. This is the paradox that characterizes the relationship between Mussolini and his political power base: The militant radicalism of the Squads that had gained power for Mussolini now hindered his efforts to consolidate Fascist state power.[6]

The Fascists' seizure of power was neither the authentic representation of the social interests of a "mass base" nor a mere repercussion of Italy's "route" to capitalism. If Barrington Moore, Jr. (1966) is correct in stating that the specific relationship between Italy's landlords and the central state affected their general stance toward the Fascists, this did not in itself determine what the Fascists in fact did to achieve their support and later win power. Neither the Fascists' actions nor the consequences of their actions were somehow predetermined historically. The Fascist Squads set out to defeat the Socialist insurgency in Italy's postwar crisis. This led to their alliance with the propertied class that, in turn, was the main determinant of the state's collusion with the Fascists. Supported by organized landlords and blessed with the authorities' indulgence, the Fascists were able to destroy—both physically and politically—the legitimately constituted Socialist provincial governments and install their own regimes instead.

On the heels of the establishment of Fascist regimes in most of Italy's northern provinces, the Fascists moved their struggle to the national level. This culminated in Mussolini's threat of a "March on Rome" in the fall of 1922 and the decision by King Emmanuel III, in October of that year, to install him as prime minister. The Fascists' strategy and concrete practices had relatively independent effects, given Italy's "route" to capitalism, in determining their own political victory and the triumph of Fascism.

NOTES

1. The word *fascio* means simply "combination." Its origin lies in the bundle of elm or birch rods bound about the lector's ax, the emblem of the authority of the Roman state, or from Aesopos' fable about the father who proved the strength of union to his sons by showing them how individually weak sticks can become an unbreakable bundle. The word had been used in Italy by various political and social associations of, for example, peasants and agricultural laborers, in the late nineteenth century, long before the emergence of Fascism.

The terms *fascisti* and *fascismo* were also current at the end of World War I and used to designate a wide range of political and social movements (Lyttelton 1987, p. 456, n.1). Until the formal establishment of the Fascist Party in 1921, the Fascists were known as the "*fasci di combattimento*." In what follows I use a lower case "f" for "fascist" or "fascists" when I refer to the generic political phenomenon, and an upper case "F" for "Fascist" and "Fascists" when I refer to the Italian political organization.

2. I use the term "origins" in the limited sense offered by the historian Vivarelli: "the actual circumstances owing to which the fascist phenomenon came to life" (1991a, p. 29).

3. These struggles and debates were to continue after the seizure of power, with the "intransigent" faction demanding the total takeover of the state's institutions by the Fascist Party, and their rivals, the "revisionists."

4. The task I set for myself in this study, to examine the effects of the political strategies in the transformation of Italy's regime and state, requires I minimize the role played by Mussolini in the Fascists' rise to power. This surely is not to say that his leadership, persona, political beliefs, and personal qualities were irrelevant to the events examined here. There are abundant studies on Mussolini, his own autobiography, and biographies written by friends, lovers, and foes, as well as authoritative studies by historians. See, for example, Mussolini 1928; Sarfatti 1925; Mack Smith 1981; and De Felice's voluminous biography (1965, 1966, 1968).

5. This was the name the *squadristi* adopted from the term for Ethiopian chieftains.

6. Indeed, "provincial Fascism" was destroyed during 1925-1928 by Mussolini and his revisionist allies, who successfully conducted a purge of the Fascist Party. The political crisis over the assassination of Giacommo Matteotti, a Socialist opposition leader, in June 1924 marked the low point of the Fascist grip on the state as well as of Mussolini's control of the Party. The intransigents—who blamed Mussolini for the "Matteotti crisis"—rebelled against his attempt to rule through a parliamentary

coalition. They demanded that he establish a dictatorship and eliminate all parliamentary opposition.

Chapter 2

The Sociological Paradigm: The Neglected Historical Sequence of Fascism's Ascendancy

Prevailing theories of fascism may be divided into three groups: (1) theories of the social and historical "preconditions" (or "origins") of fascism, which emphasize the specific constellations of class relations (Dutt [1934] 1974; Moore 1966; Poulantzas 1974), or focus on the problem of "modernization" (Parsons 1954; Organsky 1968); (2) theories of the "bearers," or the "social base," of fascist "movements," which focus on the "atomization of the masses" (Lederer 1940) or the social "displacement" that breeds "extremism" in given "social strata" (Lipset 1963; Linz 1976);[1] and (3) theories of the novelty of "totalitarianism" (Arendt 1979). The first part of this chapter analyzes these theories. In the second part, I offer an alternative logic of inquiry into the question of the rise of Italian Fascism.[2]

To reveal the underlying logic of these theories, I analyze each by answering three questions: (1) What are the crucial relationships on which the theory focuses? (2) What implicit assumptions does it make? (3) Most important for my argument: What is the significance of the "theoretical neglect" revealed by answering these questions? My purpose is to identify, for each group of theories, the specific sources of their shared theoretical neglect, that is, to reveal what these theories fail to address or explain. I do not assess the empirical adequacy or logical consistency of what they do try to explain. Hence, the following discussion is not intended, and should not be read, as an inclusive exposition, comparison, and critique of these theories.

PREVAILING THEORIES OF FASCISM: THEIR LOGIC OF INQUIRY

Analyses of the Preconditions or "Origins" of Fascism

The detailed analyses in this group are characterized by a methodology that seeks the causes of the emergence of Fascism in its social and economic preconditions. With the exception of R. Palme Dutt's work ([1934] 1974), the studies included in this group focus on the historical sequence preceding Fascism's actual emergence, whether capitalism's "extreme decay" (Dutt), its "crisis of hegemony" (Poulantzas 1974), the advent of a "revolution from above" (Moore 1966), or the strains and social conflicts accompanying "modernization" (Organsky 1968). Hence, both class analyses and theories of modernization are included.[3]

Class Analyses

The authors in this group attempt to explain the "origins" of Fascism by analyzing the class content of the social and historical conditions that preceded its emergence. The common question they address is: What are the sociohistorical conditions that led to the emergence of Fascism as a significant political organization and mass movement?

Dutt's main argument is that the causes of fascism are rooted in capitalism's crisis of "overproduction," a tendency inherent in the system. Conceptualizing the present crisis of overproduction as a crisis *of* the system, rather than merely *in* the system, is crucial for Dutt's analysis: This means that capitalism can no longer reproduce itself. Unlike capitalism's "old cyclical crises" that, Dutt argues, "permitted, after a relatively short period, the resumption of capitalist production at a higher level...the present world economic crisis is without precedent" ([1934] 1974, pp. 30, 32). To solve this specific crisis, either the "social relations of production" or "forces of production" must be sacrificed in order to preserve the other. The crisis of capitalism, therefore, allows for choice only between two social alternatives: a socialist revolution, that is, the destruction of capitalist social relations that will maintain the progressive role of the forces of production; or fascism, that is, the attempt of the propertied class to preserve capitalist social relations at the expense of the continued growth of its productive forces (pp. 44-45).

This conceptualization of the capitalist crisis also explains the crucial role Dutt assigns to socialist reformism in the emergence of fascism. Because both alternatives are structurally given, the opposition of social democrats to a revolution must mean a support of fascism. Thus, social democracy advanced the fascist alternative because it promoted the belief that the workers' interests could be accommodated within the crumbling capitalist social order. "The fascist jackal strikes only the already wounded proletarian lion. Fascism was not the weapon of defence of the bourgeoisie against the advancing proletarian offensive, but the vengeance of the bourgeoisie against the retreating proletariat, after reformism had broken the workers' ranks" (p. 119). Hence, "where the majority of the working class has followed the line of Reformism (Germany, Italy, etc.) there, at a certain stage, Fascism *invariably* grows and conquers" (p. 108, my emphasis). Fascism, then, emerged as a result of the capitalist crisis of overproduction, mediated by the ruinous effects of the social democrats' "reformist" strategies.

In Moore's study of the "social origins of dictatorship" (1966), an analysis of "fascism" itself has but a minor place, and his historical account barely reaches the period of fascism's earliest appearance. His argument is based on the basic premise that "democracy" and "dictatorship" are historical alternatives that emerge in response to the "capitalist impulse" in a specific country. Decisive in a country's "choice" between these alternatives, Moore argues, is the role played by the "agrarian classes" ("lord and peasant") as precapitalist agrarian structures are transformed in the process of the "commercialization of agriculture" (pp. 419-21). Hence, Moore identifies the coalition between large landlords and "conservative modernizers" within the state as the crucial condition precipitating the emergence of fascism.

In countries that did not experience a peasant revolution (a revolution "from below"), the "commercialization of agriculture" was accomplished by establishing "labor-repressive agrarian systems" in which landlords employed noneconomic coercion to control the labor force. Such systems, then, "provide an unfavorable soil for the growth of democracy and [constitute] an important part of the institutional complex leading to fascism" (p. 435). Another condition on the "route" to fascism is the alliance, through the state, between a politically powerful class of large landholders and emerging commercial and manufacturing interests. Where such class alliances were formed, a new "species" of authoritarian government came to power, one led by "conservative modernizers" (e.g., Cavour in Italy, Bismarck in Germany, and the Meiji reformers in Japan) who carried out a modernizing "revolution from above" as early as the 1860s (pp. 440-41).

At the turn of the nineteenth century, the semiparliamentary governments that followed these authoritarian regimes are considered by Moore as not merely the predecessors of fascism but as its hosts. "The door to fascist regimes was opened by unstable democracies (the Weimar Republic, Japan in the twenties, Italy under Giolitti)," characterized by their "reluctance or inability to bring about fundamental structural changes" (p. 438). These regimes' combination of traditional social structures with a new democratic form of government led to the emergence of fascism—which Moore loosely defines as a "pseudo-radical" and "plebeian anti-capitalism" of the lower-middle classes that is "inconceivable without the entrance of the masses on the historical stage" (pp. 447-48). Thus, in Moore's theory, the major determinants ("origins") of fascism were fully present and operative as much as a half century before the appearance of fascism itself. This assumption compels him to ignore how "the door to fascist regimes was opened," by whom, and who tried to shut it, why they failed, and how the fascists succeeded not only in entering that door but establishing a fascist regime. In short, Moore's theory ignores the actual making of fascism and the establishment of the fascist state.

Nicos Poulantzas' (1974) guiding principle for analyzing the fascist state is Thalheimer's specific analogy between fascism and Bonapartism, which he extends to support his own concept of the "exceptional capitalist state." But, contrary to Thalheimer, Poulantzas argues that once in power, fascism relinquished its own political autonomy to monopoly interests rather than representing an "autonomization of the executive"; it thereby solved the conflict between executive and monopoly capital over "capitalist hegemony." Like Dutt and Moore, Poulantzas concentrates on the historical sequence that preceded fascism's emergence. The "hegemony crisis of capitalism," he argues, was the major cause for the emergence of the fascist "exceptional state." But he also argues that the fascist state emerged in order to fulfill the functions required to resolve this crisis. The crucial relationship in this argument, then, is between fascism, conceptualized as an "exceptional state," and the extraordinary circumstances, that is, the hegemony crisis of monopoly capitalism, which produced it.

The fascist state was formed, according to Poulantzas (1974), in order to fulfill its function in resolving this crisis. "The specific historical transition to the establishment of monopoly capitalism" (p. 12) determined the global political crisis that led to the emergence of fascism and the fascist state. This functional link is also evident in Poulantzas' analysis of the four stages in the growth of fascism, stages which supposedly correspond to those of the political crisis that fascism was meant to solve: (1) the growth of a fascist party as a mass party, (2) the subsequent class alliance between monopoly interests and the petty bourgeoisie, (3) the consolidation of monopoly interests under Fascist rule, and (4) the final period of "fascist stabilization": "[F]ascism loses its facade and from now on directly exercises its own class functions" (pp. 66-67).

Given this functionalist logic, Poulantzas' analysis progresses in the opposite direction of the actual historical sequence. Instead of drawing a causal link from the "crisis" to the "state" (as in Thalheimer's analysis), he assumes an unbroken continuity from the future fascist state back to the functions it was destined to fulfill, and the antecedent crisis that the fascist state was designed to resolve. His analysis therefore proceeds in reverse: It starts by characterizing the fascist state in terms of its function in resolving the crisis of capitalist hegemony. Consequently, this essentially teleological theory attempts to explain the nature of the fascist movement by the functions of the fascist state erected by it: The course of development of fascism was predetermined by what it was to become, that is, by its future function in resolving capitalism's crisis.

Theories of "Modernization"

Talcott Parsons' (1954) analysis of fascism focuses on the consequences of modernization for fascism's mass appeal.[4] Fascism, an instance of "radicalism of the right," is distinguished from "ordinary conservatism" primarily by the mass appeal of its ideology (p. 125). Parsons inquires, therefore, into how the rapid social change spurred by modernization affected individuals' political attitudes. Fascism's reaction "against the 'ideology' of rationalization of society is one principal aspect at least of the ideology of fascism" (p. 134).

This analysis of fascism draws on Durkheim's concept of anomie, that is, "the state where large numbers of *individuals* are to a serious degree lacking in the kind of integration with stable institutional patterns which is essential to their own personal stability and to the smooth functioning of the *social system*" (p. 125, my emphasis). Focusing on the relationship between the individual's personal stability and that of the "social system," Parsons draws an analogy between fascist movements and the religious movements that emerged during the Industrial Revolution: Both, in his view, were reactions to similar systemic strains. The "differential effects" of bureaucratic rationalization and the social conflicts this process and its ideology generate led to the emergence of a fascist ideology. The "reaction against the ideology of the rationalization of society" is identified as "one principal aspect at least of the ideology of fascism" (p. 134). Thus, Parsons concludes that "the possibility [of fascism] is at least as deeply rooted in the social structure and dynamics of our society as was socialism in an earlier age" (p. 138).

It should be emphasized, though, that in contrast to other theorists of fascism who focus on individual attitudes or the "social base," Parsons is explicit about the limits of what an explanation of such attitudes can accomplish. The state of anomie can explain only the "*susceptibility* to the appeal of [fascist] movements," and is therefore an inadequate explanation of the "*actual* appearance of such movements" (p. 129, my emphasis). Nevertheless, because his explicit purpose is to demonstrate the applicability of sociological concepts (e.g., anomie and bureaucratic rationalization) to the analysis of fascism's mass appeal, Parsons does not offer an explicit conceptualization of fascism (p. 140). He mentions many of the factors referred to in other theories, (e.g., the role of the "ruling classes" and the new lower-middle class) but elaborates on them only insofar as they can be treated through his conceptual framework of anomie and rationalization as the sources of fascism's appeal.

Similarly, A. F. Kenneth Organsky's (1968) application of "modernization theory" to the phenomenon of fascism is explicitly intended as an alternative to the focus on class relationships. Basing himself on W. W. Rostow's "stages of economic growth," he offers an alternative explanation of more or less the same problem first posed by the between-the-war Marxian theorists.

Organsky views the fascist "political system [as] an episode in the modernization of the country" (p. 19). He thus aims to construct "a model that encompasses...three major patterns [that] characterize *the period preceding* the fascist power takeover" (p. 23, my emphasis). These "patterns" are rapid economic growth, large-scale mobilization (i.e., urbanization), and political mobilization, which "is particularly acute just before the fascists take power" (p. 24). His thesis is that the process of modernization, which entails both the rapid increase and "spasmodic nature" of such processes of social change (i.e., economic growth, urbanization, and political mobilization), is "particularly corrosive to the pre-fascist traditional system" (p. 30).

The "fascist formula," according to Organsky, consists of the reduction of the rate of economic growth and a decrease in social mobilization accompanied by an increasing rate of political mobilization. "A good deal is made clear about the *functions* of a fascist political system [by noting] that two of the *pre-fascist* patterns are simply altered" (p. 31, my emphasis). At the same time, political mobilization is increased, but is "deflected from its former goals," as is evidenced in "a good deal of marching, singing [*sic*] and listening to political speeches [without] involvement in the decisions" (pp. 32-33). So, Organsky argues, the fascist state emerged in order to fulfill a particular function: to resolve the social crisis of integration initiated by modernization. Nevertheless, while Organsky, like Parsons, sees the nature of the social crisis in terms of the changes brought about by modernization, his understanding of the fascist state in relation to this crisis is similar to that of Poulantzas, that is, he defines it in terms of the functions it serves in resolving the social crisis. Here, too, both the fascist movement and the fascist state loom as necessary and inevitable outcomes of their preconditions.

To conclude, theories of fascism concentrating on the precipitating conditions construct a problematic that excludes (or assumes away) the question of fascism's actual historical development after its initial emergence. What fascism becomes (or how it eventuates) is implicitly assumed to be the necessary and inevitable outcome of the conditions leading to its emergence. These theories entirely neglect the question of what determined how the fascist "ideology" and organization developed and, indeed, were transformed during the fascist era itself, or how the fascists were able to win the struggle for political power.

Theories of the "Social Bearers" of Fascism

The theories in this group invoke analyses of the "social bearers" or "social base" of a fascist movement in order to explain its emergence; the specific explanation varies with the bearers identified. Thus, the underlying logic of these theories lies in their conceptual equation of the "nature of fascism" with the nature of its social base of support. The question of "fascism" turns into a question of mass psychology, that is, of the political passions or motivations of the individuals comprising its supporters.[5]

Emil Lederer's (1940) study of the "threat of classless society" depicts fascism as a "modern political system" resting on "amorphous masses" rather than on organized classes. The "masses are...amorphous; social stratification is effaced or at least blurred. The point of unity for the individuals comprising a mass is always emotional" (p. 31). This conception of the masses results from an underlying notion of the "multitudes": "individuals who belong to different groups and who do not form a group in themselves" (p. 29).

So, Lederer's main analytical focus is on the connection between the psychology of these "masses" and their "leader." The new "modern political system" is personified in the fascist dictator; it expresses and reflects his relationship with the masses: "The masses form the substance of the movement in and through which they become institutionalized, and as institutionalized masses, *they sweep the dictator into power and keep him in power*" (p. 18, my emphasis). Hence, the dictator is, almost literally, a creature of the masses. "If everything is ripe for action, the situation will suggest to people who are apt to become leaders that they accept the challenge....When a multitude merges into a crowd, creating a psychological unity, an opportunity is offered to another type of leader—the emotional passionate man, who feels what is in the air more strongly than the crowd" (p. 39). United solely by such a subjective feeling of unity, but without any material or objective base, the "institutionalization" of the masses by the fascist movement is decisive for its evolution.

Seymour Martin Lipset's (1963) comparative study of "political extremism," which he defines as the democratic emergence of antidemocratic movements, examines the electoral support for Franco, Hitler, and Peron, who represent three "types" of "extremism." It should be noted, from the outset, that viewing "extremism" as emerging democratically overlooks the perversion of democracy that is crucial in the emergence and ascendance of Italian Fascism and, later, of Nazism. Indeed, "it is difficult," Lipset admits, "to analyze Italian political history in terms of the three types of antidemocratic politics, because of the special manner in which Italian Fascism originally came to power" (p. 165). By the "special manner" of coming to power, Lipset means the various shifts in the ideology of Italian Fascism from a "neo-Socialist" party to a form of "opportunism" seeking the support of diverse social strata.

Lipset argues that as a result of rapid industrialization, any class may find itself at the margins of the new social structure; consequently, its individual members will be inclined to support any "extremist" antidemocratic program promising to restore their "economic security and high standing in society" (p. 134). While his classification of the three "types" of extremism is based on their different class bases, Lipset argues that only one type is "real fascism": "a middle class movement representing a protest against both capitalism and socialism, big business and big unions" (p. 131). The crucial relationship here is between the effect of industrialization in creating the "marginalization" of certain social strata and its political expression in extremist ideologies. This relationship determines the political attitudes of individual members of such marginalized classes and, accordingly, leads to the emergence of social movements or parties based on extremist ideologies.

Based on the assumption that there is a "fairly logical relationship between ideology and social base" (p. 129), Lipset focuses on what he claims is "the real question to answer: which strata are most 'displaced' in each country?" (p. 136). His focus, then, is not on how fascism (or "extremism") becomes a political force, but on the individuals who become fascists (or "extremists") themselves, that is, on the historical "displacements" that convert individuals from certain social classes into "extremists." In this respect, Lipset's argument is similar to Parsons': Whether due to "displacement" or anomie, the cause of fascism is located in the effects of social and economic change on individual attitudes and on their support of fascist or "extremist" movements.

Juan Linz's comparative study of fascist movements (1976, p. 10) also focuses on social support in the explanation of fascism's emergence. He, however, locates fascism's appeal not in a particular social class and its material interests, but in its being a "political latecomer" whose populist "hypernationalist" ideology attracts the support of a variety of social classes. Although all "fascist ideologies responded to distinct political historical and national situations" (pp. 8-9), Linz argues, the decisive factor was that each was a "political latecomer." As a "political latecomer," the fascist movement had to penetrate a "political space already occupied"; this was crucial in its obtaining mass social support (pp. 4-5). The distinctiveness of fascism thus "lies in its style and in its confused vision of the future which it in many respects incorporated...[from] other ideologies and movements. The various 'antis' of fascism served to define its identity in contrast to other parties and to appeal to [their] supporters" (p. 5).

We may conclude that theories of the social bearers of fascism are based on a dual premise. First, in common with other theories, they assume that an explanation of fascism's emergence also provides an answer to its ascendance. Second, they assume that the identification of the psychology, attitudes, character structure, or social location of the supporters—or "social base"—of the fascist movement somehow, in an unspecified way, constitutes an explanation of its emergence. Whether viewed in terms of the "threat of the classless society," the "marginalization" of social classes, or popular "hypernationalism," the implication is that once this factor is present, fascist "movements" are destined to emerge. Taken together, the focus on fascism's emergence and on the mass support underlying its emergence constitutes a logic that ignores the analysis of the strategy, the specific political practices, and the struggles involved in the fascist organization's success.

FASCISM AS A "TOTALITARIAN DICTATORSHIP"

Hannah Arendt's (1979) theory of totalitarianism, like Poulantzas' theory, is distinctive in focusing on fascist rule. Yet, in accordance with their theoretical paradigm, the explanation of the practices of the fascist regime (as a type of totalitarian regime) is sought in the analysis of the fascist movement's emergence.

For Arendt, fascism is one instance of an encompassing and more significant phenomenon: modern totalitarian dictatorship. This dictatorship, Arendt claims, is a historically novel kind of rule. Borrowing from the early Marxists, Arendt argues that totalitarian dictatorships are the result of complete social breakdown: The collapse of the nation-state led to "imperialism"; the disintegration of class society led to a mass society; and the atomization and disintegration that characterize this new society led to the emergence of totalitarian parties.

Drawing on Lederer's conception of mass society, Arendt argues that the breakdown of class society and of the nation-state led to the emergence of a mass of isolated individuals for whom the only possible form of political representation was a "totalitarian movement." This movement provided the organizational base of the totalitarian dictatorship, which penetrated civil society by means of propaganda and terror. Arendt thus draws a direct causal trajectory from the origins of totalitarianism in mass society to its consequences, the actual practice of totalitarian government in power.

Furthermore, the "breakdown of the class system," according to Arendt, must precede the rise of totalitarian dictatorships. This "meant *automatically* the breakdown of the party system...chiefly because these parties, being interest parties, could no longer represent class interests" (p. 314, my emphasis). Composed of "mass organizations of atomized, isolated individuals," the totalitarian movement is dependent on the totalitarian leader. This leader, much like Lederer's dictator, "is nothing more nor less than the functionary of the masses he leads...[and] he depends just as much on the 'will' of the masses he embodies as the masses depend on him" (pp. 323, 325).

Although Arendt discusses the specific political practices of totalitarian dictatorships, she does so only in order to establish their political and historical novelty as dictatorships characterized by massive reliance on propaganda and terror. For her, this is the essential character of the dictatorship in Nazi Germany and of the Soviet Union under Stalin; this is what distinguishes these dictatorships from other autocratic regimes. Arendt's characterization of "totalitarianism in power" further accentuates the decisive role played by the "totalitarian movement" in determining the nature of these regimes.

Similar to Thalheimer's analysis of the inherent contradictions between the fascist state and the mass-based fascist party, Arendt argues that this relationship is the source of totalitarianism's internal "paradox." The "co-existence of dual authority," of the party and of the state, creates the "paradox of totalitarianism in power," which leads to the duplication of all offices of authority (pp. 390-91). The breakdown of class society that led to the emergence of totalitarian parties continues to determine the essential character of the totalitarian dictatorships erected by these parties, their "struggle for total domination of the total population of the earth" (p. 391). Arendt, similar to Poulantzas, draws a direct line from the conditions that precipitated the emergence of the totalitarian movement to a global characterization of the rule of totalitarian dictatorships.

In sum, prevailing theories of fascism share one basic assumption: No matter what the fascist organization, its political practices, ideology, actual political rule, and form of government eventually turned out to be, fascism is invariably depicted as the culmination of earlier historical processes, or as an epiphenomenal reflection or expression of its social base of support. "A way of seeing is also a way of not seeing—a focus upon object A involves a neglect of object B," as Kenneth Burke observes (cited in Merton 1987, p. 9). The focus on the question of fascism's origins or bases (object A), in itself a crucial question, has operated as a way of not seeing how fascism *became* Fascism (object B)—a way of neglecting the process unfolding from its emergence until its political ascendance. The question of the determinants of fascism's trajectory, its struggles and developments, from the time of its birth until the seizure of power and then the establishment of the Fascist dictatorship, is neglected entirely as a distinct analytical problem. How the Fascists actually took power, what Fascism became once in power, and what the Fascists did with that power—remains a "pocket of theoretical neglect." An alternative logic of inquiry may enable us to focus on what has been overlooked. This alternative attempts to correct for two problems in the predominant paradigm: (1) the conflation of the process of Italian Fascism's emergence with its actual seizure of political power; (2) the faulty conceptualization of Fascism that this conflation implies.

AN ALTERNATIVE LOGIC OF INQUIRY

The years following the initial emergence of the Fascist organization in Italy were rent by intense and violent political struggles between Fascists and Socialists. For precisely this reason, the political strategies, forms of organization, alliances, and specific tactics employed by the contending organizations in these struggles were crucial determinants of the specific character of Italian Fascism.

Accordingly, in order to understand what Fascism really was, we must analyze the specific social process behind its ascent to power: that is, why and how the Fascists, once they appeared on the historical scene, succeeded. Similarly, we must analyze not merely their supporters but the Fascists themselves. Instead of assuming that Fascism was a mature phenomenon at the time of its emergence and that it merely reflected the nature of its origins or the character of its social base, we must try to explain how it actually *became* Fascism—and this requires us to focus on the role of the Fascists in its creation.

To study the "making of (Italian) Fascism," I propose a logic of inquiry that attempts to delineate what Max Weber called "objective historical possibilities" (see also Zeitlin 1984, p. 19); in other words, what could have happened once Fascism emerged. I assume, therefore, that the course of actual historical development was neither fixed nor predetermined. The fact that a certain historical development was the one that eventually transpired does not mean, ipso facto, that it was the only one that could possibly have occurred.[6]

When applied to the analysis of the Fascists' political strategy, this means that given the historical circumstances at the time of Fascism's emergence, the question is whether a different course of action or a different political strategy was objectively available. Indeed, immediately after its establishment in 1919, the Fascist organization ran candidates for election. Following a humiliating electoral defeat, the organization abandoned the option of attaining political power by legal parliamentary means and turned to an extraparliamentary and illegal violent struggle against Socialists and organized workers. Within the same circumstances, then, different strategies to attain power and political influence were not only possible, they were actually employed by the Fascists, at least temporarily.

If we accept the possibility of alternative outcomes, the Fascists' actual seizure of political power was not the continuation of the same social process that led to Fascism's appearance or to the organization's initial establishment. Rather, it was part of a distinct, historically contingent process offering more than one possible route. This distinction is crucial. If the Fascists' initial emergence and ascent to power are seen as one and the same social process, this obfuscates the pivotal conceptual distinctions between what are empirically distinct phenomena. "Where things and their interrelations are...changing," as Frederick Engels argued, the provision of "fixed, cut-to-measure, once-and-for-all applicable definitions" can only be misleading. Rather, the "mental images, the ideas" we employ in an empirical analysis of any developing phenomenon also have to be "subject to change and transformation" ([1894] 1967, pp. 13-14) so as to adequately grasp that phenomenon. So, Fascism was neither "fixed" nor "cut-to-measure"; it was in a constant process of "change and transformation" from the moment of its emergence. As such, Fascism must be conceptualized in terms that capture the different moments of its development. And this development has to be periodized or conceptually reconstructed in terms of the unfolding drama of Fascism's self-invention—its struggle for power, its taking of power, and its use of that power.

To analyze the making of Fascism (as opposed to why it emerged, who supported it, and what produced this support), we must discover (1) how the Fascists actually took national power and, perhaps more crucially, (2) how the way they seized power affected their wielding of power. This objective, in turn, requires asking those questions we have raised before. Implicit here is the proposition that political struggles—both external, between the Fascists and their Socialist rivals, and internal, among the Fascists themselves—can be history-making events.

The general theoretical issue is, in short, the "relative autonomy" of politics, or "the possible *independent effects of political phenomena in the shaping and transformation of basic social relations*...within the objective limits imposed and the objective alternatives made possible by the existing circumstances" (Stepan-Norris and Zeitlin 1989, p. 503, emphasis in original). Even if the underlying historical conditions made possible the Fascists' emergence, these did not determine what the Fascists did following that emergence. The conditions *allowed* certain strategies to appear, but did not determine them or their historical and political consequences. The specific content of the strategies adopted by the various protagonists (e.g., the Socialists' rhetoric, the militancy of the northern landlords) were by no means the inescapable dictate of Italy's historical conditions. However, they were profound determinants of the Fascists' coming to power, and of the kind of power they wielded.

Central to the analysis of these struggles is the conception of political strategy. My conception of political strategy derives, first, from Carl von Clausewitz's definition of military strategy as the "employment of the battle as the means towards the attainment of the object of War." Tactics, in this framework, are specific modes of operation used to win particular battles aimed at achieving the strategy's major political objectives ([1832] 1968, pp. 241, 399, 192). Political strategy is thus the totality of an organization's conduct of its political struggles, that is, the multiplicity of battles (and the specific tactics employed in these battles) used as means in the campaign to attain political power.

But Clausewitz's conceptualization of strategy and tactics assumes the existence of war. The "continuation of politics," of the war between states and their organized armies, is taken for granted as the arena in which the strategy and the tactics are employed. Therefore, Clausewitz's definitions and distinctions entail elements of long-term planning. Strategy, then, as he views it, is calculated conduct, which includes the designation of specific battles and tactics, based on the certainty that their terrain is an armed struggle.

Such elements of calculation are not always directly applicable to the analysis of political strategy. The concept of political strategy, unlike that of military strategy, must account not only for the conduct of war but for the very initiation of war as the terrain in which the strategy is employed. Another view, differing from this school, defines strategy as the "means of bringing the enemy to battle" and tactics as the "means of defeating him in battle" *(New Columbia Encyclopedia* 1975, p. 2632). Here, the existence of war and of battles is not a pregiven; it is the product of the strategy itself. In this sense, the Fascists' militarization of political struggle, their campaign of extraparliamentary maneuvers and illegal violence against the Socialists, were both integral parts of their political strategy as well as one of their objectives.

However, it is crucial to remember that this political strategy, being a strategy and not a tactic, continued to evolve and to have momentous effects even after the seizure of power. One of the main tasks of this analysis, therefore, is to show the continuity between what may seem to be distinct historical sequences: the struggle for the seizure of power and the struggle for the consolidation of this power. The Fascists' political strategy includes the organization of the Action Squads; their tactic of territorial expansion through violent "punitive expeditions" against the Socialists' local and provincial centers of power; their "offensive alliances," in Clausewitz's terms, that is, alliances that involved the active collaboration with the propertied class; and their "defensive alliances," those alliances with the state authorities that colluded with the Fascists' and their allies.

Once the "enemy"—the Socialists (as well as the ruling Liberal Party)— were drawn into "war" on the Fascists' terms, then the tactic of "punitive expeditions," including the defensive and offensive alliances that supported it, were employed to defeat the enemy in actual battles. Hence, the Action Squads and their violent political strategy are crucial links in the establishment of the dictatorship. They did not wither away; instead, they developed a political identity of their own within the Fascist organization.

To understand the nature of the relationship between the state and Italy's propertied class at the time of the Fascists' ascendance, we must examine, first, the historical development of the political system of Italy's liberal state and the role of the propertied class in it. As the historian Gaetano Salvemini noted in 1942, "of the three European countries now under dictatorial rule, Russia, Italy and Germany, Italy alone had formerly a democratic form of government." This is the "first question that requires an answer": why this collapse of Italian democracy, however fragile, occurred (Vivarelli 1991a, p. 39).

NOTES

1. See De Felice (1977) for a review of the various interpretations of fascism, including the sociological and historical perspectives.

2. Another work discussing the relations between fascism and the propertied class, not discussed here, is Guerin (1973).

3. Parsons explicitly argues that the combination of fascism's mass appeal and the role played by "privileged elite groups" is, in fact, "of the very essence of the phenomenon [i.e., fascist movements]" (p. 125). However, the essay is primarily devoted to the question of fascism's appeal.

4. Elements in this critique are found in Hamilton (1982), especially chapter 2, "A Review of the Literature," pp. 9-36. His analysis of the social bases of the voters for the Nazi Party (*Nazionalsozialistische Deutsche Arbeiterpartei*, the National Socialist German Workers Party [NSDAP]) is grounded in a critique of what he terms the "Centrist Argument," that is, the identification of the lower-middle class as the NSDAP's main source of electoral support and, hence, its rise. To counter this argument, Hamilton analyzes the returns for the NSDAP, comparing the voting in rural areas with that in major urban centers. He concludes that the NSDAP vote followed religious affiliation, not class cleavages. While the Protestants tended to vote NSDAP, Catholic communities, across classes, remained loyal to *Zentrum*, Germany's Catholic Party. Following this analysis, Hamilton offers a theory of "the character of the political struggle" to explain the Nazi's success, focusing on "the role of the party's cadres, of its militants" (p. 441). According to this argument, a better key to understanding the election results than that provided by the structural position of individual voters is the specific local context of the political struggle waged by the Nazis and the specific political strategies employed by the Nazis in various social contexts that may provide.

5. On theories of "fascism and the lower-middle class," see Burris (1986).

6. This conception differs from Moore's "suppressed historical alternatives" (1978, pp. 376-97). As I understand Moore's notion, it is inextricably linked to the issue of the "moral responsibility" of individuals and the policies they make. By enjoining us to ask about individuals' choices, Moore's "alternatives" are rendered subjective policy options that may be available to some individuals but not to others. The idea of "unfulfilled historical possibilities" does not require asking why specific individuals chose one "alternative" over another, but only to establish that such alternatives were objectively possible.

Chapter 3

The Political Feudalism of the Liberal State

One of the few points of agreement found among historians of Italian Fascism is that the support of the owners of commercial estates (*agrari*)[1] was a crucial determinant in the emergence of the Fascist organization in Italy's northern provinces (Tasca [1938] 1966; De Felice 1965; Salvemini 1973; Maier 1975; Cardoza 1982; Lyttelton 1987). But how exactly did the process of commercialization of agriculture create the conditions for fascism's emergence? How did the segmentation of Italy's landowning class into northern and southern landlords affect the political hegemony of this class and the future political alliance between commercial landlords and Fascists? The theoretical questions, therefore, relate to the effect of *intraclass* struggles among Italy's landowners on the political terrain in which their future *interclass* struggles against wage workers were fought (see Stepan-Norris and Zeitlin 1989, p. 504).

This issue is directly linked to the question of the relationship between modernization and fascism. As we saw, Moore argues that the political power of the commercial landlords was a crucial condition for fascism's emergence. The alliance between the landlords and the state led to the establishment of semiparliamentary regimes that adopted authoritarian policies to protect the interests of the landed class against wage workers (1966, p. 438). These policies later developed into full-blown fascism. The rise of Italian Fascism seems to support his thesis. The Fascist organization first came forth and gained power in the country's northern regions, where commercial agriculture prevailed, and was almost completely absent in the semifeudal south. However, it was also in the commercial north that the political hegemony of the landlords declined sharply just before the rise of Fascism, while in the south, the *latifundists* maintained their political power. In contrast to Moore's logic, then, it was precisely where the political hegemony of the landlords was threatened, where they had lost direct political power, that Fascism emerged.

To solve this anomaly, we must account for the distinctions between the two segments of Italy's landed class, northern *agrari* and southern *latifundists*. The political hegemony of Italy's landlords was not determined by their alliance with the national state alone, as Moore has it. Rather, it was a product of the specific interaction between distinct forms of landlord domination on the provincial level, and the national alliance of both class segments, *agrari* and *latifundists*, with the central state on the national level. This merger of divergent class interests, associated with two distinct levels of political hegemony, the provincial and the national, may explain not only why the social conditions in the north rendered the region susceptible to Fascism's emergence, but also why Fascism was absent in the south.

The Italian political system presented the northern commercial landlords, the *agrari*, and only them, with a unique situation: Despite their relative dominance in national institutions, on the local level the *agrari* were threatened by the growing power of workers organizations that had gained control in many provincial governments. This contrast between an insurgent threat "from below," the local level, and continued political power "from above," the national level, was experienced only by the *agrari*; as described in chapters 5 and 6, it gave them the motivation to turn to the Fascists in their struggle against the workers. Most importantly, the landlords' political power in the central state gave them the influence necessary to make this support politically significant.

In Italy, the "political relevance of ownership of the means of production" (Zeitlin and Ratcliff 1988, p. 187), mainly large landed estates, is historically rooted in the nation's struggles for unification (*risorgimento*) during the mid nineteenth century. Diverse landed interests were secured through the clientele politics that guaranteed the landowning class (as well as a small manufacturing class) central state support. But the concrete political content of this class-state alliance varied with the respective, often contradictory interests of its two specific class segments, the *latifundists* and commercial landowners (Zeitlin 1984, pp. 8-9, 9n-10n; Zeitlin and Ratcliff 1988, pp. 5, 8, 9, 158, 181, 187-94, 187n-188n). In the south, the state's support was manifested in its absence from the struggle between the *latifundists* and the servile peasant population. In the commercialized north, the same class-state alliance required the state to actively interfere on behalf of the commercial landlords in their struggle against organized wage workers. However, after the War, the state did not aid the northern landlords as it had in the past. So, the local political hegemony of the northern landlords declined sharply in the period preceding the rise of Fascism, while in the south, the *latifundists* maintained their local political power. It was precisely where the direct political hegemony of the landlords on the provincial level was threatened, where they lost direct political power that Fascism emerged.

This intriguing contrast between fascism's political gains in Italy's various regions is noted by Snowden (1972). Applying Moore's thesis about the "plebeian" and "conservative" nature of fascism to the Italian case, he analyzes the "social groups that supported the Fascists in the crucial years leading up to the March on Rome." Comparing the variety of agrarian relations dominating in Italy's three main regions, Snowden reveals the relationship between various types of peasants and agricultural wage workers and the emerging Fascist organization (p. 269). This analysis shows the crucial role played by distinct forms of tenure relations in Italy's regions in explaining the composition of the movement's "mass following." The Fascists' greatest popular support was found in the north, where the crisis of modernization, manifested in "economic pressure and revolutionary challenge," was most acute and where the commercial landlords stood to lose most of their economic and political power. This was the case in the regions of "classical Fascism," the Po Valley and Tuscany. However, Snowden is careful not to trace Fascism's seizure of power to this popular support. "Fascism," he says explicitly, "was a popular force up to a point, but that point stops far short of a seizure of power....Fascism never represented more than a small minority" (1972, p. 291). This qualification makes the analysis of Fascism's support "from above" all the more crucial. The question we need to answer is: What sources of political power, other than popular support, were available to the Fascist organization?

The Italian ruling class, the *classe dirigente*, evolved and accumulated its political power beginning in 1861, with Italy's unification, until the fall of 1919, when the last election before the rise of Fascism was held. During the first decades of Italian independence, the role of the "agrarian industrial bloc in the economic and political development of Italy" was formed (Cardoza 1979, p. 172; see also Seton Watson 1967, pp. 13, 82-84; Gramsci 1971, pp. 55-113; Maier 1976; Davis 1979, p. 19; Lyttelton 1987, pp. 6-8; Cardoza 1991).

Established in 1861, Italy's unified state, under the leadership of Count Cavour, was based on an uneven political alliance between two class segments, the northern landlords and commercial interests based in the powerful kingdom of Piedmont, and the semifeudal *latifundists* of the south. In an episode of intraclass struggle between the commercial north and the *latifundist* south, the *risorgimento* defined the composition and character of Italy's governing class and the new state's political system, *trasformismo*, which this class created and dominated. It thus dictated what John Stephens terms the "black box" in Moore's thesis: the specific "mechanisms by which the existence of a relatively strong class of landlords actually influenced the political structures and events of 1870-1939" (1989, p. 1036).[2]

Following Snowden's emphasis on the regional level in explaining Fascism's support "from below," I examine the effect of regional tenure relations on Fascism's support "from above," that is, the position taken toward the Fascists by the propertied class, mainly the landlords. These regional distinctions had a direct effect on the political hegemony of the segments comprising the landed class, the *agrari* and the *latifundists*. What were the specific methods and mechanisms employed by the propertied class to secure its political hegemony over the national state and the specific forms of social domination on the provincial level?

THE POLITICAL FEUDALISM OF THE LIBERAL STATE, 1861-1918

Two major mechanisms maintained the political hegemony of Italy's propertied class.[3] The first was a severe restriction on suffrage, through extensive literacy and property qualifications. This limited suffrage prevented peasants and workers from voting and guaranteed the exclusive access of the propertied class to political power. The second, and crucial mechanism determined how the *classe dirigente* exercised its exclusive political power. This was accomplished by means of *trasformismo*, the creation of chronically shifting coalitions among the various parties representing factions of the dominant class. Literally, *trasformismo* means the "transformation" of opposition parties into members of the governing coalition. Yet, to create these coalitions and maintain a majority in Parliament, the government depended on the support of deputies who were elected by and answerable to local provincial landlord associations. *Trasformismo* thus meant, above all, an inextricable link between parliamentary politics in Rome and archaic methods of political control exercised by the preunification local oligarchies in the provinces, a situation described as "political feudalism" by W. A. Salomone (1945).

Until the electoral reform of 1911 (implemented in 1912), when property restrictions on suffrage were removed and new mass parties emerged, the almost absolute political hegemony of property and of the ruling Liberal Party remained uncontested.[4] The Liberal Party was clearly what Paul Baran terms "the ruling coalition of owning classes." It emerged in the late 1880s as a coalition of parties that opposed the authoritarian government of the ruling Conservatives, and dominated national politics, without challenge, until the end of World War I (Seton Watson 1967, p. 187).

Lacking a formal program or an established party apparatus, the term "Liberal" is applied by historians to a relatively fluid group of parties that occasionally participated in parliamentary alliances.[5] Italian Liberalism, as the historian Charles Maier puts it, was mainly (or merely) a "class concept" (1975, p. 24). It designated a relatively general commitment to constitutional government, to the monarchy, and to the "triumph of possessive individualism based on the sole principle of individual proprietorship" (Snowden 1986, p. 71; see also Seton Watson 1967, p. 246).

Before the reforms, the Liberal Party regularly won power with a narrow electorate defined by strict property and literacy restrictions.[6] To qualify to vote, a man had to be over twenty-five years of age, literate, and able to pay a minimum sum annually in direct taxes. In 1870, Italy's electorate consisted of 529,000 adult males, constituting less than 2% of the total adult population.[7] This electorate was smaller than in any other European country at the time: in France, 26.9% of the adult population were eligible to vote; in Germany, 20.6%; and in the United Kingdom, 8.8%. In 1882, an electoral reform broadened suffrage a bit: Although voting age was reduced to twenty-one and property qualifications were modified, literacy requirements were retained. The new property qualifications, based on tax payments, were precise and detailed.

Qualified voters now included property owners who paid a minimum of 19.8 lire annually in direct taxes; tenants who paid a minimum annual tax of 500 lire in rent; sharecroppers on farms taxed at least 80 lire annually; and householders who paid a minimum of 150 lire in annual rent (Seton Watson 1967, pp. 50-51). These revisions increased the eligible electorate to over 2 million, from 2% to 7% and, within a decade, to 9.8% of the total adult population.

The governing system of *trasformismo* provided the second, and critical, mechanism through which the propertied class maintained its exclusive access to, and exercise of, state power. Established by Prime Minister Agostino Depretis in the late 1870s, *trasformismo* became the enduring legacy of the Liberal state until the emergence of mass parties—the Socialist Party and, later, the Catholic Party, the *Popolari*—in the post World War I years.

Trasformismo's main objective was to obstruct the creation of a parliamentary opposition by incorporating as many parties as possible into a broad coalition. At the heart of this system were the country's sixty-nine provincial governments. The clientele politics of the Liberal state rendered the government dependent on parliamentary majorities produced by local politics dominated by patrician families and notables. Bologna's "agrarian elite," for example, embracing several old landowning families who lived in the cities, held unchallenged power at the communal and provincial levels. The province's political representatives presided over the boards of major financial institutions, the Constitutional Assembly, the political club of the landed families, and, of course, won "nearly every election" from 1860 until World War I (Cardoza 1982, p. 36).

The powers of the local governments, and thus of the landed oligarchies that controlled them, were extensive. They were the "basic political units of Italian political life" (Squeri 1983, p. 328), authorized to collect local taxes and to provide essential social services such as public health, sanitation, transportation, and education (see Seton Watson 1967, pp. 522-23; Maier 1975, p. 177; Lyttelton 1987, p. 38). The extent of power held by the provincial governments was expressed by their authority over taxation. Local taxes on foodstuffs were a major portion of the overall tax burden and fell heaviest on workers and peasants (King and Okey 1909, pp. 271-72): Two-thirds of local revenue came from taxation of food alone. The most abhorred tax was the *dazio*, a local tax of 10% to 15% imposed on flour, bread, pasta, and other staple foodstuffs. This tax system, as a Tuscan landlord acknowledged in 1907, was "a genuine regime of oppression" (Snowden 1989, p. 21).

This "oppression" was compounded by the absence of central government supervision and of any public expenditures to benefit the propertyless. The provision of public services of any kind, especially welfare services, remained at the discretion of the province's government, that is, in the hands of the landowning class (Fried 1963, p. 129; see also King and Okey 1909, pp. 263-76). Giovanni Giolitti, Italy's Prime Minister, recognized the tax system's vast inequities and soon advocated its reform.[8] The "ruling classes," he declared in a speech in 1901, spend "enormous sums of public money on their own exclusive interests, while using their over-representation in parliament to reduce their share of taxation"; at the same time they impose "a large number of taxes paid predominantly by the poor, on salt, on gambling, the *dazio* on grain and so forth." But "we have not a single tax which is exclusively on wealth as such" (cited in Mack Smith 1959, p. 214).

In addition to their direct control over local affairs, the provinces' rulers were the main anchors of *trasformismo*, its source of political stability. In exchange for its patronage, the central government would regularly strike multiple deals with local oligarchies, which provided it with acceptable candidates for deputies and guaranteed their election (Davis 1988, pp. 271-74; Seton Watson 1967, pp. 246-47).

The last master of *trasformismo* was Premier Giolitti. During his regime, the interference of government officials in the electoral process "reached unprecedented heights of brutality." The government's opponents were regularly "threatened, bludgeoned, besieged in their homes, leaders of the opposition were thrown into prison, voters were refused polling cards and favorable voters received double cards....Giolitti sold prefects in order to buy deputies" (Salvemini 1945, pp. xii, xiii). He so successfully manipulated the system that his rule was compared to that of Count Cavour: It was said that "Cavour created the constitutional state and Giolitti created the liberal administration" (Natale, cited in Seton Watson 1967, p. 251, n. 3).

Giolittismo, as the system of electoral manipulation came to be known, was based on the principle of "employing only the minimum pressure necessary to secure the minimum of reliable supporters." Such reliable support was readily found in the south. Here, as the prefect of Foggia charged in an 1890 report, politics were "confused with private interest, with profit, with greed....Neglect, waste, and maladministration...these are the words that describe the practice of nearly every commune in the district" (cited in Snowden 1986, p. 51).

Far from curbing the *latifundists'* power, Giolitti directly reinforced their control in the region. In the southern "municipal jungle" rife with rivalries between local oligarchies, Giolitti played off one faction against another; in return for votes, he allowed his favored faction to "tighten its grip over the peasantry" (Seton Watson 1967, p. 248). He delegated landlords to the offices of electors while their estate managers, the *gabolletos*, were put in charge of "delivering the vote" (Finley et al. 1986, p. 183). In Sicily, for example, "at the lowest level, the price of votes was quoted openly in the newspapers, and private armies were allowed to intimidate voters by every means up to and including assassination" (Finley et al. 1986, p. 198). Similarly, many members of successive governments in the province of Calabria, Arlacchi reportedly "owed a good part of their political success to ties with Mafia groups," which guaranteed their election to the Chamber of Deputies by "threats, extortion, and in some cases even kidnapping of electors." In return, the *mafiosi* received favors for themselves and their friends and relatives (their *cosca*) from these "men of government" (1980, pp. 117-18). The link between the almost absolute hegemony of the *latifundists* and the national government meant, in short, that "public institutions and private patronage often became inseparably interwoven" (Davis 1988, p. 271).

The *latifundists* "provided the nucleus round which [Giolitti] could build up his majority" (Seton Watson 1967, p. 247). Many of the country's political institutions, courts, and universities were staffed by sons of the southern gentry who became the "most effective evangelists of the Liberal ideology" (Davis 1979, p. 18). Here, more than in the rest of the country, the Liberals' rule, as Maier aptly puts it, was no more than a "coalition based on patronage and the enjoyment of power" (1975, p. 25; see also Neufeld 1961, p. 81).

If the deepest political corruption was in the south, it merely represented the political system in its extreme form. The modus vivendi between the local oligarchies and the central government determined the character of Italy's entire *classe dirigente*. The election of deputies in a single-member constituency tended to make "each small local group of the party into an independent entity" (Duverger 1954, p. 45); their conduct, once in office, further corrupted the political system. Leading members of the propertied class "composed virtually the whole body politic of the Italian nation" (Maier 1975, p. 24). Almost two-thirds of the members of the Chamber of Deputies were landowners or lawyers (many from landed families) "who represented wealth" (King and Okey 1909, p. 19).[9] The Liberal deputies were the "local notables, the landlords, the industrialists and business men with a taste for politics, the lawyers and the professional men, with all their dependents and hangers-on," members of the press, the intelligentsia, and officials of the Chambers of Commerce (Seton-Watson 1967, pp. 194, 246).

In terms of immediate material interest, there was a "clear symbiosis," as Cardoza puts it, between the social groups represented in the Chamber: The "well-heeled attorney...often owned sizable tracts of property in the countryside, while many sons of old landed families pursued professional or academic careers in the city" (1982, p. 37). These men were, according to some, Giolitti's *askaris*, "provincial lawyers who were well versed in local problems... politically neutral, dumb and unambitious" men whose "sole reason for being [in the Chamber of Deputies] was to give government their votes [and] seek government's patronage" for their local electors and act as intermediaries in negotiating with government departments (Seton Watson 1967, p. 247; see also Finley et al. 1986, p. 198). In the same vein, the Liberal Senator Luigi Albertini, a critic of Giolitti, argued against the "corruption of the parliamentary regime [which is becoming] deeper and deeper....What force of attraction," Albertini asked, "can public life exercise when the representative of the nation is transformed into an automaton which must go where the government wants?" (cited in Lyttelton 1987, p. 9).

The exclusive access of the propertied class to political power thus guaranteed that the Liberal government's policies were consistent with their interests. Owners of landed property as well as industrial manufacturers were almost the sole beneficiaries of official tariff and taxation policies. From the beginning of the state's unification until 1910, property taxes "fell steadily," from 125 million lire, to 106 million in 1900, to 84 million in 1910, while consumption taxes on products such as tobacco, salt, and coffee accounted for more than half of the state's total revenue (Seton Watson 1967, p. 293).[10] According to King and Okey, 54% of the tax revenue came from the "working classes," small proprietors and sharecroppers. About 10% to 20% of the average worker's wages went to pay direct or indirect taxes (1909, p. 138). In addition, protective tariffs on cereals, sugar beets, and hemp guaranteed landlords and sugar refinery owners an absolute monopoly in their home markets, which resulted in high prices for food staples (Cardoza 1982, p. 47).

The Quantitative Measures

As already noted, historically, the province was Italy's basic political and administrative unit, responsible for taxation policies, labor relations, and welfare services. A comparison between Italy's provinces (N=69) allows us to verify some of the claims about the divergent forms of social and political power held by Italy's landed class.

The political hegemony of the landlords. The political hegemony of the landowning class is measured by the electoral power of the Liberal Party.[11] The vote for the Liberal Party is calculated as a ratio of the total votes in a province. It indicates the visible strength of the propertied class and its political power in the province just before Fascism's emergence. I use these data rather than the 1919 national election results because the local elections, as discussed in detail in the following chapter, had a direct and immediate effect on the political and economic life of the province. Voting data are therefore the best available indicators of the direct power held by the propertied class over workers and peasants. This variable is collapsed into three equal categories according to the distribution of the vote among the provinces: "low," medium," and "high" (N=22 in each category). Thus, the analysis relates to the province's "structural" characteristics, that is, the dominant relations of production, and to "political" characteristics, or the rate of political participation in the 1920 elections.

Agrarian relations of production. The distinct forms of agricultural production in Italy's three geographical regions allow us to use the country's conventional division into north, center, and south as categories of social relations of production. Italy's sixty-nine provinces are divided as follows. The south, consisting of twenty-five provinces including the islands of Sicily and Sardinia, was the stronghold of *latifundismo*. Production here was carried out on great estates based on semifeudal (or seigniorial) relations between lord and peasant. The center consists of fourteen provinces in the regions of Tuscany, Umbria, and the Marches. Here production was based mainly on sharecropping, the *mezzadria* system. The north, with its thirty provinces in the regions of

Piedmont, Liguria, Lombardy, Veneto, and Emilia, was the country's most developed region and the center of industrial production. In this region, especially in the Po Valley, the predominant unit of agricultural production was the large commercial estate, employing wage labor.

Political participation. I use voter turnout as an indicator of mass political participation, the prelude to the emergence of citizenship and of political democracy (*Statistico Annuario* 1919-1921, pp. 170-72). The rate of voter turnout is calculated as the ratio of actual to eligible voters, that is, the rate of individuals who chose to vote among all those eligible to do so. The postwar elections of 1920, the first to extend universal suffrage to all males over twenty-one years of age, tested *Giolittismo*.

The right to vote, as elsewhere in Europe, one of the first signs of "the entrance of the masses onto the historical stage," indicated by the level of voter participation. Under the political circumstances of Giolitti's Italy, the rate of voter turnout also indicates the continued ability of the local rulers to manipulate elections and to prevent democratization. Therefore, a high rate of voter turnout indicates a decline in the direct power of the old local oligarchies as they could no longer control the electoral process. We should expect, then, that the level of voter turnout in the south, the epitome of *trasformismo*, to be the lowest in the country.

Agrarian Relations and Electoral Democracy

Table 3.1 shows the relationship between the regional relations of production and the rate of voter turnout in the provinces. Among the northern capitalist provinces, 57% (17 out of 30 provinces) had a high level of voter turnout. In the center, this rate declines to 29% (4 out of 14 provinces); its lowest level, 8%, is found in the south (only 2 out of 25 provinces). Correspondingly, low levels of voter turnout were most common in the south. Fifty-two percent of the southern provinces (13 out of 25 provinces) had a low level of voter turnout, whereas only 17% of the northern provinces (5 out of 30 provinces) had a similar turnout. It seems clear that the electoral reform failed to penetrate the *latifundists'* grip on the region. But in the commercial north, the new class of free wage laborers was able to exercise its recently acquired political rights.

Thus, on the national level, in accordance with Moore's thesis, the political power of the landlords did ordain antidemocratic policies. Where the coalition among a strong landed upper class, a weak manufacturing class, and the state "succeeds in establishing itself," Moore argues, there follows a "prolonged period of conservative and even authoritarian government" (1966, p. 437). In Italy, this was most apparent in the south, where the manufacturing class was all but absent and the *latifundists'* power prevented de facto implementation of universal suffrage. To understand the extent and specific form of this patrician political power, the specific nature of social domination on the local level, on which this political power rested, must be examined.

Table 3.1
Levels of Political Participation by Regional Relations of Production
in Italy's Provinces (1920), in Percentages

Region	High	Medium	Low	Total Cases
Capitalist north	57	27	17	30
Sharecropping center	29	36	36	14
Latifundist south*	8	40	52	25

*The south includes the provinces of Sardinia and Sicily.

LATIFUNDISTS AND "AGRICULTURAL INDUSTRIALISTS"

Although highly concentrated landownership was characteristic of the entire countryside, different agrarian relations of production characterized each of Italy's three geographical regions. This situation supported rendered varying degrees and forms of social domination to the landlords in the different regions.

On the eve of World War I, about 13% of Italy's population owned some land. The distribution of this class of proprietors, by holding size, is shown in Table 3.2. Altogether, 250,000 landowners, constituting about 5% of 4,931,000 "proprietors" (the total population in the 1911 census was 35,905,000), owned great estates of over 8 hectares (comprising more than two-thirds of the cultivable land). These were the largest landowners, described as "princes and barons and well-to-do townsmen." Another 342,000 proprietors (about 7%) owned parcels of 4 to 8 hectares; 450,000 (about 9%) owned 2 to 4 hectares; 614,000 (about 12%) owned 1 to 2 hectares; and 3.27 million smallholders (about 66% of all "proprietors") owned less than one hectare of cultivable land (in Neufeld 1961, p. 134 based on Leonetti; see also Schmidt 1937, p. 327; 1939, p. 6).[12]

Table 3.2
Distribution of Landownership by Size of Estate (1914)

Size of Estate	Number and Percentage of Proprietors
More than 8 hectares*	250,000
	(5%)
4 to 8 hectares	342,000
	(7%)
2 to 4 hectacres	450,000
	(9%)
1 to 2 hectares	614,000
	(12%)
Less than 1 hectare	3,275,000
	(66%)
Total number of proprietors	4,931,000

*Note: 1 hectare = 2.47 acres

The most extreme form of landlord domination, and the peasants' almost absolute economic and personal subjugation, was found in the southern *latifundia*. Here, the concentration of landownership was more extreme than in the rest of the country. Whatever land they owned was, according to a peasant saying, "not even enough to be buried in" (cited in Schmidt 1937, p. 327).

A parliamentary investigation, conducted during 1907-1910 by Giovanni Lorenzoni, described a "feudal world" in which the old aristocratic families, the owners of large estates, held a virtual land monopoly (cited in Finley et al. 1986, p. 200). A third of Sicily's total area, for example, belonged to 787 individuals. Of these, 173 individuals (many of whom were close kin) owned half of that land. Similarly, of 61,000 hectares of land in the province of Foggia, two-thirds were owned by only three families (Snowden 1986, p. 7).

The *latifundist* was an absentee landlord. According to the southern landowners' own 1904 bulletin, he was a "wealthy landowner [who] always lives far from his holdings and knows nobody except his ignorant and unreliable administrator. In fact, almost all of [our] wealthy *latifundists* do not know their properties, preferring the great cities where they enjoy their rents in idleness and pleasure" (cited in Snowden 1986, p. 14).

The laborers lived in "agro-cities," described by Snowden as "classic company towns," in dwellings built and let by the landowning families. These were, according to one landlord's description, "not suitable for use as a stable" (pp. 41, 42). The tenants were in constant debt to the landlords, who were virtually the sole lenders in the region; annual interest rates sometimes reached as high as 400%.

So great was the desolation of the southern peasants that some landlords protested against their plight: "There is no part in Italy that provides such a sad spectacle of death as ours," lamented one. "There is no other town with so many widows and orphans. Whoever works in the fields...wears himself out and cannot fail to succumb to disease, leaving behind poor unfortunate creatures with no bread and no protection" (cited in Snowden 1986, p. 57). The southern peasants were therefore subject to a "triple form of oppression": Not only landownership, but civil and military authority as well were in the same hands (Benjamin Vicuna Mackenna, referring to Chile, 1856, cited in Zeitlin 1984, p. 36, n. 34).

Two factors contributed to the *latifundists'* undisputed power in the south: the absence of central state intervention and the absence of the Socialist Party. In other words, a critical element in that control rested in the south's relative isolation from national politics. This isolation, the legacy of the struggle for unification, was crucial in maintaining the system of *trasformismo*. The absence of a central state presence guaranteed that the *latifundists* remained the sole political rulers of the region, much as they had been before unification. They ruled through the *gabolletos*, the estate managers. In turn, the *gabolletos* were answerable to the *notabili*, the local bosses, whom Liberal parliamentary representatives placed in charge in return for electoral support. The *gabolletos*, not the state police, were responsible for "public order" as they held direct and total authority over the peasants.

The second contributing factor to the south's political isolation was the absence of any peasant organizations and of the Socialist Party. Dispersed across the great estates, southern peasants had no collective organization: They lived as isolated families and never recognized their common plight as "a collective wrong" (Snowden 1972, p. 289). Yet, despite this "atomism," peasant rebellions and land invasions were endemic to the south. These, however, remained sporadic events, limited in both objectives and duration, regularly and violently repressed by the landlords' armies, assisted by central state police forces (Snowden 1972, p. 289; see also Paige 1975, p. 42).

The Socialist Movement was virtually nonexistent in the south. Its political strategy consciously and deliberately neglected the region and no efforts at organization or agitation were made (Snowden 1972, p. 290). The historian and Socialist leader Gaetano Salvemini criticized this neglect of the south as expressive of the PSI's acceptance and legitimation of Giolitti's *malavita*, the underworld's rule in the south. In 1908, Salvemini charged that "[e]ven in the Socialist party there are two Italys," and demanded that the PSI become responsible "not only for that part of the proletariat which is most developed and powerful, but also for the more backward part that which is most in need for our help" (cited in Salomone 1945, p. 56; see also Seton Watson 1967, pp. 270-71).[13] But the Socialists refused to endorse the southern peasants' strikes even when they were attacked by government troops. They denied that the strikers constituted a "real" proletariat, and further chastised the leagues for their illegal methods, their "hotheadedness," their "primitive impulsiveness," and for embarking on a "naive recourse" (*Avanti!*, September 28, 1907, cited in Snowden 1986, p. 94).[14] The end result was, in Finley's words, that the "scope for corruption was limitless" (1986, p. 183). Provincial government was nothing more than a "family affair of the propertied classes...[since] a few hundred notables and their clients were the grand electors" (Snowden 1986, p. 51).[15]

In contrast to the south, the *mezzadria* system, dominant in Italy's central region since the late Middle Ages, entailed the classic form of sharecropping (Jonsson 1992, p. 191). The powers vested in landownership under the *mezzadria* allowed the landlord direct control not only over their tenants' labor, but also over their private lives (Snowden 1989, p. 9). The unit of production was the small manor, the *podere*, carved from the landlord's estate, which constituted a relatively autonomous unit of administration and production. The *mezzadri*, the tenants living under this system, constituted well over half the population of Tuscany. Among a total agrarian population of 924,946 in that region, 540,458 (about 58%) were sharecroppers (Serpieri 1930, p. 361).

Unlike the *latifundists'* raw power and coercion, underlying the *mezzadria's* mode of production was an ideology that depicted the relationship between lord and peasant as one between "equal partners." This was manifested in the equal division between landlord and tenant of the investment in production and its product (Gill 1983, p. 166, n. 2). Behind this "official" view, however, lay the harsh reality of peasant subjugation: The *mezzadro* was not an independent, let alone equal partner of the landlord for he had no independent legal standing. Rather, he was bound to the landlord by debt and labored in virtual servitude. In addition to his 50% share in the cost of production, the *mezzadro* had to pay for tools, seeds, and machinery, which he had to buy or rent from the landlord, who owned all means of production. The *mezzadro*'s debt to the landlord passed from one generation to another, thus creating an immutable system of debt peonage.[16] In addition, tenants were obligated to provide the landlord with a certain amount of unpaid labor services annually, to transport the landlord's share of the harvest to market, to provide him with household services (e.g., wood gathering and laundering), as well as to give the landlord gifts of food on religious holidays (Snowden 1989, pp. 8-14; Cardoza 1982, p. 19).

Privileged by both economic power and by custom, the *mezzadria* landlord, in contrast with the absentee *latifundist*, was viewed as a paternal figure. This was true even on farms that were integrated into a relatively large and centralized estate that employed the *fattoria* system for "coordination of production and marketing" (Jonsson 1992, p. 207). The landlord was directly involved in and responsible for his *mezzadro*'s welfare, in addition to holding authority over his life. This regulation and control was exercised either by the landlord individually or through his *fattore*, the estate manager. The *fattore*, endowed by the landlord with the duties and power of policeman and judge, was, in practice, the highest immediate authority on the estate. The landlord— or the *fattore*—oversaw the *mezzadro*'s dress, leisure, and religious observances; the *mezzadro* could not marry or attend cafes or gaming rooms without consent, and the landlord often made him work at jobs off the estate. The sanction imposed for noncompliance was eviction (Snowden 1989, pp. 9-10).

While the concentration of landownership in the north was not as extreme as in the south, it was still relatively high. In the province of Bologna, for example, less than three hundred families owned most of the province's private property (Cardoza 1982, pp. 23-24); in Ferrara, sixty landlords controlled more than half of the province's cultivable land while employing about half of the province's landless population. The large northern estates specialized in commercial crops like sugar beets and hemp, and employed primarily wage labor, mostly migrant day laborers (Cardoza 1979, p. 172). From the last quarter of the nineteenth century on, the north also became the home of a new rural landless proletariat, "free" of traditional bonds, and of the new industrial proletariat. Manufacturing and commercial interests (e.g., chemical and machine concerns), centered in the north, were "inextricably linked" with a "burgeoning agriculture" of sugar refineries and hemp processing plants (Cardoza 1979, p. 175). The first manufacturing associations were formed between 1898 and 1902 in Genoa, Milan, and Monza by the machine and ship manufacturers (Cardoza 1979, p. 192). Like the landowners' associations, these were formed in direct reaction to labor militancy on the local level.

The most extreme effect of the commercialized agriculture was felt in the organization of wage laborers and of landowners. The northern wage laborers, both industrial and agrarian, were those whom the Socialist and trade union leaders sought to organize in the late nineteenth century. As early as the 1880s, long before the introduction of universal male suffrage and the emergence of the Socialist Party as a significant political force, the Po Valley was the site of a raw class struggle between wage workers and landlords; this was the site where one of the first organizations representing the rural proletariat in Europe was established. The Socialists gained considerable power in several northern provinces, the most notorious of which, "Red Bologna," ruled by a Socialist government since 1902, successfully undermined the landlords' traditional hold.

Italy's rural proletariat consisted overwhelmingly of *braccianti* ("arms"), as well as a small fraction of *salariati*. The *braccianti* were usually migrant day laborers, employed on a seasonal basis. The *salariati* were fixed-wage laborers, on yearly contracts, who received housing on the estate in exchange for their labor services as well as wages equally divided between cash and produce (Cardoza 1982, p. 24). In 1921, of the 5,180,329 total northern agrarian population, 135,134 (2.6%) were *salariati*, 738,678 (about 14%) were sharecroppers, and 1,616,157 (about 31%) were *braccianti*. The rest were leaseholders and property owners (Serpieri 1930, p. 361).

Unlike the *salariati*, the *braccianti*, concentrated in isolated "agro-towns," had no direct contact with the landlords. The parliamentary investigation mentioned previously described these agro-towns as crowded with workers stricken with pellagra and malaria. The workers bore a "subversive antagonism" toward their employers, whom they viewed as a "ferocious and gloomy enemy that speculated in misery and brutishness" (cited in Cardoza 1982, p. 27). Intensified migration from the south led to further deterioration as competition for scarce jobs intensified. The average day laborer could find work for only about one hundred days a year; the result was an army of chronically unemployed former soldiers (Corner 1975, pp. 3-4; Seton Watson 1967, p. 23).

Two mechanisms employed by the Socialist leagues amounted to almost complete control over the labor supply in the provinces. The most notable was the *imponibile della mano d'opera*. Based on strict discipline and universal adherence to a collective labor contract, the *imponibile* required landowners to employ a minimum number of laborers per hectare. This number was fixed in a collective labor contract between the employers and the union, according to rules "as meticulous and as closely enforced as those of a medieval guild" (Tasca [1938] 1966, p. 92).

From the employers' point of view this meant, of course, that the unions prevented them from determining wages either through negotiation or sheer manipulation of scarce jobs; they, too, were subject to severe penalties for breach of the collective contract (Snowden 1972, p. 274; 1989, p.76). Another method of control over the labor supply was the *collocamento di classe*. This was a system of centralized assignment of workers designed to guarantee an equal distribution of labor among the workers. By eliminating the competition for labor among the workers, the *collocamento*, managed and controlled by the unions, indirectly affected the employers' ability to bargain down wages (Snowden 1989, p. 49). These two mechanisms, together with strict boycotts and fines for noncompliance, practically controlled the province's labor market.

Mechanization of agriculture and production, mainly in the Po Valley, also led to the emergence of a new breed of landowners, a landed bourgeoisie. As the most important agricultural center in the country, although the Po Valley accounted for only 13% of the farmland in Italy, it produced about a third of the nation's agricultural product in 1910 (Cardoza 1979, p. 176). The commercial landlords in the region constituted a distinct segment of Italy's landowning class. Usually large leaseholders from urban centers where they were involved in industry and commerce, encouraged by government subsidies they had channeled their investments to land reclamation projects (Sereni 1968, p. 264). Being "in the business of maximizing profits by increasing production, lowering costs, and selling their crops in the most lucrative markets," the "agricultural industrialists," as Cardoza terms them, adopted new capitalist methods of production and used wage labor almost exclusively (1982, p. 49).[17]

The commercial landlords' dependence on wage labor free of traditional tenure relations rendered them particularly vulnerable to the agitation initiated by the emerging workers unions (see Cardoza 1982, pp. 54-56). Noted for combining the "pitiless greed of the modern entrepreneur...and that ancestral reactionary instinct of the landed proprietor" (Roveri, cited in Corner 1975, p. 8), this new type of landlord began to organize against the workers at the turn of the century (Preti 1955, p. 219).

The first and most militant agrarian association in the country was established in Emilia, one of the country's main agricultural regions, which covers the provinces of Ferrara, Bologna, Mantua, and Modena. In 1907, the *agrari* of Emilia extended their organization outside the region and established the first Interprovincial Landlords Federation, which soon became "the most potent class organization in the Po Valley and in all of Italy" (Preti 1955, p. 220). In the same year, Bologna's *agrari* also organized their own "defense squads." These were mobile units of "permanent strikebreakers" that were sent across provincial boundaries to guard the fields against striking workers. Similar organized landlord action took place in Parma against the Syndicalist union (Bertrand 1970, pp. 40, 42).

The growing open class struggle in the north provides the perhaps most explicit and violent manifestation of the central state's alliance with the propertied class. Refusing to recognize the legitimacy of the workers leagues, the *agrari* of Bologna, for example, demanded, and received, active collaboration from central state authorities—the police, the Army, and the prefects—that then violently suppressed the workers organizations. In 1898, the prefect of Bologna dispatched troops against workers, closed their labor organization, and arrested strikers. The Minister of the Interior went so far as to design a detailed plan to send forth "companies of soldier-harvesters," whose aim, in his words, it was "to increase the supply of labor and render strikes more difficult" in the conflict-ridden north (Cardoza 1982, p. 60; see also Neufeld 1961, p. 341).

Clearly, then, the political power of the Liberal Party rested on a diverse set of regional property relations. In the south, no parallel to the *mezzadria*'s ideology of "partnership" existed; nor was there any attempt to depict class relations as other than what they were: absolute landlord power resting on land ownership and the direct use of coercion (Snowden 1972, p. 288). At the same time, the north was the site of new capitalist class relations, characterized by the proliferation of class organizations and a fierce class struggle. We should therefore expect to find a relationship between these specific social and political realities and forms of social domination and the level of political hegemony held by the propertied class in each of the country's three regions.

Table 3.3 does show a fair though inconsistent relationship between the specific regional relations of production and the vote for the Liberal Party. In the south, 59% of the provinces (13 provinces out of 22) had a "high" vote for the Liberals, but only 9% (2 provinces) had a "low" Liberal vote. This relationship is reversed in the north. There, the Liberals received a "high" vote only in 23% (7 provinces out of 30) of the provinces, but a "low" vote in 50% of the provinces (15 provinces).

The political hegemony of the propertied class, indicated by the level of voter turnout and the vote for the Liberal Party, thus appears to be strongly related to the form of social domination maintained. Where the majority of employees were wage laborers, the commercial landlords came under pressure from an insurgent though organized workers movement, which eventually caused a decline in their political power in those provinces. In the center, the regions of *mezzadria*, the relationship, as should be expected, was mixed. While tenants were subject to the authority of the landlords, they were not as strongly organized as the wage workers of the north and did not pose a similar threat to the landlords' political power. In the *latifundist* south the landlords maintained their local political power. Throughout the political transformations of the early twentieth century and even during the post World War I social and political crisis (1919-1922), the south remained a stronghold of the Liberal Party.

Table 3.3
Liberal Party Vote (1920) by Regional Relations
of Production in Italy's Provinces, in Percentages

| | | Liberal Party Vote | | |
Region	High	Medium	Low	N
Capitalist north	23	27	50	30
Sharecropping center	14	50	36	14
Latifundist south*	59	32	9	22

* The south includes the provinces of Sardinia and Sicily.

So, the role of the central state in the determination of the Fascists' emergence was defined by and limited to its position in the class struggle between the landlords and workers. The landlords' alliance with the state, as will be argued below, became a crucial determinant in the rise of Fascism, in accordance with Moore's thesis.

But this determination materialized, historically, in various forms on the provincial level. It stemmed from the specific political mechanisms provided by this alliance in each region and, most importantly, the particular use made of these mechanisms by the northern landowning class in their struggles against the organized wageworkers. The Fascists' political struggle involved, to a large extent, the continued militancy of the local landlord organizations, which were struggling to avoid having their power snatched by the workers movement. Where the landlords' local political power was secure, as in the south, Fascism acquired no foothold. Here, there was no wage labor, no workers organizations, no need for state intervention on behalf of the *latifundists*, and no collaboration between the *latifundists* and the Fascists.

"It is always the direct relationship of the owners of the conditions of production to the direct producers...which reveals the innermost secret, the hidden basis of the entire social structure, and with it the political form of the relation of sovereignty and dependence, in short, the corresponding specific form of state" (Marx 1967 [1894], p. 791).

In Italy, this "innermost secret" rested not only in the national class-state alliance, but in the interaction between distinct forms of local relations of production dominated by distinct segments of the landowning class, on the one hand, and the dominance of property in the national state on the other. The structural weakness of the central state, namely, *trasformismo*'s reliance on local governments and electoral corruption, spelled relative political autonomy for the landlords' political organizations. This made the landlords potentially powerful allies of the Fascists and, thus, a crucial (though not sufficient) determinant in Fascism's emergence and, most importantly, actual ascendance to power.

However, these developments, it must be emphasized, were not immanent in the commercialization of agriculture. Rather, they were determined by the uniqueness of Italy's Liberal state, itself the product of the intraclass struggles of *risorgimento*. One of the state's essential characteristics was the degree to which it maintained and reinforced those preunification forms of social domination practiced by the landowning class in the provinces. This alliance between the landlords and the state was prominent in the northern and southern regions of the country. It was most evident in the south where, to repeat, it spelled the almost complete political autonomy of the *latifundists,* and where Fascism failed to emerge. On the other hand, by 1920, in the north, just before the beginning of the Fascists' "punitive expeditions," the landowning class had lost most of its electoral power to the Socialists.

The specific intraclass struggles waged during the nineteenth century within Italy's landowning class, that is, between commercial landowners and manufacturing interests on one hand and *latifundists* on the other, had a direct effect on the character (and perhaps also on the results) of later interclass struggles between landowners and organized workers. The political power placed at the disposal of the emerging Fascist organization by the northern landlords was therefore the product of the prior relationship established between the landlords and the Liberal state. This is perhaps the paradox of Italy's political trajectory from its independence until the Fascist era: The political power the landowners acquired from the Liberal state determined not only their forms of organization, but also endowed them with the political capacity to eventually destroy, or at least transform (in their alliance with the Fascists) the very state they had created and helped establish the new "Fascist state."

This analysis raises serious questions regarding the role of the Socialists in the process leading to the emergence of Fascism. The relationship between the landlords and the state examined here explains the *potential* for the rise of Fascism, but not its actual emergence. To pursue an adequate and full analysis of this issue, we must inquire into the specific and independent effects of the workers movement on the political power of the landlords. We must ask, first, whether working-class organizations attempted to affect the landlord-state alliance, and if they did, what were the odds of their success? What was the Socialists' social base of support, and what kind of policies were adopted by the Socialist Party in the provinces under its political control? What was the tactical significance of its revolutionary program? Which classes or segments thereof did the Party seek to represent, and why did this search entail the Party's neglect of the south? The answers to these empirical questions can shed light on the larger issue of the determinants of the Fascists' emergence and seizure of power. The following chapter analyzes Italy's Socialist movement and its specific political strategy from the early days of unification until the advent of Fascism.

NOTES

1. *Agrario* literally means "landowner." The term is used exclusively to refer to owners of large estates, having more than 200 hectares (see Corner 1975, p. 8, n. 2).

2. The Italian industrialists, unlike the landlords, were late to organize and employ concerted efforts to influence the government's policy. See Sarti 1971 and Melograni 1972 on the history of the General Confederation of Italian Industrialists (*Confederazione Genrale dell Industria Italiana*, CGII) Italy's industrialists' association. The special relationship between the industrialists and the Fascists is discussed in chapter 5.

3. According to Antonio Gramsci, Italy's unification was achieved through a "passive revolution": the establishment of a bourgeois state without the participation of the bourgeoisie. This concept is similar to Moore's "revolution from above" as well as to Lenin's designation of the "Prussian road." See Buci-Glucksmann 1980, pp. 54-63, for a discussion of Gramsci's and Lenin's concepts.

4. The 1911 electoral reform removed all property qualifications on suffrage, almost doubling the size of the electorate, from 3.3 million voters (9.4% of the

population) before the reform to 8.6 million (about 24% of the population) after the reform, of which 3 million were illiterate (see Seton Watson 1967, p. 282).

5. Some coalition partners, e.g., Radicals and Republicans, often opposed the leading Liberals on issues such as the monarchy's authority over the government.

6. The Italian Parliament was one of the few in Europe that did not pay its members, thus further restricting the pool of possible candidates.

7. It is interesting that even among this small group of electors, only a few hundred individuals exercised their political privilege. Until 1882, a third of the electorate "habitually abstained" from voting (Seton Watson 1967, pp. 50-51).

8. Giolitti was premier and Minister of the Interior four times before World War I (1892-93; 1903-1905; 1906-1909; 1911-1914) and again, after the war, in which he opposed Italy's participation (1920-21) (Seton Watson 1967, pp. 728-30). The period 1901-1914 is often referred to as "the Age of *Giolittismo*."

9. Italy's Senate was, formally, the upper house of Parliament; its members were appointed by the king. The Senate had little political influence and is described as a "conservative forum of the high nobility and propertied gentry" (Schmidt 1939, p. 60; see also Seton Watson 1967, p. 263).

10. In addition to the landed proprietors, Italy's industrialists—especially owners of the "three pillars of Italian protectionism," textiles, grain, and cotton—enjoyed direct government grants and subsidies (Gerschenkron 1962, pp. 79-80). For instance, the steel works at Terni was established with the government's financial aid, and both the shipbuilding and navigation industries were heavily subsidized (at 53 million lire) (Mack Smith 1959, p. 156; see also Schmidt 1939, p. 12).

11. In eleven cases the voting results of the 1919 and 1920 elections were published according to electoral colleges rather than their constituent individual provinces. A college usually comprised two or three neighboring provinces. I separated each college into its constituent provinces, and then assigned each province its college's value divided by the size of the population in that province. The provinces of Trento, Trieste and Caserta are not included because of missing data. All the electoral data are based on the results of the 1920 local elections as provided by Giusti (1922, pp. 109-10). An analysis of the 1919 national election results yields similar findings.

12. The Italian government did not systematically collect landownership data until 1929. A similar estimate based on calculations of the value of properties according to the taxes paid by their owners, is also found in Sereni [1946] 1975.

13. This view was rejected by another reformist leader, Filippo Turati. It was inconceivable, Turati maintained, that the pace of progress be dictated by the backward elements of the proletariat. The Socialist Party's commitment lay with the "progressive" elements, the skilled and semiskilled industrial workers of the north.

14. The policies of the PSI and its political strategy are discussed in detail in the following chapter. See Brustein 1991 for a comparative study of the effect of the Socialists' political power, the "red scare," on Italy's peasants, and their support of Fascism.

15. This situation remained unchanged even during the first years of Mussolini's rule. It was not until Mussolini established his dictatorship in January 1925, more than two years after the Fascist organization seized political power, that the central state extended its control to the country's southern regions.

16. In one Tuscan estate, for example, Snowden records seven tenant families who, in 1911, were in total debt of 20,654 lire to the landlord, based on a debt of 1,422 *lire* in 1895 (1989, p. 24).

17. This new approach was not well received by the old patrician families. Marchese Tanari, an aristocratic landowner of Bologna, decried this "new breed of farmers [as] characterized by a greedy industrial spirit which they are injecting into the management of the farms," and whose "principal infatuations are experimental adventures, rents and profits" (quoted in Cardoza 1982, p. 49).

Chapter 4

The Rise of the Labor Movement

In the aftermath of World War I, the secure political dominance of Italy's propertied class was challenged by an unprecedented social upheaval and the political ascendance of a militant socialist workers movement. The Socialist Party adopted a new radical program in 1919, calling for the collectivization of the land, and industrial workers' participation in factory management, a veritable "second Bolshevik revolution" in Italy.

The PSI's success in the postwar elections seemed to confirm its "revolutionary" threat. The Party had an enrollment of 200,000 members and the daily circulation of its official organ, *Avanti!*, was over 300,000 (Hughes 1967, p. 120). In the national elections of November 1919, the PSI received a third of the total votes cast and won 156 (out of 508) seats in Parliament, with 1,840,000 votes, a third of the total cast (Tasca [1938] 1966, p. 52). However, the Party's revolutionary commitment dictated its rejection of any collaboration with the "bourgeois" Liberal state. Thus, although in 1919 it was Italy's largest opposition party, the PSI refused to participate in the postwar government and deliberately abstained from national state power.

At the same time, the Party sought and gained electoral power in the provincial governments. In the local elections held in 1920, a year after the national elections, the PSI won electoral majorities in twenty-five of the country's sixty-nine provincial councils, the majority of its greatest victories being in those northern regions where commercial agriculture prevailed. The specific policies adopted by the Socialist provincial governments, together with the practices of the local unions, threatened the existing property relations, particularly the interests of the landowners in the northern and central regions. Socialist governments reinforced the effective economic power of the unions and established local quasi-autonomous regimes that came to be known as the "Red Baronies" (Seton Watson 1967, p. 524).

THE POSTWAR CRISIS AND THE RISE OF THE SOCIALIST PARTY

In the wake of World War I, Italy experienced a severe economic and political crisis. The cost of living almost quadrupled between 1913 and 1919, and doubled again between 1919 and 1920—from a base of 100 in 1913 to 365.8 in 1919 and 624.4 in 1920 (Snowden 1972, p. 270, n. 8). Prices of staple foods almost doubled between 1920 and 1921: Bread went from 0.83 to 1.41 lire; pasta from 1.24 to 2.14; and meat from 9.16 to 12.96 (Farneti 1978, p. 20). The number of unemployed rose from 102,156 at the end of 1920 to 512,260 by the end of 1921 (*Annuario Statistico 1919-1921*, p. 400). This situation also spurred the growth in affiliation with various labor-oriented organizations. By 1920, in addition to the over 2.2 million workers affiliated with the Socialist union movement, the General Confederation of Labor (*Confederazione generale del lavoro*, CGL), more than 500,000 of Italy's organized labor force were members of the Catholic Confederation of Workers (*Confederazione Italiana dei lavoratori*, CIL) (Neufeld 1961, pp. 368-69).

As elsewhere in post World War I Europe, food and coal shortages led to a wave of riots and strikes. The food riots, like other labor demonstrations throughout Italy's history, started in the northern region of Emilia in mid-1919 and soon spread to all parts of the country. "All Italy," as Tasca puts it, "was out in the streets....Indignant crowds would pour into the shops, insisting on price reductions and sometimes looting merchandise." Metallurgical and agricultural laborers, printers, textile workers, teachers, and sailors went on strike demanding wage increases. There were also so-called political strikes, as in July 1919, three months before the first postwar general elections, when the PSI organized a nationwide solidarity strike with the Russian and Hungarian Soviet Republics ([1938] 1966, pp. 18-19; see also Sirianni 1980, pp. 53-54).

Table 4.1
Number of Strikes and Striking Workers
in Post World War I Italy (1918-1920)

Year	Strikes and Strikers	Industry*	Agriculture	Total
1918	Number of strikes	303	10	313
	Number of strikers	158,036	675	158,711
1919	Number of strikes	1,663	208	1,871
	Number of Strikers	1,049,438	505,128	1,554,566
1920	Number of strikes	1,881	189	2,070
	Number of strikers	1,267,953	1,045,732	2,313,685

* "Industry," as defined by the government's statistics, includes manufacturing of goods and services, hunting and fishing.

Source: *Annuario Statistico Italiano, Anni 1919-1921*, pp. 395, 398.

The years 1919-20 were indeed the *biennio rosso*, the "Red Biennium." The CGL and the PSI organized sit-down strikes in factories throughout the country and large-scale agricultural strikes by wage laborers on the northern estates (Seton Watson 1967, p. 521). From 1918 on, as Table 4.1 shows, both the number of strikes and the number of workers striking, in industry and in agriculture, increased geometrically. In the industrial sector alone, the number of industrial strikes rose from 303 strikes involving about 150,000 workers in 1918, to 1,663 strikes involving over a million workers in 1919, to 1,881 strikes involving over 1.25 million workers in 1920. The increase in strikes in the agricultural sector was even more dramatic. Here, the number of strikes rose from 10 involving only 675 workers in 1918, to 208 strikes involving more than half a million workers in 1919, and to 189 strikes involving over a million workers in 1920 (*Annuario Statistico Italiano, Anni 1919-1921*, pp. 395, 398). The record of workers' victories was impressive: Sixty-four percent of the strikes in 1919 and 54% in 1920 resulted, according to government's statistics, in "complete or substantial" concession to the workers' demands (*Annuario Statistico Italiano, Anni 1919-1921*, p. 397).

This postwar unrest swept across the whole country. In the south, peasants organized land invasions and demanded redistribution of the land. They invaded and marked small plots of uncultivated land, and began to work them to "establish ownership." Some of the land seizures were eventually authorized by the government and distributed to newly organized peasant cooperatives (Seton Watson 1967, p. 521). But the main arena of confrontation was in the country's northern and central regions, which were the traditional strongholds of the prewar socialist movement and where the concentration of wage workers, both industrial and agricultural, was highest. In these regions the presence of the Socialist Party and the CGL was entrenched for over a generation (Seton Watson 1967, p. 298).

THE SOCIAL BASES OF THE SOCIALIST PARTY

Socialist's Mass Base of Support

The ratio of the wage workers in a province's population, both industrial and agricultural, can be used as an indicator of a potential Socialist mass base of support. This variable also indicates the structural potential for worker organization and struggle. I use this ratio as an indicator of the actual levels of unionization and strikes. The data on the social composition of the province are obtained from the Italian 1921 census (*Censimento* 1927).

(1) *Industrial workers*: This measure, provided by the census, is the number of industrial wage workers per 1,000 heads of household. The ratio is collapsed into three equal groups according to the distribution of the ratio among the provinces: low (N= 23); medium (N= 24); and high (N= 24).[1]

(2) *Agricultural workers:* Unlike the data on industrial workers, the measure provided by the census is misleading and some adjustments are required. The

census relates to "agrarian workers" as a relatively homogeneous group. This ignores the profound distinctions between the regional relations of production and the consequent differences in the social realities of agrarian wage workers in the country's three regions (see chapter 3). This variety in agrarian labor relations must be taken into account.

To more accurately measure the relative number of agrarian wage workers in Italy's provinces, we must draw two distinctions: first, between agrarian (N=41) and industrial provinces (N=25); second, among the agrarian provinces, between the north and the south. The census provides four major categories of agricultural employment: sharecroppers (*mezzadri*), leaseholders (*affituari*), farmers, and wage workers. I define a province as an "agrarian" province where the total ratio of these categories, that is, the proportion of total population employed in agriculture, exceeds 50%.

The second distinction among agrarian provinces is between the northern and southern regions of the country. In the agrarian provinces of the north, where capitalist relations of production prevailed, the relationship between agricultural wage workers and landlords is similar to that between industrial workers and industrialists. Here, agrarian wage workers constituted a "rural proletariat." In the south, on the other hand, the heart of the *latifundia* system, agricultural workers were not "proletarians." They were usually sharecroppers or leaseholders of tiny plots of land, and were hired sporadically by the *latifundists* as wage workers on a seasonal basis. Here, too, the ratio of agricultural workers to total population is collapsed into three groups, according to the distribution among the provinces: "low" (N=23); "medium" (N=24) and "high" (N=24).

Two major strikes, both in the north, exemplify the militancy of the Socialist workers movement and its direct threat to the region's employers. The largest and longest agricultural strike lasted from February until July 1920. The focus of the strike was in the province of Bologna, but it soon spread throughout the Po Valley. Sharecroppers and agricultural wage workers, organized by the *Federterra*, the Socialist Union of Agricultural Workers, demanded renegotiation of the contracts signed before the war. But the *Federterra* refused to recognize the authority of the new organization of the Bolognese landlords, the Agrarian Association, to sign new contracts, and claimed that "the workers have the right to impose their conditions of work on the employers" (Seton Watson 1967, p. 566). The employers resisted and the strike continued throughout the summer. The damage caused to the crops was so great that the government intervened to requisition the unharvested crops.

The new contracts, finally signed in October 1920 after the six-month-long strike, won the workers several important victories. These included an increase in the sharecroppers' share of the produce (from 50% to 60%); recognition of the Socialist-controlled employment offices; and, most important, recognition of these offices' authority to regulate the local labor market (Maier 1975, pp. 311-12; Cardoza 1982, pp. 287-88). By this time, however, the "devastation of the countryside was too great: [the] exasperating struggle left behind human victims, ruined crops and deep rancor" (Salvatorelli and Mira 1964, p. 168). In response to the strike, the landowners formed their first national organization, the General Confederation of Agriculture, which was to become a major protagonist in the landlords' alliance with the Fascist Squads and their struggle against the Socialists in the subsequent two years.

In September 1920, during the great agricultural strike and only two months before the local elections, the industrial workers in Turin began what came to be known as the "Occupation of the Factories Movement." This strike began with the workers' occupation of the automobile factories in Turin, and was led by the Federation of Metallurgical Workers (*Federazione Italiana operai metallurgici,* FIOM), one of the most militant unions in the country (Tasca [1938] 1966, pp. 76-78; Spriano 1964; Seton Watson 1967, pp. 562-65).[2] Initially, the occupation in Turin was a local reaction to the labor lockout initiated by the industrialists, who refused to negotiate wage demands with the workers. But the strike spread from Turin throughout the "industrial triangle" that included Milan and Genoa, and then to the rest of the country. At its height, the occupation movement involved half a million workers, most of whom (some 80%) were metal workers; the rest were engaged in the chemical, rubber, and shipbuilding industries.

The uniqueness of the occupation movement, seen as the climax of postwar labor militancy, rests in its explicitly political character. With "Red Guards" posted at the factories' gates, under red flags, workers established "factory councils" to perform managerial functions and continue production, and demanded worker representation in management. Antonio Gramsci founded the weekly *L'Ordine Nuovo* ("The New Order") as a vehicle for propagating this role of the trade unions in their struggle for the transformation of labor relations. This meant workers' control over discipline, piece rates, in short, "all power to the workshop committees" (Sirianni 1980, pp. 55-56).

But it was precisely this political character that caused a dramatic, perhaps fateful friction within the Socialist movement. The PSI and CGL leaders could not agree on whether the occupation of the factories should be declared a "political" or an "economic" strike. This seemingly formal issue was of major strategic significance. Declaring the occupation a "political strike," as the Party's leaders demanded, would place control over the strike within the jurisdiction of the PSI. This would mean the official transformation of the strike into a phase of the Party's revolutionary struggle. "Economic" strikes, on the other hand, were within the jurisdiction of the CGL, which was led by a moderate leadership. The CGL leaders opposed the acceleration of the conflict, and even threatened resignation if the strike was declared "political." While the debate over the designation of the strike was taking place, CGL leaders entered into secret negotiations with the employers. The occupation was finally declared an "industrial dispute" (Snowden 1989, p. 145).

Clearly, the deliberations regarding the revolutionary potential of the occupation are evidence of the organizers' ambivalence: "Revolutions are not made by first summoning an assembly in order to discuss whether one should or should not make a revolution," as one worker representative put it (cited in Seton Watson 1967, p. 565, n. 2). After three weeks of occupation, Prime Minister Giolitti intervened and negotiations between the unions and the employers were resumed. The CGL ordered the workers to evacuate the factories and the strikers returned to work (Tasca [1938] 1966, pp. 76-78; Seton Watson 1967, pp. 562-65). The dispute revealed a deep schism within the Socialist workers movement between the PSI's "maximalist" revolutionary cadre, and the CGL's moderate "reformist" leadership.

The PSI's radicalization began long before World War I. The most definitive victory of *massimalismo* came after the Libyan war in 1911. *Massimalismo*, together with anarchism, emerged in the period 1896-1911 in opposition to the reformists' dominance and their alliance with Giolitti. The Libyan war, initiated by Giolitti in an attempt to restore the state's prestige, induced higher rates of unemployment and raised the cost of living. The maximalists organized "food riots, barricades and violent insurrection" (Lyttelton 1977, pp. 64-65). A year later, in 1912, at its congress in Reggio Emilia, the Party expelled several reformist leaders, among them Leonida Bissolati and Ivanoe Bonomi, the PSI's founding fathers.[3] This congress marked the end of the two-year period (1908-1910) known as the "golden age of reformism" (Seton Watson 1967, pp. 366-68). The PSI endorsed a new "maximalist" program, denouncing any form of class collaboration that included parliamentary support of the government, class struggle, "absolute intransigence, and isolation at elections" were the Party's new official aims (Seton Watson 1967, p. 386).

This historical turn against the old cadre was led by a group of young radicals, most notably Costantino Lazzari, who was elected as the PSI's new secretary, as well as Angelica Balabanoff and Benito Mussolini, who were both elected to the directorate and the editorship of the Party's organ *Avanti!* (Young 1949, pp. 67-68). Lazzari was one of the most important figures in the Italian workers movement. As early as 1884, he founded the *Lega del figli del lavoro* ("League of the Sons of Labor"), which later became the *Partito operario Italiano*, and organized the *Camera del lavoro* (Chamber of Labor), activities that led to repeated arrests in the last decade of the nineteenth century. As a leading figure in the PSI's intransigent revolutionary faction, he vehemently opposed the reformists and advocated an alliance with the radical Syndicalists led by Arturo Labriola. (After the close of World War I, Lazzari demanded that Mussolini be expelled from the Party on account of his support of Italy's intervention in the war [Hembree 1982, pp. 300-301]). Angelica Balabanoff, a Russian émigré, was a member of the Party's intransigent faction and served as Mussolini's assistant during his editorship of *Avanti!* While in exile in Switzerland, Balabanoff acted as the principal contact between the Italian movement and the so-called Zimmerwald movement, and was instrumental in formulating the Italian Socialist Party's anti-war position.

The Zimmerwald movement was, according to Tasca, one of the most radical expressions of the antiwar socialist movement ([1938] 1966, p. 12, n. 1). Its first International Conference met on September 5, 1915, at Zimmerwald; thirty-eight delegates from eleven European countries attended. The Conference adopted a manifesto, *To the European Proletariat*, which, at the insistence of Lenin and the Left Social Democrats, included several basic propositions of revolutionary Marxism. It also adopted a joint declaration by the German and French delegations, a message of sympathy for war victims and fighters persecuted for their political activities, and elected the International Socialist Committee. The second International Conference was held at Kienthal, near Bern, April 24-30, 1916. It was attended by forty-three delegates from ten countries who adopted a manifesto *To the Peoples Suffering Ruination and Death*, and a resolution criticizing pacifism and the International Socialist Bureau. Lenin regarded the conference decisions as a further step in uniting the internationalist forces against the imperialist war. Both the Zimmerwald and Kienthal conferences helped unite leftist elements in the West European social democratic movement over Marxism-Leninism principles. Subsequently, these elements took an active part in founding communist parties in their countries and in organizing the Third Communist International (Lenin [1916] 1917).[4]

The PSI was the only socialist party active in a major European country to openly call for the proletariat to resist the draft: It threatened the government with insurrection if mobilization was ordered. The PSI condemned the war as imperialistic, "desired [solely] by the rich," which would necessarily lead to the reinforcement of the monarchy, capitalism, and militarism. Nevertheless, during the war, the PSI officially adopted Lazzari's demand to "neither support nor sabotage" the war effort (Seton Watson 1967, p. 436).

In spite of its radical position, the PSI was among the major proponents of the electoral reform enacted by the Liberal government in July 1919 (see chapter 3). The reform increased the electorate from 8.6 million (1913) to over 11.2 million (1919/20) (Seton Watson 1967, p. 547, n. 4). For the first time in Italy's history, a system of proportional representation in which newly defined constituencies could elect a party list of candidates was established (Maier 1975, p. 123).

The postwar call for universal suffrage and a constituent assembly, a cry that demanded revision of the system of governance and increased representation of the masses, was shared by divergent political organizations and parties that also included the new Catholic Party, the PPI (*Partito Popolare Italiano*), Syndicalists, and Fascists (Tasca [1938] 1966, pp. 14-15).[5] "Everyone who lived through the feverish months when the joy of peace was mixed with profound dissatisfaction with social and political conditions," writes the Socialist leader Pietro Nenni, "when all differences were merged into an almost mystical exaltation of the rights of those who have fought...will recall that there was never a reunion or meeting or torchlight procession without talk of the constituent assembly" (cited in Tasca [1938] 1966, p. 15).

Radicalization of the Socialist Party continued after the war. In the Party's first postwar congress, held in Bologna in 1919, the remaining reformist leaders were ousted from the Party's executive. The new maximalist leadership adopted a revolutionary program and affiliated itself with the Communist International (Seton Watson 1967, p. 548; Dutt [1934] 1974, p. 114). The Party's new program advocated the use of political violence aimed at the establishment of a socialist society, land collectivization, and industrial workers' participation in factory management. The PSI called on its members to "obstruct and paralyze the experiment of social democracy [and] the establishment of a bourgeois parliament," and to "intensify and complete the preparations for the forcible overthrow of the bourgeois state and the inauguration of the dictatorship of the proletariat" (in Tasca [1938] 1966, pp. 73-74).

The maximalist program, Tasca argues, was influenced by the Bolshevik revolution and the socialist revolts in Hungary and Germany: "These revolutionaries," he states, "wanted above all to copy Russia, and this amounted to a bemused repetition of the catchwords that the Bolshevik success had set in circulation" ([1938] 1966, p. 16). The program completed the transformation of the PSI from a reformist party—favoring collaboration with the Liberal government—into a revolutionary party that called for a "second Bolshevik revolution" in Italy.

These revolutionary goals were incorporated into the Party's electoral campaign. It called on its members to "strive in the constituencies and institutions of the bourgeois state for the intense propagation of the principles of communism, and for the rapid overthrow of these instruments of bourgeois domination" (Tasca [1938] 1966, p. 54). Three months before the elections, one PSI manifesto came close to an open call for rebellion. "The establishment of a Socialist society," it declared, "cannot be achieved by decree, nor by the decision of a parliament or a constituent assembly. Hybrid forms of collaboration between parliament and workers' councils are to be equally condemned and rejected. The proletariat must be incited to the violent seizure of political and economic power, and this must then be handed over entirely and exclusively to the workers' and peasants' councils, which will have both legislative and executive functions" (Tasca [1938] 1966, p. 54).

Undoubtedly, the electoral reform adopted benefited the Socialists. In the 1919 national elections, the PSI emerged as the largest opposition party. Its deputies were constrained, however, by the maximalists' dictates against participation in the government; hence, they confined their activities to those of a parliamentary opposition. Although both postwar Liberal premiers, Francesco Nitti and Giovanni Giolitti, offered the Socialists a position in the cabinet, the Socialists refused those overtures.

The PSI's Local Political Power

In terms of actual power, the results of the local elections that took place in November 1920 were of greater significance to the Socialist Party. The PSI gained electoral majorities in 25 of the country's 69 provincial councils and in 2,162 of the constituent 8,059 communes. Its largest victories were in the regions of Emilia and Tuscany, where 223 of Emilia's 280 communes and over half of Tuscany's 294 communes were controlled by Socialist governments. In some provinces the Socialists gained almost complete control: All of Ferrara's 21 communes, all of Rovigo's 63 communes, and 54 of 61 communes in Bologna were governed by Socialist administrations (Squeri 1983, p. 328). These electoral gains were accompanied by the growth of the Socialist unions. Membership in the CGL climbed from 233,963 in 1915, before Italy's intervention in the war, to 249,039 in 1918, to 1,150,062 in 1919, and to over 2.2 million by the end of 1920 (Neufeld 1961, pp. 368-69).

Most of the PSI's efforts, like the bases of CGL strength, were concentrated in the northern and central regions, where agrarian wage labor prevailed. Neither the PSI nor the CGL made any serious attempt to penetrate the *latifundist* south. Indeed, the Socialists' rejection of the war veterans and their alienation of small peasants exemplify the Party's position, and suggest how the Fascists benefited from the Socialists' political strategy.[6] The Socialist Party denounced the veterans as reactionaries, and provoked the small peasants by insisting on collectivization rather than redistribution of land. Because many of the veterans came from peasant families, this amounted to a dual rejection. The demobilized peasant-soldiers returned to find a labor market dominated by Socialist trade unions that had opposed Italy's intervention in the war and were now denouncing them as accomplices in that war. Rather than trying to recruit the returning peasants to their banner, the Socialists dismissed them and excluded their interests from their program.

Nevertheless, this maximalist-led line was still being debated within the PSI. Reformist leaders saw that this was clearly a disastrous course. They warned, as did Giovanni Zibordi, that the returning peasant-soldiers were turning to the Fascists "because the Socialist proletariat and the Party press have shown no sympathy at all for these proletarians in uniform." This, too, increased the Fascists' ability to organize the "middle classes," whose alienation from the Socialist cause was the product of the PSI's neglect and even repudiation of them as "bourgeois": "We give the term 'bourgeois'," Zibordi argued, "to strata that are merely middle class in intelligence, education, style of life and dress, but which are proletarians and workers with their brain" (1922, pp. 89, 91).

Similar to the Liberal Party, the vote for the PSI indicates the Socialists' visible strength and their actual political power in a province during the period immediately preceding the Fascist attacks. Nonetheless, the PSI vote is not the ideal measure to capture the intensity of the class struggle. Data on the occurrence of strikes in the provinces would be a preferable measure, both of the intensity of the struggle and of the perceived Socialist threat to propertied interests. Such data are not available on the provincial level. So, the vote received by the PSI in 1920 remains the best approximation of the Socialists' success in their struggle against the employers and the intensity of the political danger they posed on this level. The 1919 national election and the 1920 local or "administrative" elections, as we saw in the previous chapter, were the first to take place after universal suffrage to all males over twenty-one years of age had been granted (see chapter 3). Therefore, when analyzing the Socialists' ascendance, the rate of voter turnout represents an indicator of the "democratic promise" inherent in the Socialists' sweep, that is, the extent to which their political power was based on the support of the newly enfranchised masses.

Table 4.2 shows the Socialists' strength in the north and the center on one hand, and in the south on the other. The PSI received a "high" vote (over 45% of total votes cast) in 50% of the northern and central provinces. But only one of the 22 southern provinces (Bari, Apulia) had a high PSI vote. Conversely, the PSI had a "low" vote in only 7% of the northern provinces and 29% of the central provinces, but in 73% of the southern provinces.

Moreover, the militancy of the organized workers in the northern and central regions, which had participated in the great agricultural strikes and in the occupation of the factories, suggests that the PSI indeed drew most of its support from wage workers. If this is correct, we should find a strong relationship between the PSI vote and the concentration of wage workers, both industrial and agricultural. Table 4.3 shows this relationship on the provincial level.

While the relationship is not consistent, a clear pattern does emerge. Where the concentration of industrial workers was highest in the country, the PSI received a "high" vote in 39% of those provinces. Only 16% of the provinces where the concentration of industrial wage workers was "low" had a "high" vote for the PSI. Similarly, 58% of the provinces with a low concentration of industrial wage workers also had a "low" vote for the PSI, in contrast to 26% of the provinces where the concentration of industrial worker was "high."

To analyze the relationship between sagricultural workers and the PSI vote, as mentioned earlier, we must distinguish between workers in the northern and central regions from workers in the southern region. Table 4.4 shows the relationship between the concentration of agricultural wage workers and region in Italy's forty-one agrarian provinces. Controlling for the distinction in the modes of production in the northern and southern regions, we find a similar relationship to that shown in Table 4.3.

Table 4.2
PSI Vote (1920) by Regional Relations of Production, in Percentages

	PSI Vote [a]			
Regions	High	Medium	Low	(N)
Capitalist north	50	43	7	(30)
Sharecropping center	50	21	29	(14)
Latifundist south [b]	4	23	73	(22)

[a] The vote for the PSI is categorized into 3 equal groups according to the distribution of the vote among the provinces. The top third of the distribution is defined as "high."
[b] The South includes the provinces of Sardinia and Sicily.

Table 4.3
PSI Vote (1920) by the Concentration of Industrial Workers (1921)
in Italy's Provinces, in Percentages

Concentration of Industrial Workers[a]	PSI Vote			
	High	Medium	Low	(N)
High	39	35	26	(23)
Medium	42	37	21	(24)
Low	16	26	58	(19)

[a] The concentration of agricultural workers is categorized into three equal groups according to the distribution among all the provinces. The top third of the distribution is defined as "high."

Table 4.4
PSI Vote (1920) by the Concentration of Agricultural Workers (1921)
in Italy's Agrarian Provinces, in Percentages

	"High" PSI Vote						
	Concentration of Agricultural Workers[a]						
Region	High	(N)	Medium	(N)	Low	(N)	Total (N)
North	80	(5)	64	(11)	14	(7)	(23)
South	7	(15)	0	(3)	—	(0)	(18)

[a] The concentration of agricultural workers is categorized into three equal groups according to the distribution among all the provinces. The top third of the distribution is defined as "high."

In the north, where production was carried out on large commercial estates, an increase in the concentration of wage workers led to a higher vote for the PSI. Thus, 80% (four provinces out of five) of the northern agrarian provinces with a high level of agricultural workers also had a high vote for the PSI. In contrast, 64% of the agrarian northern provinces with a "medium" level of agricultural wage workers and only 17% of these provinces with a "low" concentration of agricultural wage workers had a "high" vote for the PSI. In the south, where the agricultural workers were subject to the seigniorial power of the *latifundists* and where PSI presence and organization were minimal, a high concentration of agricultural wage workers did not yield any conspicuous support for the Socialists. Only 7% of the 15 southern provinces where this level of concentration was "high" had a high vote for the PSI.[7]

Continuing this line of argument, Table 4.5 shows the relationship between the rate of voter turnout and the PSI vote in the 1920 elections. The relationship is clear and consistent. Among the provinces where the rate of voter turnout was highest (over 57.6% of the eligible voters), 68% (15 provinces out of 22) also had a "high" Socialist vote. The PSI received the same high vote in only 19% of the provinces with a "medium" rate of voter turnout, and in 13% of the provinces with a "low" rate. Similarly, a "low" vote for the PSI was inversely related to the rate of voter turnout: 57% of the provinces where the voter turnout was the lowest in the country also had a low PSI vote, whereas only 9% (2 out of 22) of the provinces where the rate of voter turnout was "high" had a low PSI vote. So, to the extent that the rate of voter turnout can be viewed as a good indicator of the political participation of the newly enfranchised masses, Table 4.5 shows a clear pattern between this process and support for the Socialists.

But the Party's postwar program and its specific declarations during the electoral campaign suggest that it aimed at being the exclusive representative of wage workers. The question is, then, whether the relationship between the PSI's electoral power and the concentration of wage workers, who now had the vote, does not conceal a different relationship, one between the Party and the more limited constituency addressed in its program.

Table 4.6 shows a regression analysis of the relationship among the level of concentration of industrial wage workers in a province, the rate of voter turnout, and the PSI vote. While the effect of the rate of voter turnout is strong and significant (β = 0.534), the increase in the concentration of industrial wage workers has no significant independent effect on the increase in the PSI vote.[8]

Table 4.5
PSI Vote (1920) by Voter Turnout (1920) in Italy's Provinces, in Percentages

Voter Turnout[a]	PSI Vote			
	High	Medium	Low	(N)
High	68	23	9	(22)
Medium	19	48	33	(21)
Low	13	30	57	(24)

[a] The concentration of agricultural workers is categorized into three equal groups according to the distribution among all the provinces. The top third of the distribution is defined as "high.

Table 4.6
Direct Effects of the Concentration of Industrial Workers (1921) and Voter Turnout (1920) on PSI Vote (1920) in Italy's Provinces

	B (SE)	β
Concentration of Industrial Workers	.053[*]	.187
	(.029)	
Voter Turnout	1.36[**]	.534
	(2.63)	
Constant	-47.26	
R^2		.34

[*]p<.07
[**]p<.01

What we can conclude is that the ascendance of the Socialist movement was integral to Italy's postwar "mood," or *diciannovismo* ("1919ism"), that "revolutionary yearning for a change" (Seton Watson 1967, p. 511). This is evident in the Party's demand for electoral reform and its decision to participate in the elections. Therefore, I suggest that despite the PSI's radical rhetoric, its call for a proletarian revolution, and its explicit contempt for "bourgeois democracy," its political ascendance were determined precisely by the introduction of democratic elections and the participation of the newly enfranchised masses.

In sum, if we measure the political power of the socialist movement in the provinces by means of the PSI vote, together with the information on voter turnout, it seems clear that the Party was supported by the political mobilization of Italy's newly enfranchised masses, the *basso popolo*. Thus, perhaps ironically, although the Socialist Party's program denounced bourgeois democracy and attempted to use democratic electoral processes only to advance the establishment of the "dictatorship of the proletariat," it was precisely this electoral process that determined its political advance.

THE SOCIALIST THREAT TO THE LANDLORDS' WORLD

"One of the most important weaknesses of the workers movement," writes Lyttelton, "was its provincialism. It was a provincialism of structure rather than attitude" (1976, p. 130). However, as we shall see in the following chapters, it may very well be that this "provincialism" was precisely what provoked the agrarians' and industrialists' response and what the anarchist Luigi Fabbri called the Fascist "preventive counter-revolution." Local organizations belonging to the workers movement definitely appear to have hurt the authority and property rights of the propertied class in the northern and central provinces (Lyttelton 1976, pp. 132-33).

In December 1920, immediately after the local elections, the League of Socialist Communes declared, as reported by the *Bandiera Rossa*, that "the Socialist administrations intend to represent the working class exclusively" in accordance with "the new communist law" that places the needs of the community "absolutely above the rights of private property" (cited in Snowden 1989, p. 170). The policies adopted in the "Socialist provinces" where the PSI had won a majority in local government indeed seemed to implement the "new communist law." "In the Socialist-administered cities," Charles Maier argues, "revolution already appeared underway. The well-born or educated, who had basked in the deference extended by the *basso popolo*, found their world of social expectations crumbling...Trolley-car service was subject now to interruptions for days at a time, and when the trams finally rolled from the yards, their crews might bedeck them with red flags of triumph" (1975, p.177).

The Socialist administrations enacted sweeping tax reforms and expanded the authority of the Chambers of Labor in labor disputes, thereby "putting into effect a new policy of income distribution" (Lyttelton 1987, p. 38). The local elections, in Cardoza's words, "added political insult to the economic injuries" caused by the unions' ongoing agitation and strikes (1982, p. 288).

The provinces of Ferrara and Bologna in the Po Valley were among the oldest and strongest bases of Socialist local power. "In no other part of Italy had the agricultural proletariat succeeded in extracting such advantageous conditions from the class of the employers" (Pittorru, cited in Corner 1975, p. 93, n. 1). According to Serpieri, "an agricultural expert and friend of property," after a year of Socialist provincial rule, the *agrari* of Bologna paid, in 1921, a total of 802 million lire in local surcharges on land as compared to 323 million lire a year earlier, before the Socialists had come into office (Snowden 1989, p. 55).[9]

The extent of the Socialists' power in the Bologna was summarized by a local landowner: "The province...is only nominally a part of the kingdom of Italy," Count Melvezzi wrote to the prefect in April 1920. "The Chamber of Labor rules and no one dares disobey its orders because everyone has become convinced that the government will not help anyone who takes the initiative in resisting the Socialist tyranny...Open and ever more frequent violations of prefectoral ordinances go unpunished—be it by the city administration or by the Chamber of Labor....The authority of this anonymous Socialist government is increasingly reinforced and in fact is the only one recognized in the province" (cited in Cardoza 1982, pp. 285-86).

The PSI and the CGL were, in effect, the two pillars of Socialist provincial power. Together, these organizations controlled a vast network of local peasant leagues, Chambers of Labor, and cooperative societies. But the CGL's leadership, as was evident in the occupation of the factories, did not accompany the PSI in its turn to revolutionary maximalism, and continued to be governed by "reformist tendencies and leaders" (Salomone 1945, p. 54). In fact, local union organizers often resented the PSI's politics and ideological radicalism. As a local leader in Ferrara put it in September 1919, just before the PSI's congress in Bologna: "The Party spends its time splitting hairs about formulae which we now believe to be superseded. Reformism, revolution? But these definitions belong to prehistoric times. The center of political gravity has moved from the political club to the league. An example is our province [Ferrara]. The political organizations no longer have either the ability or the competence to deal with economic and class questions" (cited in Corner 1975, p. 94).

The CGL was indeed a center of gravity in the provinces, and its policies directly challenged the interests of the propertied class. As was already noted, the *imponibile della mano d'opera* and the *collocamento di classe*, the mechanisms employed by the leagues, amounted to complete control over the labor supply in the provinces. The union's sanctions against workers who did not join the "Red Leagues" or who accepted lower wages were "pitiless" because their actions deprived other workers of jobs at acceptable wages: "The blackleg was boycotted, refused bread by the baker, treated as an outcast with his wife and children" (Tasca [1938] 1966, p. 92; Snowden 1972; Salvemini 1973, p. 161). Eventually, the unions' achievements—higher wages, shorter hours, and a smaller share of the sharecroppers' product—cut into the landlords' profits and led to their "flight from the land" (Snowden 1989, pp. 55, 93).[10]

In addition to the unions' control over the supply of labor, the workers' cooperative organizations controlled—and sometimes monopolized—the distribution of goods and social services. The first workers' cooperatives were established in the construction industries and were aimed at organizing workers employed in public works (Costanzo 1923, pp. 73-74). From an estimated 7,420 cooperative societies in 1915, Ruini states, there were 15,510 such societies by 1922 with over 3 million members, not including the credit and agricultural societies (1922, p.13).[11]

In the postwar years the number of cooperative societies affiliated with the Socialist National League of Cooperatives rose from 2,321 in 1919 to 3,840 in 1920, and included *over* a million members by 1921 (Neufeld 1961, p. 369). The cooperatives managed by the local Chambers of Labor fixed the price of goods and sold them in many communes through an elaborate distribution network. Thus, "landlords, shopkeepers, contractors, and middlemen of all kinds," in Tasca's words, "found their positions being daily sapped by the co-operative and municipal Socialist movement" ([1938] 1966, p. 95). In the region of Emilia, for instance, where the Socialist cooperatives were "the most flourishing in the country," the PSI-governed municipality ran its own pharmaceutical services and sold milk, meat, and bread. "It either ran or controlled food shops, restaurants, and flour-mills" (Lyttelton 1987, p. 235). By 1920, the Socialists had 86 cooperative shops in Emilia alone, with 16,800 members (Tasca [1938] 1966, p. 110). A similar development took place in Tuscany, where the Socialist cooperative alliance had a network of 34 cooperatives, with 24,700 members enrolled from among a population of 56,000 (Snowden 1989, p. 169). At the time of the Fascists' first punitive expeditions in the fall of 1920, the workers' movement constituted, as Tasca puts it, "hundreds of little republics, Socialist oases with no intercommunication, like medieval cities without their ramparts" ([1938] 1966, p. 126).

It is clear that Italian Socialism was rent by contradictions. Led by a revolutionary party that called for establishment of a proletarian dictatorship, it took part in the electoral process even though it insisted on absolute abstention from national government. At the same time, the Party took power in the country's richest and most important provinces, where it collaborated with the moderate leadership of the CGL, the organization that posed the main, direct threat to the landlords. The PSI's revolutionary rhetoric and program might intimidate the landlords on the local level but, concurrently, it led the Party to gratuitously surrender national political power to its antagonists.

This internal conflict or contradiction within the workers' movement was evident to its leaders. Reformists like Giovanni Zibordi on one hand, and anarchists like Enrico Malatesta on the other, warned against the Socialists' combining revolutionary rhetoric with incitement to violence. "The threatened revolution contained in the [Socialist] Maximalist program," Zibordi argued in 1922, "really frightened the bourgeoisie, and the weak, concessive attitude of the government towards the masses sufficed to make the bourgeoisie look to fascism for its own defence and for a substitute to the state power that was insufficient for its ends" (1922, p. 95). In exactly the same vein, Malatesta, "the greatest living Italian Anarchist," warned of the coming reaction: "If we let the right moment slip, we shall pay with tears of blood for the fright we have given the bourgeoisie" (cited in Seton Watson 1967, p. 525).

Turati's prophetic speech against the Party's call for a violent political struggle is perhaps the best statement of the Socialists' situation on the eve of the Fascist expeditions. In 1919, more than a year before the Fascists made their initial attacks, Turati addressed the Socialist members in the Bologna congress that would oust him from the Party's leadership:

> Violence is nothing other than the suicide of the proletariat; it serves the interests of our adversaries...Today they do not take us seriously, but when they find it useful to take us seriously, our appeal to violence will be taken up by our enemies, one hundred times better armed than we, and then goodbye for a long time to Parliamentary action, goodbye to economic organizations, goodbye to the Socialist Party...To speak...of violence continually and then always postpone it until tomorrow is....the most absurd thing in this world. It only serves to arm, to rouse, to justify rather the violence of the adversary, a thousand time stronger than ours....This is the ultimate stupidity to which a party can come, and involves the renunciation of any revolution (in Horowitz 1963, pp. 134-35.).

The Fascists' campaign of punitive expeditions immediately followed the local elections. In less then two years, *squadrismo* destroyed virtually all the Socialist provincial strongholds in the northern and central regions, the organizational base of its union movement, the local Chambers of Labor, and the cooperative societies. It was verily, to quote Turati once more, "a revolution of blood against a revolution of words" (cited in Seton Watson 1967, p. 575).

NOTES

   1. See chapter 3 for information about the sources. Thus, the number of provinces adds up to 75 cases because the 1921 census includes two regions (Venezia Giulia and Venezia Tridentina), containing six provinces, which were annexed to Italy in the Treaty of Rapallo in November 1920. Due to incomplete data, these provinces are not otherwise included in this analysis.
   2. The Italian Metal Union Federation, like that in Germany, was constructed as craft sections, "with a fairly high degree of sectional consciousness among the founders, coppersmiths, etc." (Sirianni 1980, p. 43).

3. Filippo Turati and other reformists voted with the majority and were not expelled.

4. This information is provided in the notes following Lenin's article.

5. The PPI was established in 1918. For the first time since Italy's unification, the Vatican approved Catholics' participation in political life and formally supported the new party. The PPI's program stressed religious freedom and extensive land and tax reforms. The *Popolari*, also in contrast with the Socialists, made some specific efforts to address the "southern question," the problem of the *mezzogiorno* (Webster 1961, pp. 52-53; Seton Watson 1967, pp. 513-14; Nazzaro 1970).

6. Brustein (1991) examines what might be called the "elective affinity" of specific types of independent farmers to the Fascist program. The Fascists, he argues, successfully gained the support of the peasantry, a social group neglected and even antagonized by the Socialists. As we shall see, the Fascists sought not only to incorporate the interests of the peasants in their rhetoric, they also recruited veterans, mainly ex-officers, for the Fascist Squads.

7. In ecological analysis, we try to infer individual behavior or characteristics from aggregate data. In this analysis, we are dealing with aggregates. Although the data confirm that the PSI's main electoral strongholds were in the northern provinces, where both agricultural and industrial wage labor prevailed, far-reaching statements regarding the position of the wage workers toward the Socialist Party cannot be made. Such inferences would be subject to the "ecological fallacy." In this analysis, we are dealing with aggregate data about the *voting patterns* in each province. An inference from these group data about the political attitudes of the *individuals* comprising the electorate in each province would constitute such a fallacy. "The basic problem in ecological analysis," in Hamilton's formulation, "stems from the fact that the aggregates are rarely pure" (1982, p. 500, n. 6). In Italy, there were no provinces with, say, 100% industrial or agricultural wage workers. Therefore, we cannot assume that the individuals who were wage workers were also those individuals who voted PSI. All we can do is make a "conservative" reading of the relationships between the patterns. (On ecological analysis, see Hamilton 1982, p. 501; King 1997).

8. The small population (N=42) and high correlations between the variables create difficulties in analyzing the same relationship with respect to agricultural workers. Based on the findings reported so far, we may expect to find a similar pattern: The level of turnout had a greater effect on support for the Socialists than did the concentration of agrarian wage workers.

9. This calculation may not be accurate. It is cited here only as evidence for the *agrari*'s subjective sense of alarm at the Socialists' ascendance. See chapters 5 and 6 for the landlords' response.

10. It is interesting to note the account written by Gino Olivetti, the secretary of the General Confederation of Italian Industry, of the development of collective agreements before and after the war. Olivetti argues that the postwar era brought a vast growth in such agreements both in terms of the number of industries covered and, perhaps more importantly, in their content and in the detailed regulation of workers' rights (1922, pp. 209-28).

11. Most of the cooperative societies were affiliated with the Socialist Party. But there were also several important "White League" societies affiliated with the *Popolare*. See Ruini 1922, p. 17.

Chapter 5

The Fascist Militarization
of Politics

There were at least three decisive turning points in the history of the Fascist organization in the years following its initial establishment in 1919; the path taken at each of these points determined Fascism's specific nature. The first was the establishment of the Action Squads in 1920 and the beginning of the systematic assaults on Socialist strongholds and activists. The second was the internal debate within the Fascist organization in the fall of 1921 over Benito Mussolini's proposed Pact of Pacification with the Socialists and the official establishment of the Fascist Party. The third was Mussolini's appointment as Prime Minister in October 1922 and the beginning of the Fascist Party's rule within Italy's parliamentary regime. At each of these points alternative paths that could have been taken in the "making of Fascism," its conduct, ideology, leadership, and political program. This chapter examines the first of these turning points, the establishment of the Action Squads and *squadrismo*, the tactic of violence.

In the two years between the local elections of 1920 until Mussolini's nomination as Prime Minister in the fall of 1922, the Fascist Squads embarked on a campaign of "punitive expeditions" throughout Italy's provinces. These expeditions, as described earlier, almost invariably resulted in the complete destruction of the workers' organizations. The Fascists assaulted striking workers and destroyed union halls and Socialist Party headquarters. In the short period of six months, 202 workers were killed and 1,144 wounded; another 2,240 were arrested (Dutt [1934] 1974, p. 124; see also Tasca [1938] 1966, pp. 102-16; Corner 1975, pp. 139-40; Salvemini 1973; Cardoza 1982 Lyttelton 1987; Snowden 1989, pp. 70-71).

The Fascists' political strategy was, in fact, determined "from below," by the military expertise of its recruits, members of the Squads and, at the same time, "from above," by the political and financial support of the propertied class and by the direct aid of the Army's High Command.

In the aftermath of World War I, Italy's Liberal governments shifted their policies in favor of a newly enfranchised electorate of workers and peasants. The social reforms enacted by these governments led to a crisis among the country's propertied class. Responding to what they saw as abdication by their own political leadership and facing an unprecedented wave of worker insurgency, the employers' associations abandoned their traditional political methods and began a drive for self-organization against the workers movement. The culmination of what can be called "bourgeois militancy" was its alliance with the Fascist organization.

CLASS ORGANIZATION, POLITICAL STRUGGLE, AND FASCISM

The origins of Fascism's political strategy raise the theoretical issue of the predetermination of political phenomena. What is the role of political organizations, mainly class organizations, in the transformation of social and political relations? And to what extent—how and under what "given" historical circumstances—do specific political strategies (i.e., class alliances, political coalitions, and tactics of struggle) determine the success or failure of political organizations? This suggests that political and historical contingencies arose *after* the establishment of the Fascist organization and, most crucially, that these contingencies, under the given "objective circumstances," had a decisive effect on the organization's eventual political triumph.

This perspective, as was discussed in detail in chapter 2, counters the dominant sociological paradigm, which emphasizes Fascism's historical and social origins. There is no doubt that the question of Fascism's origins is crucial; as Benedetto Croce puts it, "there are no bastards in history." But this may be a misleading question. Both historically and politically, the analysis of the Fascists' political organization and conduct must *precede* that of their social base of support. Before the Fascists could turn to an electorate, they had to establish themselves as a politically viable force. To understand this process we must analyze the formation of the Action Squads, their organization and their employment of violence. The Fascists did not participate in an electoral campaign; instead, they waged a paramilitary campaign and opened a real battle zone. Their objective was not to get the vote but to overthrow the legally elected Socialist provincial governments.

The significance of a struggle's conduct in transforming social and political relations urges the analysis of the protagonists' strategies. "Given a particular [historical] configuration," Adam Przeworski suggests, "a number of practices can be developed, but the *range of effective practices*, that is, of practices that can have the effect of transforming objective conditions, is determined by these very conditions" (1985, p. 68, my emphasis). While Przeworski is concerned with the conceptualization of class, his methodological framework can be applied to the analysis of Fascism. If classes are "effects of struggles," then the same should hold for their political organizations. Political struggles ("practices") may have independent effects; therefore, their dynamics, strategies, and forms of organization should be problematic. And so, rather than employing what Przeworski terms "once and for all" theoretical definitions, we can examine the actual "making of Fascism" through an analysis of its political strategy.

The specific military character of the Italian Fascist cadre was initially noted by several contemporary observers and analysts. Palmiro Togliatti, for example, argued that while fascism "comprised a movement of the rural petty bourgeois masses...it was also a political struggle waged by certain representatives of the small and idle bourgeoisie...[and] a *military organization* which claimed the ability to take on the regular armed forces" (1928, p. 138, my emphasis). Similarly, Klara Zetkin insisted that "fascism's characteristic methods [unlike ordinary bourgeois use of violence or counter-revolutionary violence by the state against the workers or the Left] combined terrorism with demagogy, and that its victory constituted a political and ideological defeat for the workers' movement, not merely a military one...Fascism was thus *a consequence, not a cause*, of socialism's political failure" (1923, cited in Beetham 1983, p. 7, my emphasis; see also pp. 105-6).

Nevertheless, we have only two sociological analyses, by Charles Tilly, Louise Tilly, and Richard Tilly (1975) and by Albert Szymanski (1973), which examine the role of violence in the rise of Fascism. As part of their account of Europe's "rebellious century," the Tillys examine the history of "collective violence" in Italy from the era of unification until the rise of Fascism. They argue that the "Fascists strong-armed their way to power in many towns" (1975, p. 122). These acts were, to a great extent, the culmination of a long period of endemic violence, beginning in 1830, in some of the country's regions. The Tillys' analysis of Fascist violence examines several distinctive factors that led to its culmination: The combined effect of postwar disturbances such as expanding organization of labor, new political alignments after World War I, the organization of industrial and agrarian employers, and the specific social problem of war veterans which led to the emergence of Fascist "punitive expeditions." But the main determinant of the Fascists' violence, they argue, was the power of the working class: The "concentration of Fascist violence in the north was due to the concentration there of its chief target: the organized working class" (1975, p. 189). This thesis acknowledges the determinative might of political action and, as the Tillys put it, "challenges the widely held idea that rapid structural change itself tends to generate protest, conflict and violence" (1975, p. 129).

Concentrating on the Marxist variant of the argument citing structural change as an inducement to violence, Szymanski argues that the Marxist theory of Fascism as a response of industrial capitalism to socialist power should be modified. His analysis of Fascist violence in Italy shows that while Fascism was, as the Marxists argued, a response to socialist political power, it was "not an industrial phenomenon" (1973, p. 401); it rose primarily in Italy's rural regions.

This argument is based on a comparison among Italy's regions (N=16), employing violence as an indicator of Fascism, votes for the PSI as an indicator of Socialist power, and the proportion of industrial workers in the region as an indicator of industrial capitalism. Szymanski finds a strong positive correlation between Fascist violence and the PSI vote but no such correlation between Fascist violence and the level of industrialization (1973, p. 401). Based on these findings, Szymanski suggests another hypothesis, which he does not examine: that the Fascist organization drew its crucial "economic and political support...from the economic elite, particularly large industrialists of Milan, Turin and Genoa," as well as "farmers" in northern Italy (1973, pp. 402, 404).

These works, together with the early insights made by Togliatti and Zetkin, provide us with a specific analytical agenda that identifies and considers the causal role of the factors neglected by the dominant paradigm: What was the nature of the alliance between the landlords and the state, the crucial axis in Moore's thesis? How, and to what extent, did it actually affect another, perhaps more significant alliance, that between the landlords and the Fascists? What were, in Przeworski's formulation, the "effective practices" employed by the Fascists? What made them "effective"? How did specific circumstances in post World War I Italy determine both the Fascists' "choice" of strategy and its effects? What was the role of the Socialists' practices in this "choice"? What practices, other than those eventually chosen by the protagonists, were available to them?

The rise of Fascism in Italy was the result of two political processes: first, the post World War I political insurgency in the provinces, which led to the second, the landlords' militancy and alliance with the Fascist Squads. This was independent of the structural characteristics of the province. Threatened by the rising Socialist Party on the one hand, and facing the Liberal government's reforms that catered to the Socialists' demands on the other, the landlords formed an alliance with the Fascists that produced the specific pattern taken by the Fascists' tactic of violence. This alliance was, to a great degree, a continuation of the landlords' prewar organizational capacity and tradition of militant, united action against the workers, a tradition not shared by Italy's industrialists. The initial question we need to answer in the development of this argument is: "Who were the executioners of this tactic of violence?"

THE MILITARIZATION OF THE FASCIST ORGANIZATION: THE ACTION SQUADS

The Fascist organization was established in March 1919. One hundred and nineteen members attended the humble inauguration of the *fasci di combattimento* in a small hall at the Piazza San Sepolcro lent by Milan's Chamber of Commerce. From the outset, the Fascist organization was characterized by political diversity. There were three major groups among its founders, who came to be known as the "Fascists of the First Hour," or the *sansepolcristi*. This "hard professional core" was comprised of revolutionary Syndicalists and Socialists or "Left Interventionists," centered mostly in Milan, who had left the Socialist Party in 1915 because of its opposition to Italy's intervention in World War I (Lyttelton 1987, p. 46; see also Roberts 1979). The second group was the organization's military element, composed mainly of Army officers and *arditi* (the brave or ardent), an organization of demobilized officers from the Italian Army's elite assault unit. The Futurists, led by Filippo Marinetti, constituted the third group. They demanded the abolition of the monarchy and represented the most radical anticlerical element. These groups were united by a strong sense of nationalism, the glorification of war, and opposition to Italy's traditional parties, both liberal and socialist (Lyttelton 1987, pp. 46-48).

Benito Mussolini was among the Fascist "Left Interventionists." He was the former editor of the PSI's official organ, *Avanti!*, and later published his own newspaper, the interventionist *Il Popolo d'Italia*, which was subtitled "a socialist newspaper" until July 1928. Other "Left Interventionists" included some of the radical leaders of Italy's prewar revolutionary struggle, such as Michele Bianchi, Edmundo Rossoni, and Alceste De Ambris, organizers of the 1913 strikes in the Po Valley and of the 1914 Red Week demonstrations. These radicals saw a genuine revolutionary potential in the social and political crisis inherent in the war. For them, Lyttelton suggested, "the famous saying of Clausewitz, 'war is a continuation of politics by other means,' needed to be reversed. The 'revolution' was to be a continuation of the war" (1987, p. 43). Indeed, apart from their position in favor of Italy's intervention in the war, these "Left Interventionists" appear to have differed little from the maximalist leaders of the PSI, whether in terms of their revolutionary fervor or their history as organizers of workers and peasants.

The influence of these radical elements on the initial character of the Fascist organization is evident in the content of the Fascist Manifesto. Written in 1919 by the Syndicalist De Ambris and the Futurist Marinetti, the manifesto was similar in many ways to the maximalist Socialist position: It called for universal suffrage, the establishment of an eight-hour workday, a minimum wage, participation of workers in industrial management, nationalization of the armaments industry, high taxation on wealth, confiscation of all the possessions of religious communities, and abolition of episcopal revenues (Tasca [1938] 1966, pp. 33-35; Seton Watson 1967, pp. 517-19).

The ensuing struggle between the Fascists and Socialists took place on a political terrain dominated by the cleavages created in prewar Italy's "interventionist crisis" (Seton Watson 1967, p. 416; Young 1949, p. 73; Cardoza 1982, p. 211). This was, as Roland Sarti observes, "one of the anomalies of the Italian political scene...that the controversy between neutralists and interventionists was even more bitter after the war than it had been before" the war (1971, p. 19).

However, the Fascists' participation in the 1919 general elections brought the new organization a humiliating defeat. Fascists in Milan, their greatest stronghold, received the support of about five thousand voters (Tasca [1938] 1966, p. 39; Lyttelton 1987, p. 45). Except for some isolated violent clashes with the Socialists (the most notorious was the burning of *Avanti!* in April 1919), up to the local elections of 1920, the movement appeared to have withered away, to represent a short-lived reaction to the postwar crisis. Mussolini himself was convinced that the movement was doomed: that it "will always be a minority movement [because] it cannot go beyond the cities" (cited in Snowden 1972).

Yet, in 1920, the second year of the Fascists' political existence, Mussolini and the Fascist leadership set out to convert Fascism into a military force. The first organized Fascist "punitive expedition" took place in the summer of 1920 in the border region of Julian Venetia. Conquered by Italy, the former Austrian region was still under military occupation when a small band of Fascists began "the work of systematic destruction of everything Bolshevik" (Tasca [1938] 1966, p. 106).

This expedition was carried out in strict military fashion. All the leaders of the Fascist Squads were Army officers still under arms or in the process of being demobilized. They divided Trieste (the region's capital) into combat zones; each zone was assigned to a Squad leader. The Squads were backed by an elaborate system of support organizations, such as health and information services, and, most importantly, a transport system provided by an officer still on active duty. The expedition resulted in the burning of the Slav Association's headquarters and the destruction of the Chamber of Labor in the city of Fiume (Tasca [1938] 1966, pp. 102-4; Togliatti 1976, p. 11; Lyttelton 1987, p. 53).

Reorganization of the hitherto small-scale association rendered the expedition to Istria and Trieste, its organization and execution, a model for the Fascists' future struggle against the Socialists. Mussolini urged the formation of "armed groups composed of 200-250 sure tried and well-armed individuals" (Lyttelton 1987, p. 52); and the general secretary, Umberto Pasella, declared the "constitution of Fascist Action Squads," as the organization's "essential task" (Lyttelton 1987, p. 46).

The core leadership of the Fascist Action Squads was the *arditi*, an organization of demobilized officers from the Italian Army's elite assault unit. The *arditi* were actively recruited by Mussolini immediately after the war. As early as November 1918, at a "victory procession" in Milan, Mussolini addressed an audience of "*arditi* comrades": "I have defended you against the slanders of cowardly philistines....With shining daggers and bursting bombs you shall wreak vengeance on the miserable wretches who would prevent the advance of greater Italy. She is yours!...Yours!" (cited in Tasca [1938] 1966, p. 24). Soon afterward, Mussolini nominated a group of *arditi* to guard the site of his newspaper, *Il Popolo d'Italia*, in Milan. They continued to be Mussolini's personal bodyguards throughout the period of the Fascists' ascendance, until his nomination as prime minister (Segre 1987, p. 49).

Historically, the *arditi*'s first organized political appearance occurred earlier, in the course of Gabriele D'Annunzio's invasion of Fiume. In September 1919, D'Annunzio, a charismatic war hero and national poet, conquered this Adriatic border city in an attempt to prevent the creation of the new Yugoslav state. Overtly defying the authority of the Italian government and that of the French and Austrian troops stationed in Istria, D'Annunzio led an army of two thousand volunteers (mainly deserters from the regular Army) into the occupied city. D'Annunzio ruled Fiume for a year, declaring it the independent "Regency of Carnaro," to be governed by his constitution, the "Charter of Carnaro"[1] (Tasca [1938] 1966; Ledeen 1971; Lyttelton 1987). This "adventure," as Farneti argues, indicates the relationship maintained between the government and the Army: Fiume was a "partial mobilization of the Army against the orders of the legitimate government, and from this point of view it was a break with the century-old tradition of an army loyal to political order" (1978, p. 16). The "Fiume Affair" signaled the beginning of what Carlo Gualtieri aptly called Fascism's "authorized lawlessness" (in Salvemini 1927, p. 57), that is, the terrorizing of "subversive" and "anti-patriotic" elements, in other words, the Socialists and the Slavs, with the tacit or explicit support of the local authorities.

The Army's High Command shared D'Annunzio's opposition to the Yugoslav state, and openly called for its subversion "by all possible means" (Lyttelton 1987). Even before D'Annunzio's invasion, General Bodoglio, the Army's Chief of Staff, ordered soldiers to suppress Slav demonstrations and to rally in the city in "an Italian show of force" (Lyttelton 1987, pp. 31-32). As D'Annunzio led his forces to Fiume, the Italian Army's regional command in Istria not only allowed his troops to cross the region, it lent them three generals and supplied them with heavy artillery, tanks, airplanes, and four warships (Salvemini 1973, p. 227). Bodoglio explicitly expressed the High Command's support of D'Annunzio. Responding to Prime Minister Giolitti's inquiry about the Army's attitude, the general telegraphed a lengthy plaudit to the cause of annexation in general, and to the "patriotic soldiers" who had deserted their posts to join D'Annunzio's forces (De Felice 1965, pp. 545-48).

After D'Annunzio's forces surrendered Fiume in December 1920, the *arditi* became Fascism's military arm. They left their mark on the Fascist organization, which incorporated the unit's rituals, uniform, and songs in addition to their tactics. During their attack on the Socialists of the Po Valley, the Fascists employed the same tactics that the *arditi* had used against the Slavs in Fiume (Tasca [1938] 1966, p. 183; Lyttelton 1987, p. 54). "The black shirt, the dagger, the club, the song '*Giovinezza*' ['Youth'], the Roman salute, the castor oil, the cruelty," in short, the *arditi*'s esprit de corps became characteristic of the Action Squads in general (Salvemini 1973, p. 292). Although the *arditi*, as a unit, broke with the Fascist organization in the summer of 1921, many of its members remained in the Action Squads and rose to become leaders of the Fascist organization (Sullivan 1981, p. 35).

In addition to the *arditi,* the Fascist leadership recruited other war veterans, mainly officers. This recruitment effort was greatly facilitated by the postwar government's policy of prolonged demobilization. Seven months after the end of the war, there were still more than 1.7 million men under arms, including 117,000 officers (De Felice 1965 p. 546).[2] Demobilization, according to Lyttelton, "increased the significance of the hard core of professional soldiers, and of the only demobilized ex-officers, NCOs and *arditi* on whom the reaction could rely" (1977, p. 67; see also Bell 1984, p. 10). Most of the demobilized recruits, as well as most of the casualties of the war, were peasants and workers who had been drafted, en masse, into the Army during the war. Thus, for instance, nearly two-thirds of all war orphans were the children of peasants and other rural poor, and about a third came from families of urban workers (Gill 1983, p. 159; Seton Watson 1967, p. 491, n. 2). Only about 5% were the children of industrialists, merchants, or professionals combined. Regardless, regular soldiers were renounced by the Socialist Party, which denied the war veterans entry into its ranks and excluded their specific interests from its program.[3]

In contrast to the peasant-soldiers, the demobilized officers became the "aristocracy of the trenches" (De Felice 1965, p. 473). They were volunteers, the "sons of the patriotic middle classes...who identified with the interventionist cause" (Snowden 1989, p. 157). Many officers had also joined D'Annunzio's invasion of Fiume, which they saw as a just and patriotic act (De Felice 1965, pp. 345-47). Umberto Banchelli, an Army officer who had joined the Fascists, described the officers' feeling toward Fascism: "The reason Fascism developed so quickly and was given a free hand was that in the breasts of officials and officers beat Italian hearts, which welcomed us gladly as we marched to the rescue. NCOs and military men competed with each other to help the *fasci*" (cited in Tasca [1938] 1966, p. 122). For the demobilized officers, then, the Fascist organization, which championed the cause of intervention in 1915 and protested Italy's "mutilated victory" after the war, was a natural political home.

The Army's High Command "powerfully assisted" the growth of the Fascist military cadre. The officers' sympathy and cooperation with the Fascists was accepted by the "higher ranks" with "cautious benevolence" (Lyttelton 1987, p. 39). A circular issued by Minister of War Ivanoe Bonomi went so far as to order officers to join the Fascists. According to this circular, "officers in the course of being demobilized (about 60,000) were...ordered to join the *Fasci di Combattimento*...for this they would receive four-fifths of their present pay" (Tasca [1938] 1966, p. 99).[4] The opposition of several government officials to the pro-Fascist attitude of the High Command provides further evidence of its appeal. A member of the government wrote to the Minister of War to protest this state of affairs: "I have been informed that the enrollment of officers and men in the *fasci* has occurred with the consent of the army corps command....A number of officers...display the insignia of the [Fascist] organization and, I repeat, many officers...take part...in Fascist punitive expeditions....All this takes place with never a correction or disciplinary action by the military authorities" (cited in Snowden 1989, p. 199).

Men with military skills and experience subsequently swelled the Fascist organization's command (Linz 1976, pp. 36-40). The Fascist leadership indeed offered the officers a special status. Local *fasci* were instructed by the Fascist Central Committee to seek out military men, especially officers, and to make them leaders of the *fasci* and as Squad commanders (Lyttelton 1987, p. 53). The Fascists also sought an alliance with the official veterans' organization, the Veterans' Association. Local Fascist organizers were instructed by Pasella, the Fascists' general secretary, to turn their *fasci* into the "vanguard" of the local associations. As a result, in some localities, the Fascists and the Veterans' Association were almost fused: The *fascio* in the city of Florence consisted mostly of veterans and was led by the president of the local Veterans' Association. In Siena, the Veterans' Association was headed by a Fascist (Snowden 1989, p. 157). When the Ferrara *fascio* was established, eight veterans (two of them *arditi*) were among its Executive Committee's nine members (Corner 1975, p. 107, n. 3). In the province of Pisa, the local *fascio*'s directorate included six former officers (Snowden 1989, p. 169).

The character of the Squads' paramilitary organization is evident in a memo circulated in mid 1921 by Italo Balbo, the leader of the Ferrara *fascio*, one of the first and strongest *fasci* in the country. "It is essential," Balbo told the Fascist secretaries in Ferrara, "that we see as soon as possible to the *regular military formation* of our forces....Only with a disciplined army shall we win the decisive victory" (in Corner 1975, p. 186, my emphasis). Balbo's circular outlined detailed instructions regarding the hierarchy and operation of this new organization. Members of the local *fasci* were to be divided into small "Action Squads," supported by "Reserve Squads" manned by older Fascist members. These were then divided into "squads," "platoons," and "companies." The squad, headed by a *capo,* was a small unit of ten men, equipped with machine-guns, rifles, and bombs. Some were special mobile units of motorcyclists and horsemen. Three squads constituted a "platoon," headed by commander and a subcommander; three "platoons" constituted a "company." The Fascist secretaries were further instructed to choose men with a military background (preferably infantry men or *arditi* ex-officers) to serve as platoon commanders (Corner 1975, pp. 184-85). By 1922, a similar hierarchy was adopted by the national Fascist organization (Tasca [1938] 1966, p. 300, n. 1).

But *squadrismo,* the systematic employment of anti-Socialist violence, required not only a military capacity but also political license. Establishing the Action Squads and capitalizing on the military skill of war veterans created the Fascist potential to engage in a campaign of violence. To utilize this potential during almost two years, the Fascists needed the collaboration and support of powerful allies. That is, without the backing of major landlords and industrialists, the Fascists would have been able to neither initiate nor carry out their violent attacks on the workers' organizations.

"ROYAL BOLSHEVISM" AND LANDLORD MILITANCY

The Fascist mobilization was, according to historian De Felice, the product of the "will of the urban and rural bourgeoisie" (1965, p. 659). This general bourgeois "will" emerged, first, as the protest of the propertied class against the policies of Italy's postwar government. In conjunction with the intensification of the economic class struggle during the "Red Biennium" of 1919-20, the electoral victories of mass parties (the PSI and the PPI) on the one hand, and the government's new pro-labor policies on the other doubled the pressure on Italy's dominant class. The propertied class found itself squeezed between the ascendance of the PSI and the trade unions and (as its members saw it) their abandonment by the Liberal government. Italy's dominant class, especially the *agrari* of the Po Valley, responded to what it saw as the "crisis of the Liberal bourgeoisie" in a drive for self-organization on the national and the provincial levels.

In the aftermath of the war, the Liberal government, representing the "parties of order," became more and more responsive to the interests of workers and peasants. In addition to the electoral reform of 1918, both postwar governments, headed by Francisco Nitti and by Giovanni Giolitti, enacted a series of welfare reforms in favor of peasants and workers, supported the redistribution of land to peasants and returning veterans, and implemented tax reforms that increased the share of taxes to be paid by the wealthy and by war profiteers. In short, the postwar Liberal government, as Lyttelton puts it, "constantly gave in" to the Socialists' demands against the employers' interests (1987, p. 40).

The first indication of a change in the Liberal government's policies appeared in its postwar rhetoric. Attempting to incorporate popular demands for radical social change, Prime Minister Antonio Salandra, and his successor, Vittorio Orlando, exalted the war's "revolutionary virtues" and promised the returning soldiers a new social order. "The war is a revolution," announced Salandra, whose government had led Italy into the war: "Yes, a very great revolution. Let no one think that after the storm it will be possible to make a peaceful return to the old order. Let no one think that the old habits of leisurely life can be resumed" (cited in Tasca [1938] 1966, p. 10). Similarly, Prime Minister Orlando promised in that same year that "this war is also the greatest political and social revolution recorded by history, surpassing even the French revolution" (cited in Seton Watson 1967, p. 511).

In contrast to these promises of an abstract better future, Giolitti, who had been one of the main opponents of Italy's intervention in World War I, specifically pointed to the interventionists' responsibility for the war's miseries. His message to Italy's dominant class was clear: "The forces of reaction," Giolitti declared, "can prevail no longer, since the privileged classes of society, which led humanity into disaster, can no longer rule the whole world alone: Its destiny must lie henceforth in the hands of the people" (cited in Tasca [1938] 1966, p. 63). In his *Program Speech* in October 12, 1919, Giolitti went on to attack opponents of the peace treaty who, he charged, were ready to "condemn Italy to...economic exhaustion in order to enrich another generation of profiteers" (cited in Clough and Saladino 1968, p. 379).

Extensive social reforms did indeed follow. The first government to lead the country in the transition to a peacetime economy was headed by Nitti. Nitti's reforms included unemployment insurance, a statutory eight-hour day, and the extension of workmen's compensation to the agricultural sector. But Nitti's policies failed to satisfy the maximalist Socialists in Parliament and they were opposed by the conservative and nationalist members of his own party. The conservatives fought Nitti's electoral reform while the nationalists were outraged by his amnesty to deserters and his government's willingness to compromise on Italy's claims to Dalmatian territory. Nitti's policies thus alienated most of the right wing without winning the support of the left (Seton Watson 1967, pp. 536-37; De Felice 1965, pp. 599-600). He was denounced by his own constituency, who labeled him the "Italian Kerensky," the individual who would open the way to a socialist revolution.

Giolitti became Prime Minister in June 1920, following the resolution of the Fiume question. Like his predecessor Nitti, Giolitti hoped to maintain the Liberals' political power by incorporating the Socialists' demands into his government's policies (De Felice 1965; Corner 1975, p. 109; Cunsolo 1991). At first, the bourgeoisie and Liberal leaders welcomed the nomination of the veteran statesman as "the only man who can resolve the grave crisis of the country" (Maier 1975, p. 181). Giolitti's uncompromising measures against the war profiteers gained him the support of the nationalists and interventionists but, again, his social reforms failed to satisfy the Socialists (De Felice 1965, p. 599; Seton Watson 1967, p. 491).

In time, Giolitti enacted an increase in the taxation of wealth, compulsory accident insurance to be financed by a surcharge on employers, and an old age and disability insurance system, the contributions to which were to be divided equally between employers and employees (Snowden 1989, pp. 53-54). The *agrari* in Tuscany, for example, where the *mezzadria* (sharecropping) system prevailed, opposed these added costs: The sharecropper, according to the secretary of the Tuscan Agrarian Association (AAT), which was established in 1919 and was one of the most powerful class organizations in the country, "has no need for insurance against disability and old age. For him, the solidarity binding the various members of our peasant families is the best form of provision" (Snowden 1989, p. 53).

Giolitti's policy against war profiteers was directed primarily against the armament and shipping industries, the main beneficiaries during the war years. He reduced state subsidies to industry and established a special commission to "investigate and revise" heavy industry's war contracts with the state. He also enacted new tax laws aimed at the wealthy, including a capital levy, an increase in death duties and expropriation of war profits, and special measures to reduce tax evasion (Seton Watson 1967, pp. 562-63, 565). All these led the conservatives to denounce Giolitti as a "traitor" and "Royal Bolshevik" (Clough and Saladino 1968, p. 379).

In addition to this legislation, aimed specifically at the propertied class, the Liberal government granted official recognition to peasant leagues and labor unions. As the Minister of Labor argued in July 1920: "To explain in a few words my idea of the co-operative movement, I will say that it is above all essential to try to secure to those depending on any industrial undertaking an opportunity of acquiring that undertaking itself by uniting for this purpose in a co-operative society. Such a co-operative society must be guaranteed the use and possession of the undertaking to which its members belong, on payment of rent; the state must encourage the workers to act along these lines" (cited in Ruini 1922, p. 15).

The new land policy was first implemented by Nitti's government. In response to the peasant leagues' demands for land redistribution in the south, thousands of hectares (estimated between 40,000 and 200,000) of land seized by the leagues were retroactively recognized by a government decree in 1919. This decree "authorized prefects to reacquisition uncultivated or insufficiently cultivated land and to cede it for four years to 'responsible cooperatives.'" In the period of September 1919 to April 1920 alone, an estimated 27,000 hectares belonging to 191 proprietors were, according to this decree, ceded and transferred to 101 peasant cooperatives (Schmidt 1938, p. 31, n. 36; Serpieri 1930, pp. 283). This land program was supplemented by the government's establishment of a formal organization of demobilized soldiers, the Veterans' Association, with a budget of 300 million lire allotted to the purchase of small holdings for the demobilized soldiers (Seton Watson 1967, p. 491).

Perhaps the most consequential action taken by the Liberal government in terms of its effect on its propertied constituency was its recognition of labor unions. This legitimated the unions' encroachment on the employers' authority to hire and fire and to unilaterally determine wages (Snowden 1972, p. 274; Seton Watson 1967, pp. 305, 523). It was an implicit threat to established property rights. The government's support of the labor unions legitimized not only their practices and demands but, most importantly, their victories (see chapter 4). Thus, in addition to increased taxation on property and support of militant and successful worker and peasant agitation, Giolitti upheld his prewar principle against state intervention in labor disputes. He refused to interfere to help the *agrari* who were beset by peasant land seizures, or to aid the industrialists during the occupation of the factories in September 1920.

The Socialists' occupation of the factories in the industrial triangle of Milan, Turin, and Genoa was, indeed, the most direct and dramatic confrontation between the government and the employers during the post World War I period. Individual industrialists demanded that the government send soldiers to evict the workers from the factories (Snowden 1989, p. 144). A delegation of industrialists to the prefecture in Turin threatened to organize their own protection if the government refused to assist them (Spriano 1964, p. 83). For instance, the Orlando brothers, shipping and electrical industry magnates from Livorno in Tuscany, wrote to Giolitti: "Despite repeated requests for protection, the government authorities...have stood aside....By now it is needless to point out that the motive of the agitations is purely political, and that the aim is to overthrow the social and political order" (Snowden 1989, p. 144).

Giolitti refused. "It is necessary to make the industrialists understand," he told the prefect of Milan on September 11, 1920, "that no Italian government will resort to force and provoke a revolution simply to save them some money. The use of force will mean, at the very least, the ruin of the factories. I place my faith in a peaceful resolution" (Spriano 1964, pp. 97-98). Giolitti held on to his program until the May 1921 elections. In his last speech to Parliament before the elections, he reaffirmed his support of worker cooperatives, land reform, social welfare, and factory councils (Sarti 1971, p. 29).

There is no doubt that the propertied constituency of the Liberal Party saw the new situation as a total breakdown of their social and political order. As early as 1917, one of the leading landlords of Bologna maintained that the old Liberal order was obsolete "in the face of new moral, economic, social and political conditions which the Great War has unleashed in Europe," and the Liberal Party "was destined to die in the great funeral pyre the war has prepared for old-fashioned notions" (cited in Cardoza 1982, p. 257). With the progression of the postwar crisis, bourgeois spokesmen articulated their sense of despair and betrayal. After the occupation of the factories, the influential Luigi Albertini, owner and editor of the *Corriere della Sera*, expressed this clearly: The "most elementary functions of government no longer exist in Milan....There is nothing, nothing, absolutely nothing, that resembles a government. People are being seized, there are thefts and homicides, everything, everything, is permitted," he told Amendola, a Liberal representative (cited in Spriano 1964, p. 188).[5] According to the agrarians' newspaper, *Resto del Carlino*, November 20, 1919, the 1919 elections "appeared to be the political liquidation of the Liberal bourgeoisie that...has governed Italy. The defeat, which is the defeat not just of the government, but of the Liberal and secular state, the crisis of a regime, and the end of a historical era, are all apparent" (cited in Snowden 1989, p. 54).

Bourgeois Militancy

The landlords, as stated, responded to the Socialists' insurgency and to the government's attempt to incorporate their socialist demands with their own political mobilization and self-organization (De Felice 1965, pp. 636-37; Salvatorelli and Mira 1964, p. 166). "Bourgeois 'defenders of order' began to take the law into their hands" (Seton Watson 1967, p. 570). If the general elections of 1919 were "the political liquidation of the Liberal bourgeoisie," the occupation of the factories in the north, continued land seizures in the south, and the Socialists' gains in the 1920 local elections were the "avalanche which is burying the rights of property" (Cardoza 1982, p. 300). An "atmosphere of battle," as Bonomi puts it, "was blowing through the countryside." Among its carriers, he argues, were the rural bourgeoisie of the Po Valley and young demobilized officers and their families, who began to talk of the necessity to defend the country from a "proletarian dictatorship." The nationalists and conservatives themselves turned to the tactic of mass protests in the streets and abandoned as ineffective more traditional institutionalized political means. They adopted the Socialists' tactic of demonstrations in the piazzas, and the walls that used to be covered with Socialist antiwar slogans were now covered with the nationalist's protests (De Felice 1965, p. 657).

These methods of "mass politics" were accompanied by the reorganization and centralization of the "political forces of the bourgeoisie" (Lyttelton 1987, p. 57): Employers established new associations, and existing ones adopted new, militant positions. To understand the effect of self-organization on the alliance with the Fascists and its effects on the tactic of violence, we must distinguish between the responses and subsequent actions of the industrialists versus the landlords.

The crucial moment in the ascendancy of Fascism, historians agree, was in its alliance with the *agrari* of the Po Valley. "The decisive impulse" in Lyttelton's words, "to an [anti-Socialist] reaction came from the agrarians," whose alliance with the Fascists had led to the expansion of the small urban organization into the countryside (1987, p. 37; see also Tasca [1938] 1966; De Felice 1966 Vol. 2, pp. 121-22; Corner 1975, pp. 108-9, 137-38; Maier 1975, pp. 311-14).[6]

The question is, then, what accounted for the distinction between the *agrari*'s relation to the Fascists and the industrialists? If, as I have argued above, the intensification of the class struggle after the war and the state's pro-labor policies were the immediate causes for the political mobilization of Italy's dominant class, why did those policies affect the two groups differently? The main reason for the *agrari*'s new, violent, reaction was the resurrection of their existing tradition of militant organization against the workers, coupled with their new opposition to the postwar Liberal government. Consequently, to comprehend the specific effect of those policies on the *agrari* requires the examination of the prewar history of the relationship between the *agrari,* the workers' organizations, and the state.

The Militant Tradition of the *Agrari*

From the outset, the alliance of agricultural workers against their employers, begun in the mid-nineteenth century, constituted a special threat to the relations of production in the northern countryside, especially in the Po Valley. As was already noted, in contrast with the semi-feudal estates in the south, agriculture in the Po Valley was based on large commercial farms, established in the second half of the nineteenth century. These modern enterprises employed mainly day laborers and cultivated industrial crops such as hemp and sugar beets (Cardoza 1979, p. 172; see also Moore 1966; Snowden 1972).

The dependence on wage workers, free of the traditional tenure relations that dominated other parts of the country, rendered the *agrari* of the Po Valley particularly vulnerable to the agitation incited by the emerging unions. Indeed, in the 1880s, the Po Valley became the focus of one of the first organizations of the rural proletariat, the *braccianti* ("arms"), in Europe. These "leagues of resistance," begun as cultural and educational movements for the workers, soon provided militant organizers of massive agricultural strikes.

For the *agrari*, noted for combining the "pitiless greed of the modern entrepreneur...and that ancestral reactionary instinct of the landed proprietor" (Roveri, cited in Corner 1975, p. 8), the rise of the Socialists was a threat to an entire way of life. And so, according to historian Luigi Preti, the first landlords' provincial organizations were established at the turn of the century in direct reaction against the labor unions and peasant leagues (1955, p. 219). Resistance to organized labor was, from the start, the raison d'être of the landlords' associations.

The *agrari* modeled their local associations after the workers' organizations. Like them, they concentrated their efforts on the communal and provincial levels; the relative strength of their local organizations grew with every increase in the "threat" from the workers. Thus, the most militant agrarian association was in the region of Emilia (which included the important agricultural provinces of Ferrara, Bologna, Mantua, and Modena), a prominent center of union organizing, strikes, and agitations. In 1907, the *agrari* of Emilia extended their organization outside the region, and established the first Interprovincial Landlord Federation which, as stated, soon became "the most potent class organization in the Po Valley and in all of Italy" (Preti 1955, p. 220). That same year, the *agrari* of Bologna organized "Defence Squads" consisting of mobile units of "permanent strikebreakers" and of "corps of volunteers" to guard the fields in several provinces against striking workers (Cardoza 1982, p. 460). Similar organized landlord actions against the Syndicalist Union took place in Parma (Bertrand 1970, pp. 40, 42; Neufeld, 1961, p. 347).

Most relevant to the analysis of the consequences of this early landlord organization to its postwar mobilization was its reliance on the central government and local authorities for assistance. The prewar governments guaranteed the *agrari* their support in the struggle against the organized workers. Refusing to recognize the legitimacy of the leagues, the landlords demanded, and received, the active collaboration of the police, the Army, and prefects who violently suppressed the workers' organizations. The prefects, actively assisted by the Minister of the Interior, dispatched troops against the workers, closed their labor organizations, and arrested the strikers (Cardoza 1982, p. 60; see also Neufeld 1961, pp. 334, 341). The state's explicit and active aid to the landlords was perhaps the main cause for the conflict's escalation after the war.

THE POSTWAR "ANTI-BOLSHEVIK" REACTION

In the postwar years, while the workers' threat "from below"—the militancy and achievements of rural workers, the electoral success of the PSI—increased, the state's support "from above" decreased. Unlike their predecessor's prewar actions, the second drive for landlord mobilization was characterized by the establishment of focused, new, and enduring organizations dedicated to the struggle against the workers. Whereas the prewar landlord actions may be characterized as state-assisted, ad hoc reactions to the workers' strikes and agitations, after the war, the *agrari* moved to create their own organizational infrastructure and political strategy, independent of the political support of the Italian government.

We should also recall that postwar developments, primarily the emergence of political democracy and the rise of mass parties, affected not only the *agrari*'s direct material interests, but also their social dominance and political power in the provinces. As Cardoza put it: The *agrari*'s "simplest pleasures—strolls through the arcaded streets...dinners in elegant restaurants, or shopping trips...seemed to depend on the good will of the new [Socialist] provincial rulers" (1982, p. 289). The fury of the *agrari*'s response should be understood as an attempt to defend themselves against what they saw as the beginning of a total assault on their social domain. "Suddenly...the country landowner who for years had been the cock of the walk, head of the commune, manager of all local and provincial bodies," in Tasca's words, "...had to reckon with the [peasant] 'League' and the [union-controlled] employment office [as well as] with the Socialist co-operative society" that set market prices on agricultural products ([1938] 1966, p. 95).

Nevertheless, the immediate significance of the postwar ascendance of Socialist provincial governments was its adverse effect on the *agrari*'s material interests. The unions' achievements and new taxation imposed on property by the PSI-led provincial governments threatened to drastically reduce the profitability of the land. In addition, both *agrari* and Socialists saw the Socialists' program of land expropriation and collectivization as a step toward a rural revolution.

The result was the *agrari*'s "flight from the land" (Snowden 1972, p. 272). In the province of Mantua, in the Emilia region, according to an account by Ivanoe Bonomi, "the established landowners...believed that the agitations of 1919 and 1920 were the portents of a Russian-style expropriation. For this reason they were induced to sell their lands at bargain prices simply in order to conserve a little money" (cited in Corner 1975, p. 155, n. 3; see also Snowden 1972). Similarly, in the province of Siena, in Tuscany, police reports describe the "massive emigration by men of property seeking to escape a systematic persecution and permanent menace" (Snowden 1989, p. 93); the whole province of Ferrara, as Corner put it, "was up for sale" (1975, p. 155; also see Serpieri 1930, pp. 484-89).[7] It is no wonder, then, that the *agrari* saw the government's defeat in 1919 as "the end of a historical era" (in Snowden 1989, p. 54).

The culmination of the struggle between the landlords and the workers came during the great agricultural strike that swept across most of the Po Valley in the spring of 1920. Historically, this was the immediate precursor to the *agrari*'s alliance with the Fascists. The strike's magnitude—its duration, the number of workers involved, and the consequent damage to the crops—led the *agrari*, like the industrialists facing the occupation of the factories, to demand that the government use force against the striking workers. But, again, the government declined to do so.

The *agrari*'s response to the state's refusal to come to their aid illustrates the extent of their resentment and sense of betrayal at the hands of their own political representatives. "The government was in no way able to guarantee...respect for property or persons," or to "maintain among the people [a] sense of respect for authority and for the law which is now totally lacking" the *agrari* of Ferrara objected (cited in Corner 1975, p. 108, n. 2). "We strongly protest the acquiescence of government towards imposition of violence [and] workers' monopoly against local landlords. We demand exemplary repression of the guilty, effective upholding of law and order, protection of private property" (telegram to the Ministry of the Interior, February 1920, cited in Snowden 1989, p. 223, n. 131). According to Serpieri, the *agrari* felt that "in the violent struggles over agricultural contracts and agricultural labor...the government is absent, or passively watches every violation of right....Thus, the conviction is widespread...among the agrarian bourgeoisie that only by their own self help, by their own force, can they protect their interests. The alternative for them is to resign themselves to the final collapse of the existing social order" (cited in Snowden 1972, p. 274, n. 21).

A similar message emerged from the Congress of the National Agrarian Association (NAA), which took place under the impact of the agricultural strike in Bologna. A "watershed in the *agrari*'s policy," the Congress expressed the explicit, formal radicalization of the employers' organizations: Although the ANA's work would now focus on local disputes with the leagues and the unions, it would likewise be directed toward "the economic and moral reconstitution of the nation" (Snowden 1989, p. 62). "We are ready to defend our rights," the *agrari* declared in February 1921, "not only to save ourselves, but also in order to defend civilization and progress...for we know that we are defending sacred personal rights and class rights" (cited in Schmidt 1938, p. 35, n. 4).

And so the *agrari* began to establish new associations or "Leagues of Social Defense." Accusing the Liberal-led government of "connivance with the Bolsheviks," Bologna's *agrari* established the Association for Social Defence (1920). This was a paramilitary organization consisting of squads of vigilantes, which the *agrari* called *volontario civile*. The alliance's purpose was to employ "whatever means necessary" against the organized workers and in defence of "the most elementary liberties" (Cardoza 1982, pp. 294-95). At the same time, an "anti-Bolshevik union" was formed in Emilia that was to represent, according to its founders, a "fusion" of "all men of order of any party...with the common intent of defence of life [and] liberty against the aggressions of the scandalous oppression of the Bolshevik mob" (in Cavandoli 1972, p. 130). It is crucial to recall that at this stage the Fascists had no role in establishing this union. In most provinces, the local *fasci* (like the Bologna *fascio*, which had at most 15 members) had hardly enrolled any members (Cardoza 1982, p. 297).

In sum, the *agrari*'s history of militant self-organization against the workers' unions, and their conviction that they had been abandoned by their government made the distance separating them from the Fascist Squads relatively small. The effect of political democracy, which led their government to implement new pro-labor policies, the ascendance of new mass parties, the continued worker insurgency, and the eventual loss of social and political power amounted, as they indeed claimed, to a crisis of the "liberal bourgeoisie." The landlords' alliance with the Fascists, discussed in the following chapter, was, to a great extent, a continuation of their already existing political strategy.

NOTES

1. D'Annunzio's co-author of the charter was Alceste De Ambris.
2. Members of both groups, peasant-soldiers and officers, probably joined the Fascists for different reasons and with different expectations. To my knowledge, there is only one systematic study (Rochat [1967] 1974) of the "social origins" of the war veterans. (See also a note by Snowden [1989, p. 34] on the lack of a social history of the Army during the war years.)
3. The Pearson correlation between the number of "soldiers under arms" in the province in 1919 as reported in the government's statistical annals, and the number of Fascist members is relatively high (r=0.38 for membership in March 1921; r=0.36 for membership in April 1921; and r=0.44 for membership in May 1921). These are correlations between the absolute number of soldiers and Fascist Party members in the province; therefore, they may not indicate a pattern. Nevertheless, in light of the Fascists' deliberate effort to recruit men having military skills, these figures— particularly the increase in the strength of the relationship with time—suggest a degree of success.
4. Although, according to Tasca, Bonomi denied issuing this circular, both Lyttelton (1987, p. 39) and Salvemini (1973, p. 118) refer to this document as if it was Bonomi's official proclamation. Whether this was the Minister's individual initiative or not, it seems that some Army High Command encouragement to join the Fascists was issued.
5. Albertini was a Conservative senator and an opponent of Giolitti. He supported Mussolini's accession to power, but withdrew his backing in 1923 and became one of the *Duce*'s most important conservative opponents.
6. Nello is explicit in his claim that the liberal and democratic right-wing parties in Pisa saw in Fascism a vehicle against the "rising tide of Bolshevism."
7. Corner and other historians who share this view draw on the data provided by Serpieri (1930, pp. 390-91). Serpieri details the increase in small proprietors during the postwar years and views this as an indication of both an emerging class of small proprietors and the large landowners' willingness to sell their land. While not conclusive, the evidence does suggest such a trend.

Chapter 6

Provincial Fascism:
The Assault of *Squadrismo*

The Fascists' paramilitary capacity, together with the political and financial patronage of the propertied class, combined to create a unique political strategy and to determine the pattern of its deployment. Demobilized military recruits supplied the Fascists with the manpower and military expertise necessary to carry out the Squads' violent actions. Local associations of the propertied class actively supported and were often directly involved in organizing and leading the Fascist locals and the Squads' "punitive expeditions" into Socialist provinces. These expeditions were greatly facilitated by the Army's High Command, which supplied the Squads with weapons, transport, and personnel.

THE LANDLORDS AND THE FASCISTS

The "offensive alliance" between the Fascists and the *agrari* developed into an open and official convergence of forces between the landlord associations and the local chapters of the Fascist organization. The distinctive element in this alliance with the Fascists was its explicit and formal character. The *agrari*'s collaboration with the Fascists was, as De Felice argues, verily an "organic link."[1] This is evident both in the range of collaboration between the organizations and in the specific forms of support the *agrari* extended to the Fascists. Their regional associations issued public endorsements of Fascism, coordinated tax strikes with the Squads to financially paralyze the Socialist provincial administrations, and organized tax funds among their members to support local *fasci*. Many agrarian leaders went so far as to actively participate in and lead the Squads' "punitive expeditions." Eventually, the *agrari*'s associations almost completely fused with the Fascist Action Squads.

The *agrari* praised the Fascists and their objectives in their newspapers and in speeches made by their associations' officials. Fascism was described as "the purest form of social defense" and the "savior of Italy"; the organization's members were, simply, "our Fascists" (Siena's agrarian newspaper, cited in

Snowden 1989, p. 226, n. 158). They were the "healthy good patriotic part of
Italian youth"; a "beautiful guardian militia," whose "young courageous forces"
symbolize "the proud awakening of the energies of the Italian race." The "youth
and force" of the Squads qualified them as the only ones capable of "arrest[ing]
the wave of madness which is breaking our Italy" and with the "right to make
claims on the future of Italy" (Corner 1975, p. 113). In short, as a Liberal
deputy from Florence put it, Fascism was a "marvelous organization" that came
to the aid of a besieged nation that "has the right to defend its institutions and
its liberties" (cited in Snowden 1989, p. 56).

Financial support to the Fascists was channeled by the *agrari* through their
regional associations. This organized, collective form of support indicates the
degree of consensus reigning among the members on the necessity of such an
alliance as well as on the tactics it should employ. In Tuscany and Emilia, the
agrari established internal taxation systems ("resistance funds" in their terms)
whose proceeds financed local Fascist chapters (Snowden 1989, p. 56). A
system of "quasi-voluntary 'taxation'" enabled regular collection of donations
from association members, with sums calculated according to the individual's
property and income. For example, in Ferrara, of the 106,276 lire collected,
60,000 lire were contributed by 32 individuals, 17 of whom were landlords. The
largest donations came from the province's large landlords and officials of the
Agrarian Association (Corner 1975, pp. 124-25). Conte Severino Navarra, "one
of the major landowners in the province and by reputation one of the most mean
and grasping," donated 15,000 lire (Corner 1975, p. 124). Other large landlords
and leaders of the province's Agrarian Association, including Vico Mantovani,
the Association's president, gave 1,000 lire each.[2] Similarly, in Bologna,
landlords signed formal agreements with the Fascists stipulating the "exact
sums which each landowner or leaseholder would contribute to pay the expenses
of [the] *fasci*'s propaganda and activities" (Cardoza 1982, p. 323; Seton Watson
1967, p. 599, n. 4). In parallel, the Bologna *fascio* established its own fund: A
circular to property owners asked for donations according to a scale determined
by the size of the property (Cordova 1970, p. 973). The Agrarian Association of
Cremona organized a campaign among its members to contribute to the local
fascio. The *agrari* collected 1 million lire which, according to the prefect, were
used to finance "the struggle to the bitter end" (Cordova 1970, p. 974).

The *agrari* also took a determined role in establishing local *fasci* and were
"active exponents of the agrarian Fascist movement" (Cardoza 1982, p. 324)
throughout the Po Valley and Tuscany. Lyttelton argues that "in provinces such
as Alessandria, Pavia or Arezzo, where no Fascist movement existed until late
1920, the agrarian associations were directly responsible for its formation"
(1987, p. 70). According to Tasca, almost every *fascio* in the country was
formed by the landlords ([1938] 1966). The first to call on the Fascists to act on
their behalf against striking workers were the Bolognese *agrari* (Lyttelton 1987,
p. 59). This alliance, according to Bologna's prefect, had the "principal aim of
forming a strong organization capable of opposing the violence that the

extremists of the Socialist Party and the anarchists were committing in the city and in the province" (Cardoza 1982, p. 302).

The culmination of the *agrari* alliance with the Fascists was in the almost complete de facto fusion of their organizations. For instance, the Agrarian Association of Tuscany (AAT) joined the Fascist organization. By this time, the AAT was already affiliated with the Tuscan Citizens' Defence Alliance, which described itself as an "anti-socialist militia," and was supported by the armaments industry and other "leading companies" in the region (Snowden 1989, p. 60). An explicitly belligerent organization, the Alliance declared that its purpose was to fight in "the war that has been declared against the bourgeoisie, to whom the world owes all its scientific, technical and political progress" (cited in Snowden 1989, pp. 133-34). The alliance also adopted the cause of the veterans, supported their demand to fire women and receive their vacated jobs, and organized "public festivities and demonstrations" in honor of demobilized units (Snowden 1989, pp. 158, 251, n. 3).

Collaboration between these organizations and the Fascists was so intense that an inspector of public security in Prato informed the Ministry of the Interior, in April 1922, that "the entire membership [of the Agrarian Association of Tuscany] belongs to the *fascio*. [It] finances the *fascio*, which has become its support and its defense" (cited in Snowden 1989, p. 225, n. 157). AAT officials went so far as to complain that the local *fascio* was draining their organization's membership. Their explanation for the landowners' turn to the Fascists points to their militancy and to the disappointment felt from their own organizations. The AAT argued that the *agrari* see "in other organizations the security...they had lacked [and] feel that perhaps they can do without their natural organization of self-defence" (cited in Snowden 1989, p. 56). Individual *agrari* leaders, including members of the nobility, became active *squadristi*. The president of the AAT became secretary of the Fascist provincial Federation, and *agrari* officials were the organizers of the *fascio* in Molinella (Snowden 1989, p. 57). "By late March [1921] landowners and professional men [in Mantua] were leading Squadrist expeditions, while former leaders of the old liberal and monarchical associations became directors of the Fascist organizations" (Maier 1975, p. 314).

In Ferrara, the *agrari* relationship with the Fascists developed into full political cooperation. They participated in a unique Fascist initiative to appeal to the province's peasantry and expand its social base of support. Under the leadership of Italo Balbo and the "ex-Wobbly" Edmundo Rossoni, the Fascists and the *agrari* formulated a joint "land program" that called for the redistribution of the land to the peasants. This program was encouraged by Mantovani, the president of the province's Agrarian Association, who described it as a "modern and healthy concept" (Cordova 1970, p. 974).[3] Joint land offices were established to distribute land donated by the large landlords (Lyttelton 1987, pp. 63-65: Segre 1987, p. 46). According to this program, by April 1921, the *agrari* had put 12,000 hectares and by September of that year 18,000 hectares (about 10% of the province's total productive land) at the disposition of the Fascist land offices. Other sources estimate the landowners' donations at 8,000 hectares (Snowden 1989, p. 96; Tasca [1938] 1966, p. 102). According to Brustein, the Fascists "proposed to transform agricultural laborers into sharecroppers, sharecroppers into tenant farmers, and eventually all three into landowners"; to do so, they attempted to transfer land from large landowners to land offices so that they could redistribute it to cultivators (1991, p. 658).

The Fascist program in Ferrara created an "atmosphere of class collaboration" between large landlords and small peasants against the "sectarianism" of the Socialists (Corner 1975, pp. 157-58). But the sincerity of the Fascists and the *agrari* was doubtful, as was the arable quality of the land. "There is no record," Corner contends, "of land actually being sold by the large proprietors" (1975, pp. 157-58; see also Tasca [1938] 1966, pp. 101-2; Cordova 1970, p. 975).[4] Nevertheless, the experiment in Ferrara remains an example of a unique, explicitly political instance of cooperation between the *agrari* and the Fascists. Here, the landlords incorporated the specific interests of the Fascist organization, that is, the strengthening of its social appeal and base of support, into their own program.

This historical evidence has generated consensus among historians of Italian Fascism regarding the role of the landlords in the Fascist offensive. Notwithstanding this agreement, analytical and theoretical question regarding the distinction between the *agrari* and the industrialists with respect to cooperation with the Fascists can be raised. Why did the industrialists not participate in the postwar "bourgeois mobilization"? If the political insurgency led by the workers' movement and the state's pro-labor policies were the main cause for the political mobilization of Italy's propertied class, why did the same cause affect the two class segments, landlords and industrialists, so differently? The answer to this question goes beyond its specific theoretical significance: It rests in the distinct organizational history of the landlords and industrialists.

THE INDUSTRIALISTS AND THE FASCISTS

The industrialists' financial support supplemented the *agrari*'s total endorsement of and collaboration with the Fascists. The main difference in the relationships maintained by the two segments was their continuity. In contrast to the "organic link" they established with the *agrari*, the Fascists' relationship with the industrialists was relatively sporadic. The General Confederation of Italian Industrialists (*Confederazione Generale dell Industria Italiana*, CGII) refused to officially endorse the Fascist organization and there was no concerted and formal alliance with the Fascists similar to that established with the agrarians (Sarti 1971, p. 18). No parallel formal organizational bond with the Fascists existed. While the number of Fascist sympathizers among industrialists increased after the occupation of the factories (De Felice 1965, p. 658), the CGII refrained from a formal endorsement of the Fascist organization until the fall of 1922, the period prior to Mussolini's nomination as prime minister.

It appears, then, that the industrialists restricted their support to sporadic albeit generous financial contributions. In addition to some essentially symbolic acts of solidarity,[5] they financed Mussolini's newspaper, they assisted Fascist candidates in the 1921 elections, and subsidized local *fasci* who organized strikebreaking activities (Abrate 1966, p. 362; also Salvatorelli and Mira 1964, pp. 164-65, 171; Seton Watson 1967, pp. 598-99n).

Individual industrial firms and their owners also contributed generously. For instance, the Perrone brothers, owners of the Ansaldo industrial complex, the Ilva Steel Works, Milan's largest steel factory, and Fiat, three of Milan's greatest industrial firms, were among the first to finance Mussolini's interventionist organ *Il Popolo d'Italia* (Lyttelton 1987, p. 211; Snowden 1989, p. 122).[6] In 1922, shipping magnates in Genoa donated 1.5 million lire to the Fascists to finance a "punitive expedition" in their city. This "March on Genoa" resulted in the complete destruction of all the worker organizations and social clubs in the city (Tasca [1938] 1966, p. 223). In Messa-Carrara, the heart of the marble-quarrying industry in Tuscany, Fascism "emerged as an instrument in the hands of the marble owners for the restoration of their unquestioned rule over their workforce" (Snowden 1989, p. 115).

The support of Tuscan industrialists was crucial to the development of Fascism in the region. The flow of "large amounts" of money from Tuscany's Industrial Association (AIT) allowed the emergent local *fascio* to "develop into a regional political force" (Snowden 1989, pp. 147-48). According to the local prefect, the association supplied the Fascists with "means of every description," and many industrialists in the province became "ardent advocates" of Fascism. This "personal, intense, and violent" alliance succeeded in replacing the militant workers of the quarries with a "docile and apolitical" workforce, supplied by the Squads, and consisting of unemployed and criminal elements (Snowden 1989, p. 114; p. 240, n. 158).

Special Fascist "funds" also received donations from industrialists. For instance, the list of donors to the "Victims of December 20th" fund established by the local *fascio* in Ferrara to support Fascists injured in a clash with the Socialists on December 20, 1920 included 450 names, among them prominent industrialists, merchants, and landlords as well as commercial and industrial firms and the sugar companies' association. The donors to a similar fund in Tuscany, established after the Socialists' "legalitarian strike" in July 1922, included the "foremost representatives of the Livorno industrial bourgeoisie" (Snowden 1989, p. 148). These donations yielded considerable sums of money. "In the first six months of 1922 the number of provinces contributing regularly [to the Fascist movement] rose from 5 to 18...The donations averaged 208,000 lire per month in October-December 1921, 193,000 in January-June 1922" (Seton Watson 1967, p. 598, n. 4; De Felice 1964, pp. 245-51).[7]

The industrialists, like the *agrari*, also gave the Fascists public support. They praised the Fascists' "youthful energy" and "magnificent agitation" in major national newspapers. In the elections of May 1921, when the Fascists were incorporated into Giolitti's coalition, the industrialists publicly endorsed the Fascists' candidates and supported their campaigns. Owners and managers of industrial firms also joined the national Fascist organization. Leading figures at Ilva became active and even "enthusiastic" Fascists. The managers of the Orlando shipyards were described as "among the most influential members" of the Fascist organization, which also enjoyed the support of Tuscany's Industrial Association's director and vice-president (Snowden 1989, pp. 149-51).

Further evidence for the industrialists' financial contributions to the Fascists comes from prefects and other political figures as well as from the Fascists themselves. So, for example, the President of the Agrarian Association of Ferrara stated publicly that "the resources of Fascism are well known to be in the wallets of every businessman, industrialist [and] landowner patriot" (Corner 1975, p. 124). In April 1921, the prefect of Florence reported that the *fascio* was "heavily supplied with funds by industrialists, property owners and merchants." In Prato, the prefect described the Fascists as "the genuine expression of...local industry [which] had it in mind to prevent the existence and resurgence of any working class organization whatsoever" (Snowden 1989, pp. 148, 238, n. 114). Perhaps the strongest evidence of the leverage of the propertied class in the Fascist organization comes from the Fascists themselves. In effect, the support of the propertied class, *agrari* and industrialists alike, was not always well received by the Fascists, especially, the revolutionary members who strongly opposed and protested the process that, they argued, was transforming the Fascists into the "body guard of the profiteers" (Corner 1975, p. 123).

But as generous and effective as they may have been, the contributions made by the industrial magnates did not amount to a concerted and formal effort parallel to that of the *agrari*. Despite this collaboration, the CGII refused to openly endorse the Fascist organization. The lack of formal CGII support of Fascism may be interpreted as evidence that the involvement of individual industrialists in the Fascist organization was only that, a function of specific economic interests and personal political preferences. Another interpretation, however, is offered by the historian Melogriani. The main reason for this hesitation, he argues, rested in the Fascists' early anti-capitalist demagogy. The industrialists' leadership, he contends, simply could not endorse the Fascists' socialist rhetoric, nationalism, and fierce anticlericalism (1972, p. 18).[8]

In retrospect, the absence of early formal endorsement on the part of the industrialists appears to be a case of tactical caution rather than the expression of a genuine position. The CGII and the Fascist organization became more closely aligned as the Fascists' success grew; hence, the CGII eventually did endorse the Fascists. In the last months of 1922, just before the Fascists' "March on Rome" and at the height of the Squads' expeditions, Ettore Conti, the CGII president, came close to making such an endorsement. Mussolini, he declared in public, was "a man...who defends the gains of our military victory, who opposes the agricultural workers' leagues, which threaten the physical safety of landowners, and imperil their goods and their crops...who trusts the elites, more than the masses...[This man] is made to order for the Confederation of Industry" (in Sarti 1971, p. 29). Indeed, after the "March on Rome," CGII hesitation toward Fascism disappeared. The King and government officials received communications from the CGII expressing its support of Mussolini. The CGII welcomed the King's nomination of Mussolini as Prime Minister and issued an "enthusiastic endorsement" of his new government. Mussolini, the declaration stated, was a leader committed to "the right to own property, the general obligation to work, the need for discipline, the advancement of private initiative [and] loyalty to the nation" (cited in Sarti 1971, p. 39).

This may partially explain the fact that Mussolini, who was far from endorsing the landlords, came forth on behalf of industry. While Mussolini referred to the landlords as "the private interests of the most sinister and contemptible classes in Italy" (Segre 1987, p. 44), he denounced "the interference of the State" in industry and its attempts to "assassinate the process of creation of wealth" (Lyttelton 1987, pp. 210-13). The nation's industrialists, who had first welcomed the Fascists merely as strikebreakers, now embraced them as political leaders.

An additional factor should also be considered. While the government's postwar policies antagonized both segments of Italy's propertied class, the respective groups' capacity to collectively respond to this antagonism was not identical. As we have seen, the landlords had a long-honored tradition of militant action against the workers and of self-organization on the provincial and regional levels. No such tradition existed among Italy's nascent industrialists, who were heavily dependent on state policies. The infant Italian industry emerging in the late nineteenth century owed its development to substantial state protectionism, nationalistic rhetoric, and imperialism (Lyttelton 1987, pp. 11-12). State protectionism, Cafagna argues, went beyond protective tariffs; it included such measures as "orders for railways, which had been nationalized in 1905, navigation bounties, and building awards for ships produced in Italian shipyards" (1973, p. 318).[9] So, although we have good reason to expect the industrialists who, like the landlords, were now deserted by the state would also react in a similar manner, they appear to have lacked the organizational capacity to do so.

Together with the alliance between the *agrari* and the Fascist organization, and the Army's assistance to the Squads, the industrialists' financial support completed the infrastructure transforming violence into the main instrument of the Fascists' political strategy. The Action Squads could now become the instruments for the reorganization of the bourgeoisie against the Socialists. By 1920, they were ready to embark on their campaign of "punitive expeditions."

THE PATTERN OF *SQUADRISMO*

Some historians of Italian Fascism argue that there was no pattern to the Fascists' violence. For example, Lyttelton tacitly accepts the thesis put forth by Dino Grandi, one of the militant squad leaders in Emilia, that the Fascists' violence was but a "*chaotic* ensemble of local reactions" (1987, p. 54, my emphasis). Implied in this view is the contention that there were multiple causes for these local reactions, and that these causes varied from one locality to another. If specific local conditions determined the intensity and direction of the Squads' violence, we may assume that any variation in such local conditions would prevent the creation of a pattern among the provinces.[10] Following Silone and Tasca, I will attempt to refute this argument and try to show that there was a pattern to Fascist violence, a pattern determined by the alliance between the Squads and the propertied class. As a result of this alliance, the Fascist Squads attacked, almost exclusively, those provinces in which the greatest threat to their allies was to be found.

Ignazio Silone, then a Socialist leader, counter-argues that there was a pattern in the Squads' modus operandi, that it was a product of the assistance and support the Fascists received from business and *agrari* organizations as well as local state authorities. Silone reports that Fascists habitually carried out "punitive expeditions" in response to "invitations" by landlords who paid for the Squads' weapons and transportation well in advance of the raids. The *agrari* would notify local police of an upcoming assault; rather than prevent the raid, the police would search union headquarters and confiscate weapons found in the workers' possession prior to it. The Squads would then enter the locality, usually at night, and often escorted by the police (in Schmidt 1938, p. 37). Tasca makes a similar argument but is even more specific: It was with "arms provided by the Agrarian Association or by some [Army] regimental stores and in trucks provided by the *agrari* that the Blackshirts would ride to their destination...[in] the country from some urban center. The expedition usually had a definite objective, which was to 'clean up' a neighborhood" ([1938] 1966, p. 103). The following analysis attempts to confirm the argument that the alliance between the *agrari* and the Fascists determined the pattern of *squadrismo*.

The "era of violence" as Tasca ([1938] 1966, p. 101) terms the Squads' "punitive expeditions," was born immediately after the local elections in the fall of 1920. Truckloads of armed *squadristi* from provincial centers destroyed worker institutions (e.g., Socialist Clubs, union offices, and press facilities) throughout the Po Valley and Tuscany. "Thousands of Fascists...with free passes on the railways, swarmed into the towns, sacked houses, looted Trade Union quarters, beat and maltreated, banished or murdered the organizers. The country was terrorized by 'punitive expeditions' which set out openly from Fascist offices in the town" (Salvemini 1927, p. 58). Organized into relatively small and mobile units of one to five hundred men, the Squads usually attacked at night. They would "rush to the buildings of the Chambers of Labor, the Syndicate, or the Co-operative, or to the People's House, break down the doors, hurl out furniture, books, or stores into the street, pour petrol over them, and in a few minutes there would be a blaze" (Tasca [1938] 1966, p. 103).

The Squads' "technique of mobile warfare" (Tasca [1938] 1966, p. 124) indicates two tactical characteristics of the Fascists' political strategy. The first is the logistic importance of the means of transportation. In Italy's relatively isolated centers of political life, with its concentration on the provincial and communal levels, the Squads' capacity to move troops from one province to another and to take the Socialists by surprise was a crucial advantage. The workers facing these attacks, Tasca argues, were as helpless as "Hanriot's gunners [paralyzed] outside the doors of the Convention on the 9th Thermidor" ([1938] 1966, p. 127). In order to move throughout a province, the Squads depended on the support of the landlords, the only ones (excluding the Army) who could supply them with the necessary vehicles to transport their armed units (Tasca [1938] 1966, p. 125; Lyttelton 1987, p. 53; Snowden 1989, p. 201). The importance of the Squads' mobility is related to the second tactical characteristic: The expeditions were not carried out by members of the local *fasci*. The "Fascists who stormed the agrarian localities came from the cities" (Lyttelton 1987, p. 53). The expansion of Fascism throughout Italy's northern provinces was not, then, an accumulation of separate and independent local developments; rather, it was the result of coordinated movement of "troops" from those provincial centers in which the *fasci* were already strongly organized and supported (Snowden 1989; Corner 1975; Cardoza 1982).[11]

This specific form of expansion, through "mobile warfare," indicates the relative weakness if not total absence of autonomous Fascist locals and the growing strategic importance of the larger *fasci* located in provincial centers, usually the provincial capitals (e.g., the cities of Ferrara, Bologna, and Florence). Indeed, most of the provinces subjected to "punitive expeditions" did see an increase in Fascist membership in the period from March 1921 through May 1922. Afterwards, the numbers seem to remain more or less stable. At the end of 1920 (before the beginning of the "punitive expeditions"), there was a total of 88 *fasci* with 20,615 members in the country. In most of the provinces, the number of Fascist members at this time did not exceed a few hundred men. This number increased steadily, from 317 *fasci* with 80,476 members at the end of March 1921, to 1,001 *fasci* with 98,399 members in May 1921. It is interesting that the intensity of the "expeditions" in Ferrara was not accompanied by an increase in membership. The province's total membership remained more or less stable from March 1921 until May 1922 (about 7,880). Yet, the number of *fasci* in the province almost doubled—from 52 in March 1921 to 95 in May 1922 (De Felice 1966, pp. 5, 10-11).

It seems clear, especially when compared with the PSI's 200,000 members and over 2 million voters that the Fascist organization, at this stage, was far from a mass-based movement. From this "technique of mobile warfare" there developed a pattern of concentric expansion of the Squads, first from the provincial centers to the remainder of the province, and then from one province to another (Snowden 1989, p. 80; Tasca [1938] 1966, p. 125). The attacks on the provinces of Grosseto and Siena, for example, could not have taken place if participation had been limited to the members of their small local *fasci* (Tasca

[1938] 1966). The importance of the provincial centers was also evident to government officials. A "constant stream" of communications went from central state officials to the prefects, urging them to "prevent the Fascists from driving about in lorries spreading panic and alarm" (Snowden 1989, p. 184). These attacks by the mobile Squads in Tuscany were so grave that they provoked Prime Minister Giolitti's personal intervention. "The prefect of Pisa calls to my attention," Giolitti told Florence's prefect, "that all the Fascist incursions in his province originate [in Florence]," and that "armed gangs of Fascists from this city and from Prato are roaming about Pistoia committing violence against an unarmed population" (cited in Snowden 1989, pp. 184-85). [12]

The first wave of systematic intra-provincial expansion took place in the province of Ferrara, under Italo Balbo's leadership. [13] The Squads' expeditions through the province were described as a "blitzkrieg" (Cardoza 1982, p. 341). Between February and April 1921 alone, an estimated 130 "punitive expeditions" took place in Ferrara, which led to the destruction of Socialist property and acts of personal violence against leading Socialists. The Fascists destroyed about forty Socialist properties, including Chambers of Labor, league offices, and cooperatives. They searched for "the most prominent Socialists" in the area, then beat or killed them (Corner 1975, p. 139). By April 1921, all of Ferrara's twenty-one communes (municipal governments under Socialist rule) were overthrown by the Fascist Squads (Tasca [1938] 1966, p. 102).

The Ferrara Squads soon became a model for Fascists throughout the country (Cardoza 1982, pp. 316-17). From there they expanded into the provinces of Mantua and Veneto to the north, and Ravenna and Bologna to the south (Corner 1975, pp. 137-38; see also Cardoza 1982). Although not as spectacular as in Ferrara, the Fascists' expansion in Bologna was no less effective. Beginning in April 1921, the Squads destroyed some 35 Socialist holdings in the province; they intimidated and regularly assaulted elected Socialist officials. By the end of the year, according to the Bolognese Chamber of Labor, 557 workers were arrested, 1,936 injured, and 19 killed in the province (Cardoza 1982, p. 377). As in Ferrara, the expeditions led to the overthrow of Socialist officials in all but two of the province's communes.

Again, in Florence, south of Bologna, the Fascist center there was described as "the most savage and arrogant [squadrismo] that ever took root in Italy" (Spriano, cited in Snowden 1989, p. 70). "Florentine Fascism," according to the head of the local Squads, was "conscious of being the Father of Tuscan Fascism...[the Florence fascio] hurried where there was need. With its best men it shielded its comrades in every quarter. It defended, it raised up, it encouraged, it struck and it punished" (Tasca [1938] 1966, p. 125). In Tuscany alone, 137 incidents of violence were initiated against Socialist institutions, including raids on People's Houses, Chambers of Labor, cooperative societies, and other workers' social establishments (Tasca [1938] 1966, p. 120).

There is no doubt that the landlords and employers benefited from the Fascists' violence and their destruction of worker organizations. They were now able to turn back the clock and annul their collective bargaining agreements with the Socialist-led unions. For example, after a two-month campaign of Fascist violence against the Socialists, the *agrari* of Ferrara suspended their agreements with the unions. They began to hire labor on the basis of prewar conditions, thus undoing most of the workers' gains achieved since the war (Corner 1975, p. 145). For instance, the prefect of Mantua reported in a telegram to the Ministry of the Interior on March 1922, that "the landlords of the province no longer intended to honor their signature. The idea penetrated that the Fascist cudgel would suffice to defend their interests and sweep away the labor headquarters and peasant leagues and bring back the old individual contract between proprietor and laborer" (cited in Maier 1975, p. 318).

Data on incidents of Fascist violence in the provinces, based on information gathered by the Socialist Party and retrieved from the Socialists' archives, are provided by the historian De Felice. De Felice lists the aggregate absolute number of incidents of Fascist attacks on various Socialist targets in each province from November 1920 until May 1921 (1966, pp. 36-39). It goes without saying that the source of this data hardly makes them ideal. This is a methodological shortcoming that cannot be overcome because, quite simply, these are the only provincial data we have on the frequency of Fascist violent attacks that are amenable for comparison. However, the methodological problems may perhaps illuminate a more crucial aspect about the PSI's activists: The very fact that the Socialists, while under repeated violent attack by the Squads, found it worthwhile to try and keep records of these incidents provides us, in itself, a sharp if not tragic contrast between the Socialists' and the Fascists' political strategies. While the Squads were attacking, the Socialists were counting and recording these attacks.

The data do not provide a measure of the "quality of violence," such as the number of persons involved, the extent of the property damage, or the number of injuries and deaths. In the absence of such data, I use the absolute number of violent incidents to indicate the Fascists' ability to repeatedly attack in specific provinces. The frequency of violent incidents is thus a rough indicator of the Fascists' ability to initiate and continue to engage in political violence. The ability to do so is independent of the damage or injuries caused by each attack. I do not standardize the rate of violence by, for example, the size of the province's population. This would require the untenable assumption that the meaningfulness of any single incident varied with the province's size, that is, that an incident in a "small" province meant "more" than a similar incident in a "large" one. (Counting the "incidents" implicitly equates them, though they might have been far different in "intensity," a characteristic for which we have no data.)

The level of Fascist violence in a province is classified into three categories: "Chronic" violence is defined as at least fourteen incidents, or at least two incidents per month, for the period between November 1920 and May 1921 (N=25); "recurrent violence" is defined as seven to thirteen incidents of violence, or at least one incident per month (N =14); "sporadic violence" is less than one incident per month (N=28) and includes provinces that experienced no incidents (N=6). In some tables, the frequency of Fascist violence had to be dichotomized. There, I collapsed the categories of "recurrent" and "chronic" violence into one category of "frequent" violence. "Frequent" violence thus is defined as the occurrence of at least seven incidents of violence, or one incident per month.

The historical narrative about the Fascist expeditions suggests a pattern in their mobile warfare: the Fascist attacks concentrated in Italy's northern and central regions, while almost entirely neglecting the country's south. Table 6.1 shows the regional variation in the Fascist violence. Among the 32 provinces in the capitalist north, 53 percent (17 provinces) display the highest rate ("chronic") of Fascist violence, 29 percent of the central provinces (4 out of 14) reveal a similar rate of violence, whereas only 16 percent of the provinces in the *latifundist* south (4 out of 25) show the same rate. Similarly, the occurrence of a "sporadic" rate of Fascist violence was highest in the south. Sixty-eight percent of the southern provinces (17 out of 25) had a "sporadic" rate of violence, whereas only 31 percent of the northern provinces (10 out of 32) had a similar low rate of violence. It appears, therefore, that the Fascists concentrated their attacks in the capitalist north and failed to penetrate the *latifundist* south.

This pattern in the Fascists' mobile warfare brings us to the question of what caused the regional variation in the Squads' violence. Why were some provinces attacked while others were not? What were the social and political characteristics of the attacked provinces, and can they explain the Fascists' strategy? The arguments raised by Silone and Tasca provide the historical and political trajectory that created this pattern: The northern provinces were attacked because they were Socialist provinces.

Table 6.1
Incidence of Fascist Violence by Regional Relations of Production (1920-1921), in Percentages

Region	Level of Fascist Violence*				
	"Chronic"	"Recurrent"	"Sporadic"	(%)	(N)
Capitalist north	53	16	31	100	(32)
Sharecropping center	29	36	36	100	(14)
Latifundist south	16	16	68	100	(25)
Total (N)					(66)

* "Chronic" violence refers to 14 or more incidents of violence (two incidents or more per month) in the province during the period November 1920 to May 1921; "recurrent violence" refers to 7 to 13 incidents of violence (at least 1 incident per-month) during the same period; "sporadic violence" refers to fewer than 7 incidents per month, including provinces with no incidents during this period (N=6).

If we accept the argument that the *agrari*'s alliance with the Fascists influenced the direction of *squadrismo*, we should expect the Fascists to target those provinces where the PSI had considerable electoral strength, especially where they actually governed. Table 6.2 shows the relationship between the PSI vote and the frequency of Fascist violence in the province. Among the provinces where the vote for the PSI was highest, 68% (15 out of 22) were subjected to "chronic" Fascist violence. Alternatively, "chronic" violence occurred only in 23% of the provinces with "medium" or "low" PSI vote. Similarly, the occurrence of "sporadic" Fascist violence (the most infrequent attacks) was inversely related to the size of the PSI vote: Sixty-four percent of the provinces where the PSI vote was lowest in the country and only 14% of the provinces where the PSI vote was highest were subjected to "sporadic" (or no) Fascist violence.

Universal male suffrage, instituted for the first time in Italy's history in 1919, renders the PSI vote a good indicator of the political status of its constituency, the newly enfranchised working class. The PSI vote, therefore, represents two aspects of political power: the Party's popular support (and legitimacy) and its actual political power on the provincial level. Indeed, as we have seen (chapter 4), the provinces where the proportion of wage workers, both industrial and agricultural, was high also tended to have a high PSI vote. This requires us to distinguish between two further aspects of the Socialists' strength: the PSI's actual political power, indicated by the vote, and their social base, the wage workers.

An examination of the PSI vote alone cannot exclude the possibility that the Fascist Squads targeted the Socialists' political and economic organizations in addition to their social base, the workers themselves. The ratio of wage workers in industry and in agriculture indicates the potential Socialist power in the province. The PSI vote may therefore indicate the possibility of distinguishing the "structural" (or "constant") potential of insurgency among the province's working class from its actual political manifestation.

Table 6.2
Incidence of Fascist Violence (1920-1921) by PSI Vote (1920)
in Italy's Provinces, in Percentages

PSI Vote[*]	Level of Fascist Violence				
	"Chronic"	"Recurrent"	"Sporadic"	(%)	(N)
High	68	18	14	100	(22)
Medium	23	32	45	100	(22)
Low	23	14	64	100	(22)
Total (N)					(66)

[*]The vote for the PSI is categorized into three equal groups according to the distribution of the vote among the provinces (N=22 in each category).

To confirm that the frequency of Fascist violence was indeed determined by the PSI's organized political power in the province and not by the size of the Party's social base, we have to examine the alternative hypothesis that the Fascists attacked provinces where the PSI's social base was relatively dominant. Table 6.3 shows the results of a regression analysis of the effects of PSI vote, voter turnout, and concentration of agricultural (Model A) and industrial (Model B) wage workers on the frequency of Fascist violence. The regression shows that the numerical presence of wage workers had no significant effect on the frequency of Fascist violence. Here we have an important distinction between the relevance of the province's class structure and the process by which Fascism rose. In spite of the strong relationship between the proportion of wage workers (both agrarian and industrial) and the vote for the PSI (chapter 4), we see that this relationship did not affect the rate of Fascist violence in the province. The increase in the frequency of the Fascists' attacks followed the increase in the Socialists' actual and visible political power as rulers or as significant contenders for rule in the province. The regression results indicate that the attacks were not against the workers per se, but against the political organization and power of the Socialists.

Nevertheless, the explicit political mobilization of the newly enfranchised workers and peasants, I argue, was crucial in determining which specific province was to be subjected to Fascist violence. The rate of voter turnout in the elections is, in itself, a fair indicator of the province's level of political insurgency. Therefore, it is reasonable to likewise view the rate of voter turnout as a visible threat to the propertied class. The fact that a high proportion of the new electorate took advantage of its new political rights as citizens and chose to go to the polls indicates the insurgent mood characterizing province. But, as we already know, the provinces where voter turnout was high also tended to have a high PSI vote. The rate of voter turnout further demonstrates the Socialists' ability to mobilize the population (i.e., getting the voters to vote) as well as the extent of their popular legitimacy. For these reasons we should expect that in those provinces where the PSI was both strong and popular it would constitute a greater threat to the interests of the propertied class. Such an enlarged threat would increase, in turn, the likelihood that the *agrari* would resort to the violent means offered by the Fascist Squads. Indeed, as Table 6.3 shows, the effect of the political variables, that is, the PSI vote and rate of voter turnout, also had a strong and significant effect on Fascist violence. In Model A (agricultural workers), B=0.848 for voter turnout and B=0.326 for PSI vote. In Model B (industrial workers), B=0.914 for voter turnout and B=0.315 for PSI vote. So, to the extent that the rate of voter turnout was indeed a threat to the interests of the propertied class, we find a clear pattern in the employment of violence. The higher the rate of active political participation in the province, the more likely the occurrence of Fascist attacks in the province.

A more detailed picture of these relationships is revealed in Table 6.4. If Socialist provincial governments were the targets of *squadrismo* (Table 6.2), we should expect that in those provinces where such governments claimed to represent the political will of their electorates, there would be a greater likelihood of attack by the Fascist Squads. The highest rate of Fascist violence should therefore occur in provinces where a high vote for the PSI was accompanied by high voter turnout. Table 6.4 shows the relationship between voter turnout and the incidence of Fascist violence and the effect of the PSI vote on this relationship. In all provinces, independent of the PSI vote, 95% of the "high" turnout provinces were subjected to "frequent" Fascist violence. Only 26% of the provinces with "low" voter turnout experienced a similar level of violence.

Table 6.3
Direct Effects of the Concentration of Agricultural Wage Workers
(Model A), Industrial Workers (1921) (Model B), Voter Turnout (1920)
and PSI Vote (1920) on the Incidence of Fascist Violence (1920-1921)
in Italy's Provinces

	Model A		Model B	
	B (SE)	ß	B (SE)	ß
Agricultural wage workers	.029 (.024)	.133		
Industrial workers			-.043 (.033)	-.143
Voter turnout	.848*	.311	.914** (.351)	.335
PSI vote	.326* (.144)	.305	.315* (.141)	.295
Constant	-48.08		-37.83	
R²	.29		.29	
N	64		64	

*p < .05
**p < .01

Table 6.4
Fascist Violence (1920-1921) by PSI Vote (1920) and
Voter Turnout (1920) in Italy's Provinces, in Percentages

	Incidents of "Frequent" ("Chronic" or Recurrent") Fascist Violence							
	PSI High		PSI Medium		PSI Low		All Provinces	
Voter Turnout	(%)	(N)	(%)	(N)	(%)	(N)	(%)	(N)
High	100	(15)	80	(5)	100	(2)	95	(22)
Medium	75	(4)	60	(10)	43	(7)	57	(21)
Low	33	(3)	29	(7)	23	(13)	26	(23)

The relationship strengthens if we consider the effect of the PSI vote: The higher the level of voter turnout and of the PSI vote, the higher the incidence of Fascist violence. Practically all fifteen provinces where both the PSI vote and the rate of voter turnout were "high" were subjected to "frequent" Fascist violence. But in the thirteen provinces where both levels were low, only 23% were subjected to the same level of violence. Controlling for the level of the PSI vote, we find the same relationship within each category of voter turnout. The rate of "frequent" Fascist violence among the "high" PSI provinces drops in relation to the level of voter turnout—from 100%, to 75%, to 33%. The same trend is discerned in the remaining "medium" and "low" categories.

The findings presented here reveal a clear pattern in the Fascists' employment of the tactic of violence. Fascist violence followed the level of political insurgency in the province and the threat it posed to the landlords, the Fascists' allies. The Squads attacked Socialist provinces, but refrained from attacks on provinces where the Liberal Party (supported by and representing the propertied class) held local power. In these Liberal provinces, where no collaboration was spawned between the landlords and the Fascists—meaning that their coordinated opposition to Socialism was absent—attacks by the Fascists were rare.

This is significant both analytically and historically. Analytically, it shows that for the Socialists, as for the Fascists, the relevant level of analysis is that of the organization and its strategy. It cannot be reduced to the level or number of potential individual electoral supporters. Although the Socialists' political strategy led them to seek (and win) the support of the workers, this aspect of their power was not significant in terms of the Fascist reaction. Historically, this finding refutes Grandi's position: It is clear that the Fascists' violence was indeed characterized by a distinct pattern and that this pattern was determined by the level of the Socialist threat in a province. If we conceptualize voter turnout as an indicator of the Socialists' hold on power or of the province's political insurgency, *squadrismo* can be characterized as the effort to eliminate the most rebellious strongholds in the country. The insignificance of the ratio of the working class, the strong effect of the PSI vote, and the level of voter turnout support and further specify Szymanski's claim, mentioned in the previous chapter, about the role of Socialist power in determining Fascist violence.

This analysis of the Fascists' militarization of the political struggle urges a revision in our conceptualization of Fascism. It was surely, as Przeworski suggests, an "effect of struggle." Whatever its ideological appeal to specific strata, at the time of its ascendance to power Italian Fascism was, first and foremost, an organized anti-Socialist, anti-democratic paramilitary organization sponsored by the organized propertied class. Military organization and capacity, together with the political and financial patronage of the agrarian and industrial segments of the bourgeoisie, combined to create a unique Fascist political strategy and to determine the pattern of its deployment. Local associations of the propertied class actively supported and were often directly involved in organizing and leading the Fascists' locals and the Squads' "punitive expeditions" into the Socialist-controlled provinces. Demobilized military recruits supplied the Fascists with the necessary manpower and military expertise. Finally, the Army's High Command supplied the Squads with weapons, transport, and personnel.

Once we understand the process by which the Squads achieved their immediate aim, the destruction of the Socialist organizational structure, the questions become: What should they have done next? How did their tactic of violence affect the Fascists' takeover of provincial political power? If their "offensive alliances" with the propertied class were crucial in determining their tactic of violence, the Fascists needed a "defensive alliance" with the authorities of the Liberal State to transform this tactic into a vehicle for the seizure of the power to rule.

NOTES

1. See Banti (1988) for a different view: Comparing the organization and role of "agrarian elites" in Prussia and the Po Valley, Banti argues that this thesis applies only to Prussia.

2. See Corner 1975, p. 124, for a detailed breakdown of names, occupations, and amounts donated, as published in the Fascist paper *Il Balila*.

3. Mussolini claimed that Mantovani's letter is an "historical" document that affirms the role of Fascism in the liberation of the peasants (Cordova 1970, p. 975).

4. The author of this Fascist *agrari* program was a landowner who, together with Italo Balbo, was the editor of *Il Balila*, where the program was first announced.

5. As was noted earlier, the hall where the Fascists' founding convention took place, in the Piazza San Sepolcro in Milan, was lent to the movement by the local Association of Industrial and Commercial Interests (Tasca [1938] 1966, p. 33).

6. In July 1918, Mussolini changed the subtitle of his paper from "a Socialist newspaper" to "the newspaper of combatants and producers." Some believe this indicates the increased influence of the industrial interests that financed the paper (Mack Smith 1981, p. 32).

7. These figures are based on De Felice's (1964) study of the financing of the Fascist organization. It should be noted that this study draws only from data regarding the financing of the Fascist Central Committee in Milan, and thus does not include information on the support received by specific *fasci* in the various provinces, which never reached the Milan center (in Lyttelton 1987, p. 210).

8. According to Melograni the industrialists also had ideological reservations based on the Fascists' early pro-labor rhetoric (1972, p. 18), although this does not disqualify consideration of their organizational capacity. See De Felice's detailed study of financial contributions to the Fascist organization; Abrate 1966, p. 362; Lyttelton 1987, pp. 210-11; Snowden 1989, pp. 114, 147-51, 238, n. 114, 115, 122, 240, n. 158; Tasca [1938] 1966, p. 223; Seton Watson 1967, p. 598; Salvatorelli and Mira 1964, pp. 164-65, 171.

9. Rueschemeyer et al. also argues that this protective state policy created in Italy an alliance similar to the famous iron and rye alliance in Germany (1992, pp.103-4).

10. This is also the conclusion reached in Petracchi's study of the development of

Fascism in Pistoia. He suggests that the violence that erupted between the Fascists and the Socialists was the result of local, even personal rivalries rather than an expression of a coherent strategy and organization.

11. The dependence of the Squads on their mobility through and from provincial centers is related to the often-mentioned distinction, emphasized initially by Gramsci, between "urban" and "agrarian" Fascism.

12. Clearly, such communications also testify to the government's attempt to curb Fascist violence. I discuss the relationship between state authorities and the Fascists in chapter 7.

13. This, of course, came after the initial, "sporadic" phase of *squadristi* violence in the borderland regions. See Faustini 1992 on the Fascist raids in Trentino that were aimed specifically against the local press.

Chapter 7

The State's Alliance with the Fascists

Italy's central government, led by the Liberal Party, colluded with the Fascists first passively, by its absence from the scene of struggle, and then actively, by incorporating the Fascists into the governing parliamentary coalition. By doing so, the government legitimized the Squads' tactic of violence and the political achievements the Fascist organization gained from it. At the height of this collusion, the Liberal government not only failed to defend legally constituted Socialist local governments when besieged by the Fascists, they verily aided and abetted the Fascists: Ministerial decrees proclaimed the dissolution of Socialist governments, and prefects who vilified the Fascists as alleged Bolshevik accomplices were discharged. The Liberal government replaced these prefects and provincial governments with commissioners favorable both to the Fascists and to the employers' organizations.

The analysis of the Fascist seizure of power raises two problems in Moore's thesis. First, Moore's analysis simply stops too early, long before the Fascist organization itself was established, and before it embarked on its struggle for power. Second, and related to the first, Moore's state-landlord alliance plays a relatively minor and indirect causal role: It explains only one of Fascism's "precipitating conditions" but not its actual rise. Moore's focus on the historical sequence that preceded the Fascists' emergence leaves us with a conundrum. We do not know, for example, why the Giolitti regime failed, and how the Fascists succeeded not only in gaining admission to but, more pointedly, overthrowing his Liberal government.

If social classes, as Moore argues elsewhere, arise out of "an historically specific set of economic relationships and...the class struggle [is] the basic stuff of politics" (1958, p. 116), then we should explain the Fascist takeover in terms of this class struggle (see also Przeworski 1985, pp. 67-68; Zeitlin 1984). I try to show in the following two chapters that "Moore's alliance" played a greater role in Fascism's rise to power than his own thesis allows. It was not only a "condition" for middle-class support of Fascism; it paved the way to the Fascists' seizure of power. The transformation of local alliances between Fascists and landlords into a national alliance between Fascism and the central state that culminated in the incorporation of the Fascist organization into the ruling Liberal Party was possible because of the "first" pre-Fascist alliance between the landlords and the state. It was therefore was a major, albeit indirect determinant in the Fascists' seizure of power and in Italy's transformation from a parliamentary democracy into a Fascist state.

To understand this development we must answer at least two central questions. The first: What were the determinants and effects of the collusion of the provincially based security forces (including the Royal Guards)[1] with the Fascists? This requires us to revert to the pre-Fascist era. For, as Moore notes, it was during the first years of Italy's independence and unification that the crucial set of social and political relationships, namely, the dependence of the political authorities on the propertied class, was established. The second: What were the Liberal government's policies toward the Fascist organization and the causes for incorporating the Fascists into its ruling coalition?

The historical evidence for the relationship between the Fascists and the provincial and central state authorities relates to almost every branch of the state—the police force, the Army, the judiciary, the magistrates, the prefects, and the national government itself. These relationships held during the Squads' expeditions and subsequent seizure of power. The Fascists' attacks on Socialist institutions and leaders were directly assisted by the entire provincial apparatus of the Liberal state. At first, the security forces "openly supported" the Fascist "punitive expeditions"; later, they collaborated in their taking of power (Tasca [1938] 1966, pp. 102-3; Silone, cited in Schmidt 1938, pp. 36-37).[2] A parliamentary committee appointed by Giolitti in November 1920 to investigate the Fascist violence found that "the local authorities were not adequate," and showed "benevolence" toward the Fascist organization, which also enjoyed the support of "a large part of bourgeois public opinion [and] the sympathy of the local authorities and police agents" (De Felice 1965, vol. I, p. 657).

Two political events facilitated the collusion of the provincial authorities with the Fascist organization: First, as discussed in chapter 3, despite the political transformations that followed World War I, the propertied class retained its power in the Liberal state's executive branch and bureaucracy, and continued to control government policies in the provinces. Second and closely related, the local authorities had long been hostile to the Socialists; this antipathy antedated by decades the emergence of the Fascist organization. Hence, once an alliance was forged between the propertied class and the Fascists, this hostility toward the Socialists easily turned into full-blown collaboration with the Squads.

THE TRADITION OF COLLUSION

Despite the postwar electoral reforms and the electoral gains of the two new mass parties—the PSI and the *Popolare*—the propertied class continued to dominate the state's executive structure. This was a consequence both of the persistence of *trasformismo*, especially Giolitti's reliance on the traditional methods of clientelism, and of the PSI's political strategy. By refusing to join Giolitti's government, by limiting its national struggle to the parliamentary arena, and by concentrating its organization and agitation in the northern provinces, the PSI failed to use its substantial mass representation in Parliament to gain access to the state executive.

As of the turn of the century, Giolitti made several attempts to "domesticate" the reformist Socialists and include them in his cabinet, but the Socialists rejected his offers. In the years 1908-10, the "golden age" of reformism, several contacts between Socialist leaders and Giolitti were initiated. Filippo Turati, the PSI's leader and head of its parliamentary group at the time (he was removed from the Party's executive in 1919), wrote to Anna Kuliscioff in 1908 that he saw in Giolitti "the only serious statesman we have in the Chamber, the only real radical in temperament" (cited in Seton Watson 1967, p. 270). Three years later, Giolitti invited Leonida Bissolati, a founder of the reformist faction (he was expelled from the Party during the 1912 Reggio Emilia congress), to join his government; in 1920, he again offered the Socialists a cabinet post, this time to Turati. However, neither PSI leader accepted, mainly for fear of losing Party support (Seton Watson 1967, p. 562; Maier 1975, p. 183). Thus, the state's bureaucracy and government ministries remained in the hands of the *classe dirigente*. Giolitti continued to rely on his old political network of local clienteles, particularly the prefects, who acted as his liaisons with local men of power.[3]

The relationship between local and national government in Italy is crucial to this issue. Italy's model of local autonomy followed that of France, and was applied first to Piedmont and then to the rest of the state in the 1860s (Spencer 1932, p. 202). The prefectoral system of the postwar era was, to a great extent, "Giolitti's creation" (Maier 1975, p. 315). Appointed by the central government, the prefects were the highest political authorities present in the provinces. They even had the authority to annul the decisions of the provincial governments and, with the approval of the Ministry of the Interior, to remove those governments. In short, as Maier puts it, "The Italian system copied the centralization of the French, but did not endow its civil service with the same jealous independence" (1975, p. 315). Situated between the prefects, who were in charge of the provinces, and the local government was a prefectoral council appointed by the central state "to advise the prefect in all matters of administration." Within the council, two members composed a *giunta,* which was joined by four members selected by the elective council. The *giunta* of local notables supervised the provincial communes and operated as a countervailing force to the prefectoral council and the prefects (Spencer 1932, pp. 203-4). And so, given the landlords' and the nobility's open support of the Fascists, the space available for provincial officials, including the prefects, to act against the Fascists—assuming they wanted to—was limited. Indeed, in those rare instances in which individual prefects did attempt to take action against the Fascists, they were opposed by local men of property, who eventually saw to their expulsion.

The prefects were themselves usually members of the "upper reaches of the bourgeoisie and aristocracy" (Snowden 1989, p. 191; see also Fried 1963, p. 126;

Seton Watson 1967, p. 598, n. 2). Even if they were not personally men of property, the prefects were dependent on the province's notables. Their authority and ability to "reward and punish" was based, to a large extent, on their "good relations" with industrialists, landlords, and merchants who "could be instrumental in making or breaking a [prefect's] career" (Snowden 1989, p. 191). "Traditional solidarity" therefore existed between the prefects and the men of property in the provinces (Fried 1963, p. 148). Both tended "to regard the threat of the left as the main danger of the hour" (Snowden 1989, p. 186), and both saw Fascism as their "deliverance from Bolshevism" (Lyttelton 1987, p. 157). The prefects' intimacy with the propertied class, Salvemini argues, was simply a "gnawing cancer" in Italy's political life (1945, p. xii). This was true of most other higher provincial authorities that were hostile to the worker organizations and to the PSI. Indeed, many high officials, such as the chiefs of police (*questore*) in the provinces of Lucca, Massa, and Siena in Tuscany had personal links with the Fascists through those members of their families who were members of the Fascist organization (Snowden 1989, p. 192).

Long before the postwar ascendance of the workers' movement, prior to the emergence of the Fascist organization, local organizations of the propertied class and the provincial authorities actively cooperated against worker organizations and Socialist agitation (Dunnage 1989). The 1896-99 wave of worker unrest and violent strikes exemplifies the extent and power of this collaboration. The total number of strikes and strikers was without precedent. They were joined in some places by peasant rebellions against grain dealers. Battles between protesters and police spread throughout the Po Valley in the north, and peasants attacked local estate administrators in the south. "Almost every week the peasants of some southern commune revolted in protest against taxes or the price of grain or lack of land" (Seton Watson 1967, p. 189).

The government's response, the Socialists claimed, amounted to a "systematic campaign of intimidation." This wave of "sweeping repression" lasted, with varying degrees of intensity, for three years. Martial law throughout the country was imposed; special "tribunals" were established to "punish the rioters," and hundreds of newspapers were closed (Cardoza 1982, p. 65, n. 137).[4] The focus of the struggle between the state's forces and the Socialists was in Milan where, in May 1897, three days of "bloody fighting" left 80 people dead and 450 wounded. In Bologna, the prefect mobilized troops against striking workers; the police compiled a "list of subversives" and conducted repeated searches in league offices and homes of strike leaders. The Socialist electoral union of Bologna was closed. Striking women were jailed en masse and Socialist leaders were arrested for "enticing hatred between the social classes, rebellion, and crimes against the right-to-work laws" (Cardoza 1982, p. 60). Practically all the labor organizations in the country were dissolved and 828 "political offenders," including "most of the prominent Socialist leaders as well as numerous Republican and Radical politicians" were imprisoned. Included among the "thousands of indiscriminate arrests," were Turati, Kuliscioff, and Bissolati, the future leaders of the PSI's reformist wing (Seton Watson 1967, p. 193). The government issued a decree, the *Comprehensive Coercion Bill*, which established penal colonies for political prisoners. This law also placed further restrictions on public assemblies, and allowed the courts to dissolve any organization threatening "to subvert the social order and the constitution" (Cardoza 1982, pp. 64-65).

This wave of repression was unusual only in its intensity. The prefects continued to act on behalf of the ruling party and the propertied class and against the workers' organizations in the aftermath of World War I. The entrenched anti-Socialist position of the provincial authorities is evidenced in their routine actions on behalf of the employers during the Red Biennium. Tuscan prefects regularly allowed the police to harass strikers and protect the "right to work" of strikebreakers brought in by the employers (Snowden 1989, p. 187). In 1919, during a general industrial strike in the province of Brescia, the police "intervened to combat unionists and enlist peasant blacklegs." The employers also received assistance from the Army, which provided them with war surplus lorries to transport over 1,600 scabs from the countryside to their factories (Kelikian 1986, p. 84). Similar phenomena appeared in the south. In the region of Apulia, the landlords, "in collusion with the authorities," regularly employed gangs of *mazzieri* (clubs, cudgels), who forced workers to vote for the landlords' candidates in the elections (Tasca [1938] 1966, p. 117). In Sicily, it was the active cooperation between "organs of the state" and the "armed power of the local *Mafiosi*" that was "decisive in the killing, capture or neutralization" of rebellious peasants (Arlacchi 1980, p. 117). The similarity between the government's anti-labor actions and its pro-Fascist position a generation later is obvious. As would occur in the postwar collusion of officials with the Fascists, the main executors of these repressive policies were the prefects.

THE COLLUSION OF THE PROVINCIAL AUTHORITIES WITH THE FASCISTS

The provincial authorities' collusion with the Fascists was, first of all, a continuation of their existing alliance with the propertied class. The police and the Royal Guard, which were directly responsible to the prefects, regularly collaborated with the Fascist Squads. This was evident in virtually every province invaded by the Squads. As we already saw, the Fascists' mode of territorial expansion was facilitated by their ability to transfer their troops rapidly from one province to another; they could not have done so without the collaboration of the police and the Army. In the wake of Fascist violence, the central government banned the "circulation of lorries," and use of such means to transport the Squads required a special license. Despite this, the Fascists were able to move freely both inside the provinces and, later, between the provinces, with the connivance if not collaboration of the police and the *carabinieri*, who ignored the central government's ban. In Tuscany, for instance, "trains and lorries filled with armed Fascists were able to converge upon the city from centers throughout the region...without once encountering police resistance [or] a single arrest [or] a weapon being confiscated" (Snowden 1989, p. 201).

The collaboration between the state's security forces and the Fascists ranged from passivity in the face of their attacks on Socialist leaders and PSI and union property, to arrests of workers and Socialist activists who resisted the attacks and, finally, to open and active participation in the Squads' expeditions. In addition to providing the Squads with means of transportation, *carabinieri* and Army officers informed them of the location of Socialist organizations as well as searched the Socialist leagues and confiscated arms prior to Fascist attacks. Often, *carabinieri* openly escorted the Squads as they marched through the towns (Snowden 1989, pp. 193-200; Cardoza 1982, p. 361; Maier 1975, p. 322). In Ferrara, the first province taken over by the Fascists, the chief of police was a notorious Fascist sympathizer, and "it was the police who did the work of the Fascists for them" (Corner 1975, p. 119). In fact, the Fascists of Ferrara openly relied on the *carabinieri*'s preemptive action both against Socialist institutions and leaders and against the *Popolari*.[5] In the final months of 1921, the *carabinieri* confiscated the Socialists' arms and notified the Fascist Squads, whom they actually accompanied into town. They then "turned a blind eye" to the assaults on the Socialists and the unions. Socialist leaders who attempted to organize resistance groups against the Fascists were systematically arrested (Corner 1975, pp. 202, 141, 205-6). The same pattern was repeated throughout those areas in which the Squads carried out their "punitive expeditions."

The Army often armed the Squads and even actively participated in their expeditions. Throughout Tuscany, Army officers, "fully armed and in uniform," joined the Fascists' assaults (Seton Watson 1967, p. 576; Snowden 1989, p. 203). In Foiano, the local police and military provided the Fascists with trucks, machine-guns, and heavy artillery; in July 1922, four trucks full of Royal Guardsmen accompanied the Fascists in a mass demonstration (Salvemini 1927, p. 93). From July to September 1922 alone, hundreds of Army officers, including several generals, who had officially enrolled in the Fascist organization, took part in the organization's ceremonies or sent Mussolini telegrams, which were published in *Il Popolo d'Italia,* expressing their support (Salvemini 1927, p. 96; see also Snowden 1989, p. 157; Tasca [1938] 1966, p. 121).

The active role taken by the police and the Army was particularly evident in provinces where the workers resisted the Squads' assaults. An eyewitness description of a Fascist expedition to Pontlagoscuro, a commune in Tuscany, in March 1921 exemplifies the general pattern of collaboration between the police and the Fascists. "The Fascists are accompanied in their expeditions by lorries full of police, who join in singing Fascist songs....An expedition of more than a thousand Fascists terrorized the country with night attacks, fires, bomb-throwing, invasion of houses, [and] massacre under the eyes of the police...[who were] doling out arms and ammunitions....For two days a combined picket of Fascists and police searched all those who arrived at the Pontlagoscuro station, allowing only Fascists to enter the country" (cited in Tasca [1938] 1966, pp. 121-22). Tasca reports that in Siena in February 1921, workers were attacked by a joint force of Fascists, police, and two hundred Army troops ([1938] 1966, p. 116). In Livorno, in March 1921, workers built barricades in the streets to defend the local Chambers of Labor from the Fascist Squads. The Fascists retreated and then returned to the scene equipped with heavy artillery, armored cars, and tanks supplied by the Army; they then smashed through the workers' barricades (Snowden 1989, p. 78; Tasca [1938] 1966, p. 115). Three months later, in June 1921, in the province of Grosseto, during "one of the three most violent *squadrist* exploits" in the country, local residents battled against an army of one thousand *squadristi* who, according to official police reports, were assisted in their "work of terror" by high-ranking military and police officers (Snowden 1989, p. 201). During this same period, in Florence, the Fascists encountered barricades put up by the workers, and were forced to retreat. However, in a second attack, reinforced with a "large patrol of Royal Guards, a battalion of infantry, numerous *carabinieri* and two armored cars," they defeated the workers (Snowden 1989, p. 78).

The extent of the collaboration with the Fascists is further revealed in correspondence from the Ministry of the Interior with several prefects who tried to prevent the Fascist violence. A secret memorandum from the prefect of Bologna, Cesare Mori, to the Minister of the Interior, dated October 1921, reports of his difficulties in containing the Fascists' violence on account of police refusal to cooperate, a result of the sympathy felt for them. "Despite my repeated recommendations and instructions," Mori complained, "the authors of this [Fascist] violence, all well known and pointed out by me on various occasions, have never been arrested" (cited in Cardoza 1982, p. 361). A public inspector in Tuscany also complained to the Ministry of Interior that his orders were not followed by the police: "It is sufficient to note that of the thirty-three arrest warrants personally issued by me in all secrecy, only four were executed" (cited in Snowden 1989, p. 202). The effect and potential danger of this union between Fascists and armed officers was noted in 1922 by the Socialist leader Zibordi, who warned against the "moral and material solidarity with Fascism of the officers and NCOs." This, Zibordi charged, meant "solidarity with an armed organization operating outside the law, a state arisen within the state and sometimes against the state, a veritable military sedition" (1922, p. 89).

Like the police, the courts also refrained from legal action against the Fascists while enforcing the law against the Socialists. Some of these policies were initiated or approved by central government officials. Rome, Maier argues, "was willing to delay any effective repression" of the Fascists' violence (1975, p. 322). For instance, Minister of Justice Luigi Fera circulated a letter among the magistrates urging them to "shelve their records" of Fascist crimes (Tasca [1938] 1966, p. 129). In Bologna, judges "tended to view Fascist illegality with a sympathy that sharply contrasted with their harsh treatment of Socialist offenders." Moreover, the courts and prosecutors initiated their own legal offensive against the Socialists; they charged that fines imposed by the Socialist unions constituted acts of "criminal extortion" (Cardoza 1982, pp. 356, 382). In consequence, the peasant leagues in Bologna were "effectively decimated" and, in one commune, the entire leadership was arrested and persecuted "for assaults and extortion committed against those who did not belong to the Red Leagues" (Cardoza 1982, p. 357).[6]

The records gathered by the Socialist Party, as reported by De Felice, provide additional evidence of the judicial system's benevolence toward the Fascists. In addition to the number of incidents of violence in each province, De Felice also reports the number of police arrests and releases of Fascists and Socialists. The police arrested 396 Fascists and 1,421 Socialists during the period between fall 1920 and May 1921. In some provinces the disparity was even greater. In Alessandria, for example, which experienced 21 incidents of violence, the police arrested 174 Socialists but only 12 Fascists; in Bari, with 30 incidents of violence, they arrested 137 Socialists but only 9 Fascists; in Ferrara, with 49 reported incidents of violence, they arrested 110 Socialists but only 33 Fascists (1966, vol. 2, pt 1, pp. 35-37). Later in 1921, Syndicalists and Anarchists formed the *Arditi del Popolo* (they were not supported by the Socialists), a self-defense group dedicated to combating Fascism. Their actions, Maier tells us, "prompted more government circulars to prefects and police for 'public order' than did the Fascists" (1975, p. 330).

However, it is interesting to note that the collusion with provincial authorities took place in violation of specific government laws and regulations. The central state's penal code forbade the formation of "armed companies" and "armed assemblies." It further ordered local authorities to occupy the headquarters of these groups, confiscate their arms, and forbid any bearing of arms. Violators were to be reported to the authorities. But, according to Tasca, local authorities applied these regulations, especially the "disarmament of citizens," only to the workers' organizations, not to the Fascists: "Nothing was ever found in Fascist headquarters" ([1938] 1966, pp. 193, 169). When Ivanoe Bonomi (who became premier after the 1921 elections) attempted to take forceful action against the Fascists, provincial authorities deliberately sabotaged his efforts. The prefect of Ferrara, for instance, delayed acting on reports of violence until it became "too late to permit Mori [the prefect in charge of the whole region of Emilia] to send forces to intervene against the Squads" (telegram to Bladier, cited in Corner 1975, p. 205). The inspector general of Siena reported in November 1921 that the judicial proceedings against perpetrators of violence were "slow, long, almost inert...for long periods there is no outcome...particularly against the Fascists" (cited in Snowden 1989, p. 263, n. 52). The Ministry of the Interior sent a stream of telegrams to various prefects, protesting their inaction and urging them to take measures against the Fascists. In April 1921, in one such telegram, Giolitti personally warned Olivieri, the prefect of Florence, that the judges' laxity in allowing Fascist "murders [to] go unpunished is the most subversive action possible." He admonished the prefect to prevent pressure from being exerted on judges—and to see that these acts were "energetically repressed" (cited in Snowden 1989, p. 184).

The prefects, for their part, blamed the security forces whose overt sympathy with the Fascists, they argued, prevented them from taking any action against the Fascists. This, according to the inspector general of Siena, was the product of the Fascists' "good will" and respect for the armed forces (Snowden 1989, p. 193).[7] But, in reality, the collaboration of the police with the Squads typically continued with the support and encouragement of the prefects. Several prefects were open Fascist supporters, among them the prefect of Rovigo, the "Fascist prefect *par excellence*," who publicly declared in July 1921 that "Fascism was a necessary dike against the arrogant encroachment of bolshevism" (cited in Snowden 1989, p. 189). Provincial magistrates openly expressed their support of the Fascists and defended the Squads' violence as a justified response to violence perpetrated by the Socialists. "The dominant note of Fascist excesses," as one official put it, "is violence against things; that of communist excesses is the thirst for blood"; the Fascists' "youthful enthusiasm" was a welcome response to the "arrogance of communism" (cited in Snowden 1989, p. 198).

The experiences of the aforementioned Cesare Mori, appointed prefect of Bologna in February 1921, perhaps best illustrate how the alliance of the propertied class with the Fascists, together with the sedition among the state's security forces, subverted the authority of the central state when it attempted to suppress Fascist violence. Mori was one of the few prefects who forcefully tried to resist the Fascists. During his first months in office, more arrests took place and more warrants were issued against Fascists than in any other province in the country (De Felice 1968, pp. 35-39). He was then put in charge of the entire region of Emilia, with orders to control the Fascists and to prevent other prefects, such as Bladier in Ferrara, from collaborating with them (Corner 1975, p. 187). However, in May 1922, "leading business and commercial figures" showed their support of the *fasci* by informing the government that they were breaking off relations with Mori (Cardoza 1982, p. 383). By the summer of 1922, Mori had become "an outcast and a virtual prisoner in his own headquarters." A central government inspector reported that "Mori is in a very difficult and painful situation. He is isolated, removed from any contact with the citizens....He cannot leave the perfectural palace and travel in the city streets since at least he certainly would be insulted and booed...Among the class of businessmen, industrialists, and the bourgeoisie in general, no one intends to maintain any relations with Mori; no one ascends the steps of the prefecture" (cited in Cardoza 1982, p. 384). Mori was removed from his post in August 1922, transferred to the south, and appointed prefect of Palermo.[8]

Regarding the prefects' cooperation with the Fascists, its significance lay not only in their compliance with the violence but, more decisively, in their sanction of Fascist takeovers. For instance, when the Fascists of Bologna occupied the Socialist cooperatives there, the prefect expressed his approval by appointing an interim commissioner to administer the cooperatives (Cardoza 1982, p. 159). In Cremona, when Roberto Farinacci, the local *squadrist* and future leader of the intransigents forced the local administration to resign in July 1922, the prefect accepted his move with alacrity (Seton Watson 1967, p. 607; Lyttelton 1987, p. 80). By the fall of 1922, the prefect had appointed commissioners to replace most of the Socialist communal administrations in Bologna; these commissioners simply allowed the Fascists free rein in their jurisdictions and permitted the landlords to resume their former posts as mayors (Cardoza 1982, p. 347).

The preceding account leads us to conclude that the political power of the propertied class in the provinces and its support of the Fascists account, in large part, for the central government's lack of forceful action against the Fascists and for the resurgence of the prewar pattern of collaboration with the government against the worker organizations. Such a conclusion, however, would only be partially valid. It was, as we shall see, the ambiguous and contradictory policies of the Liberal government, led first by Giolitti and then by his successors Bonomi and Facta, which transformed the ad hoc support of provincial authorities into formal legitimation, followed by the invitation to join the central state itself (Snowden 1989, pp. 183-84).

THE INCORPORATION OF THE FASCIST ORGANIZATION INTO THE LIBERAL PARTY

As we saw, central government policy toward the Fascist organization, unlike that of the provincial authorities, was characterized by ambiguity: Its assistance of the Fascists was therefore inadvertent. Both Giolitti and Bonomi attempted to halt the Fascist advance in the provinces, although Giolitti was the architect of the most explicit act of central government collusion with the Fascist organization, namely, its incorporation into the Liberals' National Bloc *(Bloccho Nazionale)*. By this act, as De Felice argues, Giolitti lost his credibility as the restorer of order (1966, pp. 25-26; Lyttelton 1987, p. 40).

To repeat, in the early months of the Fascists' expeditions, Giolitti tried to halt their advance. He replaced several chiefs of police and prefects who had shown Fascist sympathies, and gave specific orders to local authorities to act against the Squads (Cardoza 1982, pp. 381, 383). For example, in response to the Fascists' burning of the premises of the Socialist paper *Difesa*, Giolitti wrote to the prefect of Florence: "I am amazed that the security forces have not acted vigorously to prevent [this] devastation." Giolitti demanded that the prefect identify and prosecute those "responsible for the inaction of the police" (cited in Snowden 1989, p. 259, n. 1). In January 1921, Giolitti ordered the prefects of Bologna, Ferrara, and Modena, the provinces hardest hit by the Squads, "to revoke all permits to bear arms and to ban temporarily any public rallies, meeting and ceremonies." When Visconti, the prefect of Bologna, failed to comply with these orders, Giolitti replaced him with Mori, an already acknowledged opponent of Fascism (Cardoza 1982, p. 380, see p. 116).

However, such actions were insufficient. The Fascists' violence continued, and, as we have seen, so did the collusion of the provincial authorities. Early in 1921, while *squadrist* leaders were engaged in a bloody struggle against the Socialists and power had been taken in four of the country's provinces (Cremona, Ferrara, Rovigo, and Trieste), Giolitti dismissed Parliament. He reestablished the National Bloc, the Liberal Party-led electoral coalition formed during the 1920 local elections. Giolitti then called for new national elections and invited the Fascist organization, together with the Nationalist Party and several liberal-democratic groups to join this coalition. Filippo Meda, a leader of the PPI, and Alfredo Frassati, the director of *La Stampa* and ambassador to Berlin, who were both Giolitti's advisors, argued against this step. Under the new system of proportional representation, they argued, Parliament would not attain stability by new elections. On the contrary, the entry of the Fascists might lead to further fragmentation (Maier 1975, pp. 325-26). Their reading of the situation, as we know, proved to be true.

The 1921 election campaign was dominated by terror and fear. According to *Avanti!*, "workers were attacked and searched before entering the electoral rooms," and "were loaded on lorries, beaten, threatened, and forced to vote for the Bloc" (Corner 1975, p. 180, n. 1). Other, non-Socialist sources provided similar accounts: "Fascists with clubs were responsible for dozens of deaths on polling day alone, and they had rendered Socialist propaganda completely impossible over large areas" (Mack Smith 1959, p. 345). The violence was so extensive that it provoked Giolitti's protest. He wrote thusly to the prefects of Emilia, Rovigo, Bari, Foggia, and Turin in April 1921: "Fascist violence during the election is a great offense and dishonor to the country. A chamber elected with violence has no moral authority." He lamented that provincial authorities calmly accepted the Fascist offenses, and ordered the prefects to replace the responsible heads of the police forces and to telegraph him personally with the names of the *carabinieri* officials and the Royal Guards (De Felice 1965, p. 603). But the Fascists' intimidation and terror continued. "It proved difficult," Charles Maier notes ironically, "to curb [Fascist] excesses while the prefects were overseeing coalitions of Liberals and Fascists under government sponsorship" (1975, p. 326); to say the least, under such circumstances "prefects and police were not disposed to interfere too much with Fascist supervision of the polling" (Corner 1975, p. 180).

Despite the violence and fraud, the election failed to provide Giolitti with the majority he expected, and he resigned in July 1921. But it did help the Fascists. They obtained nearly fifty thousand votes throughout the country and thirty-five seats in the Chamber (Maier 1975, pp. 326-28; Seton Watson 1967, pp. 587-89; Brustein 1991). By then, numerous deputies and ministers, most notably the new premier Ivanoe Bonomi, were constrained by their affiliation with the Fascists during the election campaign. In many localities, full integration took place between the Fascists and the Liberals (Corner 1975, p. 181). When Bonomi attempted to act against the Fascists, they reminded him of his own collaboration with them. For instance, the *ras* of Cremona, Roberto Farinacci, helped Bonomi recall one of "the many episodes" of his assistance to the Fascists. "It was Prime Minister Bonomi—our candidate—who placed his motorcar at the disposal of the Fascists, who that very same night were to destroy the cooperative stores of Poggio Rusco. And in the marvelous days of the electioneering struggle of 1921 we saw him marching under our standards and we attended his meeting and guarded him with our bold 'Blackshirts'" (cited in Salvemini 1973, p. 320). The distinctions between the Liberals and the Fascists had blurred, if not disappeared.

Why had the Liberal government vacillated and why had it failed to resist the Fascists when the organization was still a minor force in the provinces? Unlike the entrenched opposition to Socialism that characterized provincial authorities, Giolitti (and his predecessor Nitti) had a record of positive welfare policies and was known for his refusal to repress workers on behalf of the landlords and industrialists, and for his support for postwar electoral reform. This record is sufficient to eliminate the possibility that Giolitti knowingly and intentionally acted in support of the Fascist organization. So what can explain his failure to contain the Fascists' advance?

GIOLITTI AND MUSSOLINI: THE COUNTERFACTUAL QUESTION

Historians have offered several interpretations of Giolitti's motivations. His policy toward the Fascists, especially their incorporation into the National Bloc, they argue, was largely a result of the Prime Minister's underestimation of the organization's power as well as of its ultimate objective (De Felice 1966, pp. 605-7; Seton Watson 1967, p. 577). Giolitti, Tasca states, had hoped to use the Fascists against the Socialists and thereby lure reformist leaders to his coalition. Similarly, Corner argues that by allowing the Fascists to gain influence, Giolitti hoped he could use them to weaken the Socialists and the *Popolari* and to force them to join his government on his terms (1975, p. 179). Mack Smith agrees that Giolitti's "positive electoral support" was a "key factor" in the Fascists' 1921 entry into Parliament; however, he also views this support as an "uncharacteristic error of judgment" on this veteran leader's part (1989, p. 245). That Giolitti underestimated the Fascists is suggested by his remark, made to the British ambassador during the May 1921 elections, that the "Fascist candidates are nothing but fireworks; they will make a great deal of noise but nothing will come out of it" (Tasca [1938] 1966, p. 333, n. 1; also in Seton Watson 1967, p. 588).[9] After the elections he lauded the "entry into political life of the *Fascisti* Party, represented by thirty members [in Parliament], for the most part young and combative," as "a real benefit to the country" (Giolitti 1923, p. 445). Giolitti's policy was thus first of all a continuation of the old politics of *trasformismo*: the incorporation of political rivals into the ruling coalition. But if this sheds light on his view of the Fascist threat, it obscures the main determinant of the government's actions toward the Fascists, especially Giolitti's continuous but failing attempts to mobilize the provincial authorities against them.

What Giolitti's thoughts and considerations concerning these policies were, we cannot know. Did he consider deploying troops against the Fascist Squads? Nary a historian provides information on this, nor does any reference to this appear in Giolitti's own memoirs.[10] If he did consider such an action, why did he decide against it? Was he indeed hoping to win the support of the Socialists and the *Popolari?* Did he really underestimate the strength that the Fascists had already achieved through their alliances with the propertied class and its support by the armed forces? These are matters of informed speculation at best.

To probe more deeply into the sources of the government's actions, we should ask what would have happened if the central government had withheld support from or had actually opposed the Fascists. Such questions require us to ask, first, whether the Liberal government was interested in following this alternative policy. Did Giolitti and his successors, Bonomi and Facta, want to halt the Fascists' advance in the provinces? Only if the answer to this question is positive can we proceed to ask whether an alternative policy was at all possible. That is, if the government had decided to halt the Fascists, would they have been able to mobilize troops against them, and would the Army have obeyed such orders? If such mobilization was feasible, then the question it raises becomes: Would this have halted the Squads' advance and prevented their taking power in the provinces?

However, the initial counterfactual question—the possibility of an alternative state policy toward the Fascists—I submit, is not legitimately counterfactual (Elster 1978, p. 185). It could not have happened in the real past. By the May 1921 elections, six months after the beginning of the Action Squads' expeditions in the provinces, the penetration of the Fascist organization into the provincial strongholds of the Liberal state was a fait accompli. In the interim, short as it was, Liberal deputies had been supporting the Fascist organization, aiding the Squads' expeditions in the provincial towns, and defending their actions.

As early as the fall of 1920, Marchese Tenari, a senator, mayor, Liberal deputy, and scion of one of Bologna's most illustrious families expressed his support of the Fascist organization. "I ask myself," Tenari wrote in his letter to Facta, "if we should not enroll in the *fasci*. They are violent and impulsive, but they are also idealists and bring us some fresh air, and if there will have to be a civil war, old as I am, I will fight with them" (cited in Cardoza 1982, p. 303). A Florentine Liberal deputy was, according to his own testimony, "the organizer ...of a financial consortium...which subsidized the principal patriotic initiatives in the province, and gave the *fasci* several hundred thousand lire" (cited in Lyttelton 1987, p. 482 n. 39). As already mentioned, in Florence, the center of the Tuscan Agrarian Association (AAT), Liberal deputies "toured the region to argue the Fascist cause...presided at ceremonial occasions and participated in public demonstrations of pro-Fascist sympathy" and proclaimed in Parliament in March 1921 (when the wave of "punitive expeditions" was already underway) that "'the nation has the right to defend its institutions and its liberties, and the marvelous organization of the *fascisti* is contributing to this end' as it is 'the purest form of social defense'" (Snowden 1989, p. 56). Again, in Cremona "all the local 'constitutional' parties joined the Fascists' demand that the town council be dissolved, and the prefect submitted to this demand" (Maier 1975, p. 319).

What makes the counterfactual question of an alternative policy toward the Fascists by the central government illegitimate is the fact that to mobilize the Army against the Fascists would have meant the government's forceful repression of its own social base, the landlords. The latter were, from the outset, closely allied with the Fascists and with the state's provincial apparatus, the government's institutional link to this base. Such an argument does indeed constitute an absurdity because it implies that the government would have been willing to commit political suicide.

The historical evidence thus suggests that the Fascist organization was regularly aided by its provincial alliances with the propertied class, expressed by the direct action taken against Socialist provincial governments as well as uncooperative prefects, the active collaboration of the Army and the police forces, and the collusion of provincial state authorities. The Fascists' "offensive alliance" with the propertied class and their "defensive alliance" with the Liberal state's authorities led to a shift in their objectives. Their struggle was thus transformed from an ad hoc anti-Socialist tactic into a struggle for the seizure of power. Their goal was no longer limited to the destruction of Socialist civil organizations but to overthrow legal Socialist provincial governments. If this is so, the crucial question to be asked next becomes: To what extent were the

Fascist takeovers dependent on collusion with the state authorities? The following chapter attempts to do so.

NOTES

1. The Royal Guard was a special riot police unit established by Nitti in 1919. The *Arma dei Carabinieri Reali* was the state's police force, responsible to the Ministry of Interior.

2. It may be that the motivations of each force differed, but the nature of their assistance and its effects were similar (see Snowden 1989, pp. 190-91).

3. This point is also relevant to the conceptualization of the Liberal state and the attempt to locate the roots of Fascism in the analysis of its structural or institutional weakness. This is the core of Vivarelli's work (1991). Like Moore, Vivarelli seems to neglect the role of the organized workers as well as that of the political transformations in the period following World War I.

4. The first and most severe action proposed by the government was the call by Sidney Sonnino (then Minister of the Treasury) to disarm "the permanent armies of the extremist parties," strip the Chamber of Deputies of its power over the government, and strengthen the king's executive powers. This action was not adopted (Cardoza 1982, p. 65).

5. The Fascist Squads burned down the headquarters of the local Catholic League, although it was only 300 yards away from *carabinieri* headquarters (Corner 1975).

6. In the Italian legal system, prior to a public trial a case was first brought before an examining judge and the public prosecutor. From the data presented by De Felice, it seems that many of the Fascists brought for preliminary examination by the prosecutor were never brought to trial (see Salvemini [1973, p. 313, n. 17] for details on this judicial procedure).

7. Some prefects asked Giolitti for armed reinforcements, but they were not made available.

8. A case similar to Mori's is that of Achille De Martino, the prefect of Brescia. De Martino, too, attempted to conciliate the agrarians and the Socialists, and later attempted to curb the Fascist terror. He was replaced only after Mussolini's nomination as premier (Saija 1985).

9. As late as 1924, two years into Mussolini's premiership, the King still maintained that Fascism "is not serious, it will not last" (in Tasca [1938] 1966, p. 333, n. 1).

10. Giolitti's *Memoirs*, written in 1922, contain only this single reference to the Fascists' emergence, as quoted above.

Chapter 8

The "March on Rome":
The Seizure of Power

After the Fascists had broken a nationwide Socialist strike in August 1922, Mussolini declared: "In forty-eight hours of systematic warlike violence, we won what we would never have won in forty-eight years of preaching and propaganda" (cited in Seton Watson 1967, p. 609). Mussolini's assessment of the effectiveness of his organization's use of violence against the left—whether out of self-delusion or to deceive others—is misleading. For it was by no means through their use of "systematic warlike violence" itself that the Fascists won power. Rather, as the following analysis of the determinants of their taking of power in the provinces reveals, the Fascists never "seized power" so much as they were handed it, with the support of the propertied class, through the connivance or collusion of the Liberal state's administration.

So, the central question addressed here is how did the Fascists use both their illegal and extraparliamentary tactic of "punitive expeditions" and their "offensive alliances" with the organizations of the propertied class to seize state power in the provinces? How, in other words, was the Squads' violence transformed from a targeted anti-Socialist tactic into a vehicle for acquiring political power? The answer to this question entails answering two other, more limited, questions: What did the Fascists do with their initial tactical success after they had destroyed the Socialist organizations and institutions? What kind of organizations did they try to establish in the provinces, and what were their objectives? This chapter focuses, then, on the development of the Fascists' political strategy after they had realized their initial objective of destroying Socialist institutions, and on how this led to their taking of provincial power.

From the unification of Italy until the electoral reforms of 1911 and 1918, the propertied class had possessed exclusive access to state power (see chapter 3). The allegiance of central state officials stationed in the provinces and of elected provincial governments to the interests of property was taken for granted. But after the war, the advent of the Socialist Party as a major force in the electoral arena enabled Socialists to attain office in many communal councils and provincial governments, an achievement that often entirely stripped the propertied class of its accustomed hold on these institutions. At the same time, given the structure of Italy's state, the Socialists' grasp on local power was limited because they also had to answer to Rome's appointed provincial authorities and agents.

The local political power, economic ascendancy, and social dominion of propertied families had long been indissoluble. Their members were accustomed, as we have seen, to the unchallenged sway of property, to the deference and even obeisance of their social inferiors. But all of these interrelated aspects of their class hegemony were now being called into question by the rise of the Socialist movement. In many provinces, especially in the north and the center, the unions and the PSI not only challenged the economic power of the propertied families but, as we saw earlier (chapter 4), they also took a modicum of control over the labor market itself out of the employers' hands. The very social world of the propertied class, notably that of the landed gentry, was now in the throes of change, threatened and in danger of being undermined.

CLASS HEGEMONY AND THE SOCIALIST THREAT

The pattern of Socialist ascendance and the stability of propertied hegemony differed dramatically among Italy's major regions. The north, the center, and the south each had their own distinctive, characteristic relations of production (chapter 3). The more a region was penetrated by commercialization, the more the cash nexus between "master and man" replaced patriarchal bonds or seigniorial domination (as with sharecropping and renting in agriculture). Similarly, the more the relations of production came to approximate the class relations characteristic of capitalism (that is, private enterprises employing wage labor), the less stable if not actually eroded became the hegemony of a region's propertied families.

With the expansion of suffrage and the increasing participation of the newly enfranchised masses in the electoral arena, the stability or, alternatively, decline of the dominant class was now reflected in one, singularly public measure: the relative hegemony of the Liberal Party as indicated in the electoral balance between the PSI and the Liberal coalition.

Measuring Liberal Hegemony

The Liberal Party was Italy's dominant center of political power by far; as we have seen, the propertied class constituted, almost exclusively, its pool of candidates at the same time that, through its local hegemony in the provinces, it mobilized much of the Liberal electoral base. Hence, the ratio of votes for the Liberal-led coalition's candidates to the votes for the Socialist candidates provides us with a useful indicator of the relative strength of the classes they represented. Put differently, the electoral balance in a province indicates the stability of, or threat to, the hegemony of the propertied class as represented by the hegemony of the Liberals.

Other possible measures are a simple continuous variable measuring the margin between both parties and, simply, the PSI vote itself. However, my underlying premise is that there is a qualitative difference between the levels of control exerted by the Liberals in the provinces already under their rule. That is, I assume that there is significant variance within the Liberal-led provinces in terms of the security of the control exercised by the dominant class. The provinces where the Liberals ruled with little or no challenge (as in the south, where the Liberals received as much as 90% of the total vote) are qualitatively distinct from those provinces where their hegemony was challenged or even threatened by a relatively large Socialist opposition. Therefore, the variable of voting margin reflects two distinctions that capture this political reality: first, between provinces where the Liberals received a greater vote than the Socialists, and second, within each region, according to the margin between both parties.

The Regional Liberal Hegemony

As Table 8.1 shows, the regional pattern of Liberal hegemony is deeply etched, running from south to north in a sharply rising curve of relative strength. In the *latifundist* south, where seigniorial relations prevailed, the Liberals had a "wide majority" in 59% of the provinces. (In only one southern province, Caltanisetta, Sicily, did the Liberals receive an electoral minority.) An almost diametrically opposed picture is found in the capitalist north, where the Liberals failed to attain a wide electoral majority in any of the provinces; in the sharecropping center, they held a wide majority in only 14% of the provinces. The Socialists, on the other hand, held an electoral majority in 40% of the provinces in the north, in 14% of those in the center, and none in the south.[1]

Clearly, then, the hegemony of the propertied class, represented by the Liberal Party's relative electoral power, was directly related to the form of social domination in the region. Where, as in the north, the mass of employees were wage laborers, the capitalists were subject to the pressures and even insurgency of an organized workers' movement. The erosion of their hegemony was reflected in proliferating provincial Socialist electoral majorities or pluralities. One or the other was attained in over half of the northern provinces. In the center, the regions of *mezzadria*, the relationship was far more mixed. Tenants and sharecroppers were still largely subject to the immediate authority of the landlords, and were not as organized as the northern wage workers. But in the wake of the struggle to organize peasant leagues in the region, the Socialists began to establish substantial electoral strength. Hence, the PSI obtained an electoral majority or plurality in over a third of the central provinces. In none of the *latifundist* provinces did the PSI have a majority, and they had a plurality in only 5% of those provinces. There, the hegemony of the propertied class remained stable and secure.

Table 8.1
Liberal Hegemony (1920) by Regional Relations
of Production in Italy's Provinces

Relations of Production by Region	Liberal Hegemony*					
	Liberal Wide Majority	Liberal Narrow Majority	Liberal Plurality	Socialist Plurality	Socialist Majority	(N)
Capitalist north	0	33	13	13	40	(30)
Sharecropping center	14	21	29	21	14	(14)
Latifundist south	59	14	23	5	0	(22)

* I identify the electoral balance as follows: a Liberal "wide" majority existed in provinces where the Liberal Party received over 50% of the votes and had a "wide" margin (see below) over the PSI. A Liberal "narrow" majority existed where the Liberal Party received over 50% of the votes but had only a "narrow" margin over the PSI. A "wide" margin is defined as a margin above the median margin of Liberal to PSI votes, and a "narrow" margin as below the median in all those provinces in which Liberal candidates won a higher vote than did Socialist candidates. A Liberal plurality existed in provinces where the Liberals received more votes than did the PSI. A Socialist plurality existed in a province in which PSI candidates received more votes than did the Liberals or any other party's candidates. A Socialist majority existed in a province in which the PSI received over 50% of the votes.

HEGEMONY, COLLUSION, AND THE PATTERN OF FASCIST VIOLENCE

An analysis of the pattern of Fascist violence shown in Table 8.2 reveals that the growing instability and erosion of Liberal hegemony tended, though roughly and unevenly, to coincide with the rising incidence of that violence. Thus, as expected, Fascist violence was concentrated in those provinces where the Socialists governed with an electoral majority: it was chronic in only 20% of the provinces where the Liberals held a wide majority. Conversely, and here the pattern is somewhat clearer, the more stable and secure the hegemony of the propertied class in a province, the greater the probability that the incidence of Fascist violence would be low, or merely "sporadic." In those provinces where the Liberals held a wide majority, 67% experienced no more than sporadic Fascist violence. Nevertheless, sporadic violence occurred in 41% of the provinces (N=29) where the Liberals held either a narrow majority or plurality, and a bit less where the Socialists had only a plurality, as compared with an incidence of sporadic violence in only 14% of the provinces where the Socialists held an electoral majority.

What explains this approximate, inverse association between the incidence of Fascist violence and Liberal hegemony? Clearly, it took no special ingenuity for the *squadristi* to identify and thus target the provinces where the declining Liberal hegemony, reflected in the general level of worker organization and insurgency, favored the Socialists. This was especially true where the Liberals had a governing majority. In fact, as we know (chapter 7), the propertied class, threatened as they were by Socialist power, not only invited the Squads into those provinces, they often personally participated in anti-Socialist assaults.

But, again, as the earlier presentation of the historical evidence has shown, the connivance if not collusion of the provincial authorities with the *squadristi* was crucial for the continuation of the attacks. The police and other security forces, subject to the authority of the provincial prefects, not only did not prevent the Squads' expeditions, they often directly assisted them. Furthermore, on the rare occasions when the *squadristi* were arrested and tried for their violent attacks on the lives, property, and institutions of the Socialists, local judges released them unpunished.

Of course, the Fascists also found a welcome embrace among the dominant families, even in some of the provinces where the Liberal hegemony was relatively stable. Those provinces were, apparently, also being subjected to growing Socialist agitation as well as worker organization and militancy. This would account, then, for the unevenness of the association between the Liberal hegemony and the incidence of violence.

The Concentration of the Working Class

To rephrase our findings, working-class organization and militancy had its own independent effects in provoking the Fascist reaction in the provinces, irrespective of the level of Socialist electoral ascendancy or the degree of propertied hegemony. Inasmuch as we have no data on the number of strikes or strikers or of union members on the provincial level for these years, the relative concentration of workers, whether industrial or agricultural, remains the best available indicator of the objective possibilities or potential for labor organization and struggle. This assumption permits us to use the concentration of industrial and agricultural workers in a province as a proxy measure for the actual levels of unionization and strikes. Both measures are expressed in ratios of the number of workers per thousand households in the province.

Table 8.2
Fascist Violence (1920-1921) in Italy's Provinces by Electoral Balance
of Liberals versus Socialists (1920), in Percentages

Electoral Balance	Incidence of Fascist Violence			
	Chronic (%)	Recurrent (%)	Sporadic (%)	(N)
Liberal wide majority	20	13	67	(15)
Liberal narrow majority	44	19	37	(16)
Liberal plurality	8	46	46	(13)
Socialist plurality	37	25	37	(8)
Socialist majority	79	7	14	(14)

Nonetheless, a regression analysis (OLS) of the effects of Liberal hegemony and of the relative concentration of industrial workers on the incidence of Fascist violence in Italy's provinces does not bear out my hypothesis. Alternatively, as expected, each category of Liberal hegemony has a significant inverse effect on the incidence of violence in industrial provinces when compared to the effect found in the omitted category of provinces where the Socialists had an electoral majority. The concentration of industrial workers per se has no such significant independent effect (see Table 8.3). This, I suggest, may reflect the lesser strength of the Squads and their reduced ability to mobilize against workers in the cities as compared to the situation in the countryside, where the *agrari* acted as the Squads' protectors and sponsors. Unlike the factory owners faced by unionization and worker demands for better wages and working conditions, the *agrari* saw burgeoning organization among their own formerly quiescent agricultural laborers and sharecroppers as a threat to their entire social world (as argued in chapter 6). The *agrari* had a history of self-organization, and they could actively recruited the Squads as their allies against these perceived threats and against the Socialist leaders.

As Snowden suggests with reference to the Fascist advance in Tuscany, "there was a rough correlation between the degree of agrarian unrest and the persistence of reports of complicity by the authorities" with the *squadristi* expeditions (1986, p. 195). Accordingly, we may hypothesize that the relative concentration of agricultural workers, insofar as they were unionized or already involved in struggles against their rural employers, had an independent effect in determining the incidence of Fascist violence.

Table 8.3
Logit Estimates of the Effects of Liberal Hegemony (1920) and the Concentration of Industrial Workers (1921) on Fascist Violence in Italy's Provinces (1920-1921)

Liberal Hegemony	B	β
Liberal wide majority	-32.74^{**} (6.68)	$-.670$
Liberal narrow majority	-26.63^{**} (6.42)	$-.557$
Liberal plurality	-31.38^{**} (6.85)	$-.591$
Socialist plurality	-19.21^{*} (7.72)	$-.306$
Concentration of industrial workers	$-.043$ (.033)	$-.144$

Intercept: 45.74
R^2: .349
N=64
* $p < .05$,
** $p < .01$

Note: The model compares the effect of each category of Liberal hegemony to the effect of the omitted category of Socialist majority.

The evidence is consistent with this hypothesis. Although each of the four categories of Liberal hegemony has a significant negative effect on the incidence of Fascist violence, the relative concentration of agricultural workers per se in a province has no measurable effect, in either direction, on the incidence of violence (Table 8.4, model A). But this is not so once the region of the country is taken into account (Table 8.4, model B) as well as both the nature of the property relations and the extent to which the countryside had been the scene of worker organization and struggle.

In this regression analysis (Table 8.4, model B), the north, where wage labor prevailed in agriculture, and the center, with a mix of sharecropping and wage labor, are combined and compared to the *latifundist* south, where seigniorial relations between master and man endured. In the combined category, the concentration of agricultural workers has a significant independent effect (β = 0.358) on the incidence of Fascist violence. With these controls for region and concentration of agricultural workers, each of the four categories of Liberal hegemony continues to have a significant negative effect on the incidence of Fascist violence.

Table 8.4
Logit Estimates of the Effects of Liberal Hegemony (1920)
and the Concentration of Agricultural Workers (1921)
on Fascist Violence in Italy's Agrarian Provinces (1920-1921)

Electoral Balance	Model B		Model A	
	B	β	B	β
Liberal wide majority	-46.42** (8.98)	-.838	-31.90* (12.09)	-.576
Liberal narrow majority	-37.05** (8.16)	-.716	-32.11** (8.43)	-.620
Liberal plurality	-43.41** (9.11)	-.713	-31.05* (11.37)	-.510
Socialist plurality	-27.65** (10.01)	-.395	-23.89* (9.97)	-.342
Concentration of agricultural workers	.048 (.036)	.171	.100* (.046)	.358
Northern and central regions	--	--	18.54 (10.67)	.399
Intercept:	36.67		5.29	
R^2 =	.50		.54	
N =	39		39	

*p<.05
**p<.01

THE FASCIST SEIZURE OF PROVINCIAL POWER

How, then, do these variables enter into the determination of the Fascist seizures of power in the provinces? This process occurred in three distinct phases. The first phase was the Action Squads' destruction of the worker organizations. The second was the Fascists' move to establish their own economic organizations, the Fascist labor unions or National Syndicates. In collaboration with employers, they coerced workers into joining the Syndicates as part of their common objective of restoring the prewar pattern of provincial labor relations. The third phase was, again with the cooperation of the propertied class and the collusion of provincial and national officials, the Fascists' actual taking of power in the provinces and, subsequently, of the state itself (Salvemini 1973, p. 320). In distinguishing these "phases," we appear to be suggesting that the third phase was the Fascist organization's deliberate objective. That is, that their strategy of militarizing the political struggle against the Socialists—through the punitive expeditions, the "offensive alliances" with landlords and industrialists, and the "defensive alliances" with provincial authorities—was, from its inception, aimed at the seizure of power.

Some statements, mainly pronouncements made by Mussolini and *squadristi* leaders, would seem to support this view. For instance, Italo Balbo, the *ras* of Ferrara and one of the Fascist organization's major leaders, declared that "we have not only broken down the resistance of our enemies, but we also control the departments of the state. The prefect has to submit to the orders I give him in the name of the Fascists" (Tasca [1938] 1966, p. 188). Mussolini himself announced, a week before the May 1921 national election in which Fascist candidates ran as members of the coalition led by the Liberal Party, that "the final goal of our impetuous march is Rome" (Seton Watson 1967, p. 587).

However, I suggest that it is doubtful that the Fascists organized their punitive expeditions, from the outset, with the aim of taking power. Rather, the articulation of this objective, together with its requisite mobilization and organization, were products of the Fascists' political struggle against the Socialists. Only manifest success in rooting out Socialist strongholds could have made the establishment of Fascist power feasible. So, the Squads' terror against the Socialist organizations was a "first phase" only in the sense that other, analytically distinguishable phases followed. Taken chronologically, they constitute the Fascist organization's struggle for political power.

Furthermore, there is a fundamental difference between the determinants of Fascist violence and those of the provincial takeovers. The Fascists' violent destruction of Socialist unions and institutions was experienced exclusively by the Socialist leaders and their working-class constituency. But the Fascists' government takeovers affected the entire political and economic life of a province, including that of the propertied class. This indicates that the Fascists' ability to employ violent means against the workers did not ensure that they would become the new provincial rulers. To turn their tactic of violence—originally a means of anti-labor and anti-Socialist intimidation—into actual control of an entire province required a "defensive alliance" with the authorities in addition to their "offensive alliance" with the landlords. Liberal state collusion was requisite for both destruction of legally constituted Socialist provincial governments and establishment of Fascist regimes in their place.

The Fascist National Syndicates

The Syndicates served a dual purpose. They allowed the Fascists and *agrari* to control the workers, but they were also crucial instruments in the Fascists' seizure of provincial political power. The "fortunes of agrarian Fascism," and its eventual "political predominance" in the northern regions, as the historian Luigi Preti argues, depended to a large extent on the Syndicates' ability to control the workers. Or, as Corner puts it, "syndicalism and squadrism were essentially different methods of achieving the same result—the subjugation of the agricultural workers" (1975, p. 213).

Like the Squads, the Syndicates were sponsored and sustained by the active collaboration of local employer organizations: They compelled workers to become Syndicate members while they offered the employers "the best of both worlds." They contained and repressed workers' grievances and left the *agrari* free to dictate the terms of agricultural employment (Cordova 1970, pp. 975-76). This situation was obvious to state officials. The provincial commissioner in Ferrara reported to Rome in June 1922, that a "tight link" now bound the "*agrari* and the Fascist Syndicates, a link [with]...essentially political content" (Corner 1975, p. 219). Similarly, the prefect of Florence observed that "behind the Fascist Syndicates stand the agrarians...who are seeking above all to profit from the situation in order to destroy the [Socialist] organizations" (Cardoza 1982, p. 368).

The Syndicates were, in reality, often initiated by the employers. Following the Fascists' initial attacks, the *agrari* of Tuscany, for instance, explicitly proclaimed the need for a new phase. This was put rather bluntly in an editorial printed in the *Difesa agricola* in November 1921: "Repressive means alone are not enough to bring beclouded minds to reason....We must oppose propaganda with propaganda, and spread with the benevolent forms of class solidarity, the feelings of law and order and of morality" (cited in Snowden 1989, p. 62). In Ferrara, employers supported the Syndicates' demand that employment in the *Bonifica*, the state-sponsored land reclamation projects, be reserved for their members only. In this way "money provided by the state was in fact being used to strengthen the political hold of the Fascists" (Corner 1975, p. 213).

Coercing workers into joining the Syndicates was generally a joint undertaking of the Fascists and the employers, who made membership in the new unions a requirement for employment (Snowden 1989, p. 102; Corner 1975, p. 164; Tasca [1938] 1966, p. 109). How crucial this collaboration was for the Syndicates is shown by what happened when such collaboration was absent, as in the case in the Brescia. There, both the industrialists and the landowners who supported the *Popolare* refused to yield to the Fascists' demand for the Syndicates' exclusive representation of the workers. Consequently, the Fascists could not compel workers to join. Even as late as December 1922 (after Mussolini's nomination as prime minister), the *fasci* in Brescia were still unable to break the employers' resistance (Lyttelton 1987, p. 160).

Brescia, however, was the exception that proves the rule. Much more typical were the actions taken by employers in Grosseto, shipyard owners in Livorno, and *agrari* in Bologna. In Grosseto, according to the Fascist press, employers agreed not only to "guarantee work to those enrolled" in the Syndicates, they also committed themselves to pay members a "wage sufficient to meet the cost of living" and to provide them with the opportunity to purchase "articles of first necessity at prices and conditions below the market level" (Snowden 1989, p. 65). In Livorno, shipyard owners granted the National Syndicates exclusive representation of their employees (Snowden 1989). In Bologna, the *agrari* divided the workers by offering favorable individual contracts to those who deserted the Socialist agrarian leagues (Cardoza 1982, p. 367). Such contracts, also in force in Piacenza, Milan, and Parma, "allowed the parties to add to the contract special or individual clauses...[which] were not to be subject to the jurisdiction of the responsible organizations, nor to the Commission of Arbitration" (Tasca [1938] 1966, pp. 195-96).

If the employers could make membership in the Syndicates a matter of economic survival for the workers, the Fascists simply made it a matter of their physical survival (Lyttelton 1987, p. 217; Seton Watson 1967, p. 547). The Fascists made efforts to paint their Syndicates as genuine alternatives to the Socialist unions, but few workers joined them voluntarily. Rather, the relatively rapid growth of membership in the Syndicates occurred because the chief "labor organizers" in the provinces were also the leaders of the Fascist Squads. They employed the same tactic they had employed to destroy the Socialist unions prior to establishing their own Syndicates. "Socialist leagues frequently voted," as they did in Ferrara, "to join the *fascio* and take on the name of '*Syndicato Autonomo*' at the point of the gun." There, the Socialist League of Agricultural Workers transferred en masse to the Fascist Syndicate, which could boast of more than forty thousand members by June of 1921 (Corner 1975, p. 164-65).

Under similar threats of violence, the Socialist leagues in Tuscany "passed wholesale into the labor organization of the *fasci*" (Snowden 1989, p. 64). In Bologna, the leaders of the *Federterra*, the sharecropper leagues, were forced "under the barrel of a gun" to repudiate the contracts they had won earlier and to call on their members to join the National Syndicates (Cardoza 1982, p. 355-56). Under compulsion, membership in the Syndicate, including growing numbers of sharecroppers as well as wage workers, rose from 160 families in the beginning of 1921 to 3,000 by the end of that year, and gave the Fascists control over the majority of Bologna's laborers (Cardoza 1982, pp. 362, 316).

Even before the Socialist provincial governments were themselves overthrown, this cooperation between the National Syndicates and the employers' associations succeeded in destroying the most important Socialist achievements made in the provinces: acceptance of the principle of collective contracts, institution of arbitration, and regulation of the distribution of labor. The new contracts between the Syndicates and the employers either restored pre-Socialist labor relations or regressed them even further (Seton Watson 1967, p. 574; Salvemini 1936, p. 5; Maier 1975, p. 314).

That the Fascist Syndicates were designed from the outset to benefit the employers—despite some rhetoric to the contrary—is evident from the content of these organizations' new labor contracts. The Tuscany Syndicate's 1922 contract with employers, for example, was a complete reversion to the old landlord-tenant relations. It reinstated not only the employers' economic power but, perhaps more importantly, the employers' supervision over their tenants' private lives. The contract ruled that "the entire tenant family was legally tied to the *podere* [the family farm] and only the landlord could give permission for the size of the family to be modified."

Economically, the expenses of cultivation were again to be divided equally between the partners (rather than the reduced shared of 40% obtained for the tenants by the Socialist league) and a release from the obligation to provide insurance was obtained for the landlords. Management of the estate was again to be the proprietor's exclusive prerogative. The arbitration boards established by the Socialists were abolished, and all disputes over the interpretation of agreements were now to be "referred for solution to the local, provincial or national agrarian and tenant organizations" instead of to the union bodies, the practice under Socialist rule (Snowden 1989, pp. 68-69).

Another potent nonviolent weapon of the rich against the Socialist governments was the tax strike. For example, in Ferrara, as early as April 1921 (that is, a month before the national election and only five months after the beginning of the Fascists' punitive expeditions), a tax strike organized by the Agrarian Federation led to the resignation and dissolution of the Socialist provincial government and Socialist communal commissioners. Pugliese, the prefect (not to be confused with General Pugliese), then appointed new commissioners who were "known to be either Fascists or strongly favorable to Fascism at the time of their appointment" (Corner 1975, pp. 176-67). These appointments required and received Rome's approval.

Elsewhere, in Bologna, in August 1922, taxpayer leagues headed by the leader of the province's Liberal Association (who had been secretary to Sidney Sonnino) withheld their communal tax payments until the Socialist communal councils were removed (Maier 1975, p. 320). Similar tax strikes occurred in many provinces, municipalities, and communes. With official collusion, they brought down the local Socialist governments and communal councils, which led to the installation of Fascist regimes in their place.

In general, the National Syndicates rejected any demands made by Socialist union leaders that encroached on managerial prerogatives, such as worker participation in the management of an estate. Instead, they sought "substantial" monetary rewards to individual members and benefits, such as hospital insurance, based on "merit and talent" (Snowden 1989, pp. 64-6). In short, the pacts negotiated by the Syndicates avoided infringement of landowner property rights and encouraged the fragmentation of the peasantry as a class, thus making the *agrari* "the cocks of the walk" once again (Cardoza 1982, p. 421). Thus, the employers' collaboration with the Syndicates paralleled their active assistance to the Fascists in their takeover of provincial political power from the Socialists. The Syndicates, so it was hoped, would serve the interests of the propertied class by helping to permanently erase the Socialist threat.

The Takeover Data

In the following analysis I focus on the twenty-five Fascist provincial takeovers that occurred prior to the "March on Rome" and Mussolini's nomination as premier in October 1922. I define *takeover* as the overthrow of the pre-existing provincial government and the installation of Fascists or elements favorable to the Fascists in the provincial administrations. These takeovers are listed and located on a map of Italy by Adrian Lyttelton (who based the classification of each takeover on province and region).

The nature and use of these data require some elaboration. First, Lyttelton's map is devoid of any commentary, nor does he say specifically what he himself means by "takeover." Second, Lyttelton does not indicate the source of the data contained in the map. The data provided were verified against information contained in local studies of specific provinces. Indeed, the only case I found that was omitted from Lyttelton's map is the province of Bologna. In addition, as the scope of the sample is appropriate (it includes all the provinces in Italy), these data may be considered valid although certainly not ideal (see Zetterberg 1965, pp. 128-30). Finally, as in the case of De Felice's information on Fascist violence, these are simply the only data we have.

A different, conceptual, problem relates to the classification of the takeovers. Lyttelton classifies the takeovers into so-called "stages" in the seizure of provincial power: (1) the period before the general elections of May 1921; (2) the period opening with these elections and closing with the Socialist general strike of July 1922; (3) the period in the aftermath of this strike until the "March on Rome" (October 1922) and Mussolini's accession to national power.

This periodization is determined by two suppositions, neither of which I consider tenable: first, that these national events had an independent effect on the Fascists' ability to take over the provinces, and second, that the likelihood of a Fascist takeover in the second or third stage were independent of the events in the preceding stages. I know of no convincing evidence, however, that national events determined local capacities for a takeover (nor does Lyttelton so argue).

The Coefficient of Collusion

Stated simply, the question is: Was there a pattern to the Fascist takeovers in the provinces? And, if there was, does it accord with the hypothesis that the relative stability of class hegemony and the odds of a Fascist takeover were closely (and inversely) related. The electoral balance favoring the Socialists, as we saw earlier, tended to coincide, approximately and unevenly, with the rising incidence of Fascist violence. But the pattern here with respect to the association between the Liberal hegemony and Fascist power is quite distinct.

As Table 8.5 shows, this pattern is clear and consistent, and precisely in accord with my first hypothesis. The lower the level of Liberal hegemony in a province, the greater the odds that the Fascists would seize power there.[2] The Fascists took over 86% (12 out of 14) of the provinces where the Socialists had received an electoral majority, and 50% (4 out of 8) of the provinces where they obtained an electoral plurality. In contrast, in the fifteen provinces where the Liberals enjoyed a wide electoral majority, the Fascists took power in only one province. Put differently, some three-quarters of the twenty-two provinces where the Socialists had participated in governance, whether on the basis of an electoral plurality (8 provinces) or electoral majority (14 provinces) were taken over by the Fascists.

This finding is also consistent with the argument that the Fascists could not take power on their own and probably did not "take" it at all: They were handed it, or allowed to keep it, only where both the propertied class and state officials were interested in their doing so. This argument can be tested more directly by assessing the effects of both the level of class hegemony and the extent of Fascist violence in determining whether the Fascists took provincial power.

Table 8.6 shows, as before, a relationship that is fully consistent with this argument. Holding constant the incidence of Fascist violence, the odds of a Fascist takeover were directly related to the level of Liberal hegemony. Where the incidence of violence was frequent (that is, "chronic" or "recurrent"), and where it was merely sporadic, the odds of a Fascist takeover increased as the Liberal hegemony declined.

In contrast, the odds of a Fascist takeover dropped steadily and sharply as the Liberals' hegemony increased. For instance, all but one of the dozen provinces where violence was frequent and the Socialists had an electoral majority fell to the Fascists. But, given the same amount of violence, the Fascists took over in only one of the five provinces where the Liberals held a wide majority. Where Fascist violence was sporadic, they succeeded in taking over none of the ten provinces with either a wide Liberal majority or the six provinces with a narrow one. Nevertheless, the Fascists were allowed to take power, with the same low amount of violence, in two of the five provinces where the Socialists held either an electoral plurality or a majority.

The data imply that one factor allowing the Fascists to turn their assaults on the Socialists into paving stones on the road to power was the acquiescence or actual collusion of state officials. Where it was missing, as it surely was in the provinces where the Liberals ruled unchallenged and the hegemony of the propertied class was secure, the Fascists simply failed to take power.

Table 8.5
Fascist Seizure of Power (1921-1922) by Liberal Hegemony
in Italy's Provinces (1920)

Electoral Balance	Fascist Seizures of Power	(N)
Liberal wide majority	7	(15)
Liberal narrow majority	25	(16)
Liberal plurality	31	(13)
Socialist plurality	50	(8)
Socialist majority	86	(14)

Yet, it seems certain that Fascist violence did matter because at every level of Liberal hegemony, the odds of a Fascist seizure of power were considerably greater where their violence was frequent rather than sporadic. The issue is, I believe, what logical inference can be made from the relationships revealed here even if they do not contradict our main conclusion? How can we explain that even in the small number of provinces where the Liberals ruled unchallenged and which witnessed repeated, frequent Fascist attacks, the Fascists did not take power? Put simply, in the absence of the collusion with officials, were the outcomes of the Squads' violence limited by their fighting capacity alone?

Another (perhaps more precise) estimate of the magnitude of the independent effects of Fascist violence versus the Liberal hegemony on the Fascist takeovers is provided by a logit (logistic regression) analysis. Table 8.7 shows the odds of a Fascist seizure of power in each of the top four categories of Liberal hegemony compared to the odds in the omitted category, namely, the provinces where the Socialists had an electoral majority.[3] This analysis shows that when the incidence of Fascist violence is held constant, the odds against a Fascist takeover in those provinces where the Liberals held a wide majority, as compared to those in which the Socialists had an electoral majority, are roughly 60 to 1 (alternatively, the odds favoring a Fascist takeover were 0.017).

Table 8.6
Fascist Seizure of Power (1921-1922) by Liberal Hegemony (1920)
and Fascist Violence in Italy's Provinces (1920-1921)

Electoral Balance	Frequent Fascist Violence		Sporadic Fascist Violence	
	(%)	(N)	(%)	(N)
Liberal wide majority	20	(50)	0	(10)
Liberal narrow majority	40	(10)	0	(6)
Liberal plurality	43	(7)	17	(6)
Socialist plurality	60	(5)	33	(3)
Socialist majority	92	(12)	50	(2)

Note: "Frequent" violence includes the categories of "chronic" and "recurrent" violence (over seven incidents of violence during the period November 1920 through May 1921).

Table 8.7
Logit Estimates of the Effects of Liberal Hegemony (1920)
and Frequent Fascist Violence (1920-1921) in Determining
the Fascist Seizure of Power in Italy's Provinces (1921-1922)

Liberal Hegemony	Logit Coefficient	Odds Multiplier
Liberal wide majority	-4.06*	
	(1.39)	.017
Liberal narrow majority	-2.99**	
	(1.09)	.050
Liberal plurality	-2.90*	
	(1.15)	.054
Socialist plurality	-1.53	
	(1.20)	.204
Frequent violence	2.62**	
	(.94)	13.83

Intercept: -.146
Chi-square (df): 35.11 (5)
N = 65
* p < .05
** p < .01

Overall, the odds favoring a Fascist takeover increase sharply, controlling for Fascist violence, as Liberal hegemony decreases. Thus, where the Liberal Party ruled with a narrow electoral majority, the odds *against* a takeover are 20 to 1 (the odds *in favor* of a takeover were 0.05). Where the Liberals held only a plurality and shared power with the Socialists, the odds against a takeover were a bit less, 18.5 to 1 (the odds *in favor* of a takeover were 0.054).

Finally, where the Socialists had an electoral plurality, the odds against a takeover went down to 5 to 1 (the odds in favor of a takeover were 0.204.) At the same time, as the contingency table also shows quite clearly, with Liberal hegemony held constant, the net effect of the incidence of Fascist violence on the odds of a Fascist takeover was also substantial. The odds that the Fascists would seize provincial power where their violence was frequent rather than sporadic were 14 to 1. Thus, the paramilitary capacity of the Fascists surely mattered but it was insufficient, by itself, to bring down Socialist governments.

The political terrain on which the Fascists and Socialists fought was never neutral, and victory was in no way determined by the size of their political constituency, their social base. An indirect indication of this is given by a logit analysis, which shows that the concentration of industrial workers had only a slight independent effect on the odds of a Fascist takeover (Table 8.8).[4] In other words, with this variable controlled, the measurable change in the independent effects of Fascist violence and the Liberal hegemony is minimal.[5] Nor did the number of Fascist cadres matter. A "high" number of members in the Fascist provincial organization on the eve of the first wave of takeovers, May 1921, had virtually no independent effect on the odds of a Fascist takeover (Table 8.9).[6]

Table 8.8
**Logit Estimates of the Effects of Liberal Hegemony (1920), Frequent Fascist
Violence (1920-1921) and the Concentration of Industrial Workers (1921) in
Determining the Fascist Seizure of Power in Italy's Provinces (1921-1922)**

Liberal Hegemony	Logit Coefficient	Odds Multiplier
Liberal wide majority	-4.00*	
	(1.40)	.018
Liberal narrow majority	-2.96**	
	(1.10)	.0517
Liberal plurality	-2.97*	
	(1.17)	.0511
Socialist plurality	-1.58*	
	(1.19)	.20
Frequent violence	2.70**	
	(.97)	14.96
High concentration of industrial workers	.417	1.51

Intercept: -.372
N = 65
Chi-square (df): 35.42 (6)
* p < .05
** p < .01

Once more, as the historical evidence suggests and the findings of my own
analyses tend to confirm, the decisive factors in this process were the Fascists'
"offensive alliances" with the propertied class and their "defensive alliances"
with local and national officials and Liberal political leaders. The "offensive
alliances" provided their bloody assaults with approval, sponsorship, and active
participation by "respectable" men of property.

However, this support, while necessary, was insufficient to turn the
Socialists' defeat in this one-sided civil war into a Fascist political victory.
Instead, it was the "defensive alliances" that determined the pattern of the
Squads' punitive expeditions and violence. That is, if the Fascists were to take
power, "defensive alliances" with local and national authorities were requisite.
This, I believe, is the logical inference to be drawn from the quantitative
analyses presented here. Were it possible to obtain systematic data on the degree
of state collusion and to enter them into our equations, the "coefficient of
collusion" would be salient.

In sum, as we have seen, only rarely did the state's higher officials actively
seek to stop the Fascists' advance; when they did, they found themselves
socially reviled, politically isolated, and rendered ineffective by both their
superiors in Rome and their subordinates in the provinces.[7] Neither the police
nor the Army acted against the Squads. Indeed, the collaboration of high Army
officers and *carabinieri* commanders together with Giolitti's own incorporation
of the Fascist organization into his ruling Liberal coalition, aided and abetted
(as leading historians of Fascism have likewise suggested) the Fascists' so-
called seizure of power.

Table 8.9
Logit Estimates of the Effects of Electoral Balance, Liberals vs. Socialists, Frequent Fascist Violence, and the Concentration of Industrial Workers (Model A) and Fascist Membership, May 1921 (Model B) in Determining the Fascist Seizure of Power in Italy's Provinces

Electoral Balance	Model A		Model B	
	Logit Coefficient	Odds Multiple Coefficient	Logit Coefficient	Odds Multiple Coefficient
Liberal wide majority	-4.00**	.018	-3.94**	.019
	(1.40)		(1.43)	
Liberal narrow majority	-2.96**	.0517	-2.93**	.053
	(1.10)		(1.09)	
Liberal plurality	-2.97*	.0511	-2.79*	.061
	(1.17)		(1.18)	
Socialist plurality	-1.58*	.20	-1.57	.207
	(1.19)		(1.21)	
Frequent violence	2.70**	14.96	2.53**	12.64
	(0.97)		(0.981)	
High concentration of industrial workers	.417	1.51	—	—
"High" Fascist membership	—	—	.252 (0.770)	1.28

Intercept Model A: -.372   Intercept Model B: -.238
Model A Chi-square (df): 35.42 (6)   Model B Chi-square (df): 35.21 (6)
Model A N = 65   Model A N = 65
* p < .05
** p < .01

Note: Fascist membership is defined as the ratio of members enrolled in the Fascist organization in May 1921, to the number of eligible voters in the province. "High" Fascist membership is defined as the top third of the distribution of this ratio among the provinces.

In brief, the Fascists' successful establishment of "local tyrannies" in the provinces was determined not merely by their "warlike violence" but by the overall collusion of the Liberal state itself. This collusion rested on the weakness and ambivalence of the central government toward the Fascists and, most importantly, on the class allegiance of the provincial officials who carried out this policy. The influence if not absolute sway that the propertied class held over the political authorities made it possible for the *ras* to establish de facto provincial Fascist regimes (see Tasca [1938] 1966, p. 108; Seton Watson 1967, p. 606; Salvemini 1973, pp. 307-9; Corner 1975; Maier 1975; Lyttelton 1987, pp. 54, 78-80).

The "March on Rome": The Provincial Road to National Power

Still, the shift of the Fascists' struggle from the provincial to the national arena was not complete until the fall of 1922, that is, only after the Squads had destroyed the majority of the provincial Socialist organizations and secured their hold in most of the northern provinces. The pivotal events occurred during the parliamentary crisis that followed Giolitti's resignation from the government. The dramatic culmination of this phase was Mussolini's Fascist *coup de main*, the "March on Rome".

By October 1922, the Fascists controlled most of Italy's northern provinces. Their political victories on the provincial level were the main determinant of their ascendance to state power on the national level. Their show of strength made them a political force that the Liberal government, in the midst of a deep parliamentary crisis, could not resist. Supported by the employers' organizations, the armed forces, and the central government, the King chose to exercise his power and to nominate Mussolini to serve a one-year term as prime minister.

The Fascists' seizure of power, personified by Mussolini's appointment as prime minister, was the direct outcome of the now explicit and formal collaboration of the Liberal government with the Fascists. It was preceded by the dramatic threat of a "March on Rome." In Farneti's words, this act was "essentially political, not military, and from this point of view the 'March on Rome' was the conclusion of a strategy based on the exercise of violence and, above all, on the enfeeblement and division of forces of the political alignment" (1978, p. 26). Mussolini's open threats to seize power in Rome marked a profound transformation of the Fascists' objectives. Their struggle was now directed not against the Socialists but against the Liberal state per se. The objective of this struggle, in Mussolini's words, was to "put the masses in action to make an *extra-parliamentary crisis* and come to power" (Lyttelton 1987, p. 83, my emphasis).

In August 1922, Mussolini announced that the "March on Rome" had begun, if not strictly from the standpoint of insurrection, at least from a historical perspective: "[A]t this very moment a new political class is in the process of being formed, to which will be confided...the difficult task of governing...the nation" (cited in Tasca [1938] 1966, p. 255). Concurrently, Mussolini announced the establishment of the Fascist Militia, organized on a national scale, and in overt defiance of state authority (Lyttelton 1987, p. 82; Tasca [1938] 1966, p. 178).

The "March on Rome" was planned in advance in a strict military fashion. The close collaboration between the Army's command and the Fascists was evident in the presence of three generals among the group that had planned the March (Lyttelton 1987, p. 83). In the last days of October 1922, while negotiating with several political parties over the formation of a new government, Mussolini appointed a quadrumvirate, including General Emilio De Bono, *squadrist* leaders Cesare De Vecchi and Italo Balbo, and Party Secretary Michele Bianchi to draw up a plan for the March (Tasca [1938] 1966, p. 266). They divided the country into twelve military zones, and assigned each one to a Squad leader. The plan called first for the occupation of public buildings in the provinces and then for the mobilization of three columns to enter the capital (Lyttelton 1987, p. 85).

By this time, as we have seen, the first stage of this plan was already underway. The prefectures of Perugia, Pisa, Mantua, and Cremona were taken over, and provincial communications centers, railway stations, and telegraph offices were occupied by the Squads (Lyttelton 1987, pp. 89-90; Tasca [1938] 1966, pp. 301-4). Elsewhere, the Fascists began to target state officials and institutions as objectives on their road to national power. But the second stage, the military occupation of the capital, never took place. This was partly due to the government's rather belated but effective measures against the Fascist mobilization. Prefects were ordered to hand their power over to local Army units, and a military force of 12,000 men under the command of General Umberto Pugliese was deployed outside Rome to block the Squads' entry into the city (Lyttelton 1987, p. 85; Seton Watson 1967, p. 625).

In a strict military sense, "March on Rome," as Lyttelton argues, proved to be a "colossal bluff" (1987, p. 87). However, politically, the aborted march was successful: While the Fascists were gathering on the outskirts of Rome, Prime Minister Luigi Facta resigned and King Emmanuel III appointed Mussolini in his stead.[8] Only then were the blackshirts allowed to enter the city and to march to the palace and greet their leader, Mussolini, as the newly appointed Fascist head of government (Tasca [1938] 1966, pp. 296-99).

NOTES

1.   Clearly, these relationships were partially a product of the political strategy of the PSI and its selection of agricultural laborers and workers as targets for its organizing drives. See chapter 4 for an analysis of this strategy and PSI neglect of the south.

2.   Lyttelton notes (without elaboration) that "Fascists had made little inroads by 1922 into Liberal strongholds" (1987, p. 108). Obviously, the findings presented here are consistent with this observation.

3.   In the following logit regressions, I use listwise deletion.

4.   "High" is the top third of the distribution, "medium" the middle third, and "low" the bottom third. The latter two-thirds are collapsed into a single "not high" category and compared with the "high" category in the logit analysis.

5.   A perhaps more appropriate indicator of the size of the Socialists' working-class constituency would have been the concentration of agricultural workers because it was this group's struggle against the *agrari*, under Socialist leadership, that most provoked the Fascist reaction. But these struggles were waged predominantly in the north and, to a lesser extent, in the center. So, as detailed in chapter 4 (see also Table 4.4), a region would have to be under Socialist control in order to assess the effect of the concentration of agricultural workers on the odds of a Fascist takeover. This analysis cannot be done here because nearly all of the Fascist takeovers also occurred in the country's north and center regions (of the twenty-five takeovers, only two were in the south.)

6.   Fascist membership refers to the number of members registered with the provincial Fascist organization as of May 1921, which was also the highest membership

recorded before the takeovers began (see De Felice 1966). But even this figure is inflated for by this time, many "members" had been involuntarily recruited by the threat or use of violence against them. Indeed, the distinction between the Fascist organization and the Fascist Syndicate, whose members (as we saw earlier) were mainly if not entirely coerced into joining, was often blurred by the Fascist secretariat that recorded these figures (Lyttelton 1987, p. 71). The size of the Fascist membership is measured here as a ratio of the number of members to the number of eligible voters in the province (which is the same denominator used in the measure of voter turnout in chapter 4). A "high" Fascist membership refers to the top third of the distribution of members by province; "not high" refers to the bottom two-thirds. The logit analysis compares the "high" to the "not high" category.

7.   The actions and consequent fate of such men, who sought to honorably fulfill their sworn duties but failed, is exemplified by Cesare Mori, the prefect of Bologna, whose case is discussed in chapter 7.

8.   The Army's High Command, according to De Felice, played an important role in the king's decision to nominate Mussolini as Prime Minister. In late October 1922, the king met with Generals Diaz, Giardino, and Pecori Giraldi, as well as Admiral Thaon de Revel, who told him, according to De Felice, that "the army will do its duty but it would be best not to put it to the test" (1966, pp. 361-62).

Chapter 9

The Internal Contradiction
of Fascist Rule

The question of what determined the Fascists' seizure of political power is inseparable from that of the specific nature of their organization. This means we need to show how—and why—the Fascists seized power, but also what Fascism became. How exactly did the historical content of the Fascists' route to power—the initial form of their organization, the political alliances forged to sustain this organization, and the tactics employed against the Socialists—determine the character of their ideology and the contours of their organization? The Fascist Party that took power in 1922 was not the same political organization operating in 1919. If there had been an "unfulfilled possibility" of Fascism evolving into something other than what it eventually became, what were the specific moments of its creation. More specifically, how did the Fascists' *external* struggle against the Socialists as well as, eventually, against their own allies shape the nature of their *internal* struggles?[1]

We have seen that the Fascists' "offensive alliances" with the landlords were an integral part of their extra-parliamentary, paramilitary, political strategy. The postwar ascendance of the Socialist Workers' Movement and the establishment of "Red Baronies" in the country's northern provinces drove the militant organized landowners of the north and center into an unofficial covenant with the *squadristi* and into support of the punitive expeditions in Socialist-controlled provinces. The landlords' political hegemony also allowed the formation of the Fascists' "defensive alliances" with the Liberal state. Due to their continued control over official institutions, the landlords secured the collaboration and collusion of state authorities with the Fascists. This gave the Fascists the freedom to destroy Socialist organizations with impunity and to overthrow Socialist provincial governments. They could then install their own "local tyrannies" in their place. At the same time, the provinces governed by the Liberal Party, where the hegemony of the propertied class was secure from any Socialist threat, remained virtually untouched by the Fascists' Squads. By the time of the "March on Rome," and of Mussolini's appointment as prime minister by the King, the

Fascists had reversed the tide of Socialist insurgency that had swept the country since the end of World War I.

This political strategy affected the Fascist organization in two major respects. First, the alliance with the landlords led to a shift in the Fascists' own objectives: It transformed the Fascists' struggle from an ad hoc anti-Socialist tactic into a full-blown war for state power. They ceased being satisfied with the elimination of the Socialists as a civil or a political force and now turned to wrest power from their ally, the Liberal government. The second, more salient effect was that the strategy of violence forged a path leading to the creation of the Squads as a distinct, internal "intransigent" faction within the Fascist organization itself. As such, the Squads came to challenge not only the dominance of the original Syndicalists and ex-Socialists, but also Mussolini's personal authority.

THE NEW PARTY AND ITS LEADERSHIP

Two major internal events and associated conflicts characterized the period of the Fascists struggle for power: Mussolini's Pact of Pacification with the Socialists, signed on August 3, 1921, and the establishment of the Fascist Party, the *Partito Nazionale Fascista*, PNF, in November 1921. The three-month interim between the two events was crucial for the transformation of Fascism into a phenomenon far different from what it had been upon its emergence.

The factions formed about these issues and their conflicting positions shed some light on the organization's internal dynamics, especially on the rising influence of the Squads. Here we see the formation of what Antonio Gramsci called the "two Fascisms." In an article in the *L'Ordine Nuovo*, written at the height of the debate over the Pact, Gramsci described the formation of the Fascist factions as a "rift" between the urban "petty bourgeois" nucleus of the *fasci di combattimento* and the "bands, created and armed by the big landowners" (August 25, 1921, p. 86). Gramsci was accurate in his prediction that "Fascism will get out of the crisis by splitting. The parliamentary part headed by Mussolini...will necessarily point itself towards collaboration with the Socialists and the *Popolari*...the intransigent part...will continue with its characteristic anti-proletarian activity....The crisis will only signal the exit from the *fasci* movement of a faction of petty bourgeoisie..." (August 25, 1921, p. 86). A similar view was expressed by Agostino Lanzillo, a leading Fascist intellectual who opposed the Squads. Lanzillo claimed that urban Fascism did have some "general and reasonably well-defined" elements in its ideology, but that it could not check the avalanche of agrarian Fascism (1922, p. 225).

To understand why both Communist and Fascist observers agree on this issue, we have to recall the history of the Fascists' initial appearance. When the Fascist organization was established in the midst of Italy's postwar crisis, it was composed of three major groups: the revolutionary Syndicalists and Socialists or the "left interventionists," centered mostly in Milan; the *arditi;* and the Futurists, led by Filippo Marinetti (see Chapter 5). These were the "Fascists of the First Hour," or, the *sansepolcristi*. The Fascists' participation in the first postwar general elections (1919) resulted in a humiliating defeat. In Milan, their major stronghold, the Fascists received a little less than 2% of the votes cast (about 5,000 out of 270,000) (Tasca [1938] 1966, p. 39).

By the fall of 1920, the organization appeared to have withered away. Although some isolated violent clashes occurred between the Fascists and the Socialists (the most notorious was the Fascists' burning of *Avanti!* in April 1919), the Fascist organization practically ceased to exit. A year later, the militarization of the Fascist organization and the establishment of the Action Squads led to the Fascists' penetration into the countryside and the creation of a new cadre rooted in provincial centers. This new cadre, Lanzillo argues, was nothing but a "cruel and implacable movement of interest" (1922, p. 226). In the course of the punitive expeditions and the weaving of an alliance with the landlords, the *squadristi* developed their own distinct groups of allies and supporters, independent financial and political resources and, consequently, singular political objectives (Lyttelton 1987, p. 106).

The autonomy of the provincial Squad leaders became evident in the course of the debates conducted within the Fascist organization over the Pact of Pacification and the establishment of the Fascist National Party. The Pact called for "immediate action to put an end to the threats, assaults, reprisals, acts of vengeance, pressure, and personal violence of any description" by either organization against the other, and for the "mutual respect" of "all economic organizations [i.e. the Fascist and Socialist labor unions]." The Futurists and Syndicalists, as well as others hostile to the intransigents led by Mussolini himself, favored this attempt at reconciliation with the Socialists. The Pact was signed in August 1921 by Mussolini together with other representatives of the Fascist organization, leaders of the Socialist Party, and the General Confederation of Labor. The event was witnessed by members of the Chamber of Deputies (Tasca [1938] 1966, pp. 148, 147; Lyttelton 1987, pp. 72-3).

It was no secret that by agreeing to the Pact, Mussolini and his followers had hoped not only to control the violence of the Squads against the Socialists but also to contain the Squads' growing influence within the Fascist organization. In August 1921, Mussolini bluntly stated what he expected from the Pact. The treaty, he said, "also settles the internal Fascist crisis, in the sense that henceforward the political element [i.e., the leadership in Milan] will have a clearly marked supremacy over the military [i.e., the Squads]" (cited in Tasca [1938] 1966, p. 149; see also Maier 1975, p. 330). In his statement, Mussolini was explicit about his opposition to the provincial Fascists and his contempt for their landowning allies. During negotiations over the Pact, Mussolini condemned provincial Fascism as "no longer liberation, but tyranny; no longer protector of the nation, but defense of private interests and of the dullest, deafest, most miserable cast that exists in Italy" (in Corner 1975, p. 193 n. 5). But the intransigents continued to oppose the Pact. In response to its signing, the Squad leaders unleashed a wave of protests. The Fascist bosses of its "capitals," Italo Balbo of Ferrara, Roberto Farinacci of Cremona, and Dino Grandi, the new boss of Bologna, joined forces to repudiate the Pact. Henceforth, the intransigents would employ methods similar to those used against the Socialists to confront opponents in their own organization and Mussolini's leadership. They organized meetings in their provinces that condemned Mussolini's new "parliamentary timidity," which they presented as a betrayal of the Fascist revolutionary mission. Posters appeared in Bologna denouncing Mussolini as a traitor to Fascism; the local *fasci* in Florence and other cities dissolved local chapters in protest against the Pact and Mussolini's leadership (Tasca [1938] 1966, pp. 149-152; Seton Watson 1967, pp. 593-4). This led Mussolini, in mid-August 1921, to tender his resignation from the Fascist leadership. Dramatic as this gesture was, it did not bring the provincial leaders into line. They remained united in their rejection of the Pact.

Eventually, the Squads prevailed. Mussolini withdrew his support for the Pact in exchange for the intransigents' support of his motion for the formation of the Fascist Party. In March 1921, Mussolini had insisted that Fascism was an "anti-party movement": "Fascism is not a Church. It is more like a training ground. It is not a party. It is a movement....We are the heretics of all Churches" (Lyttelton 1987, p. 44). Now, only eight months later, the Fascist third national congress in Rome approved the motion to establish the Fascist National Party. Mussolini hoped that a hierarchical organization, with ties to the Fascist parliamentary representatives elected in the May 1921 elections, would secure his leadership and control over the new party (Tasca [1938] 1966, pp. 161-163).[2]

This compromise exacted its price. The new program clearly reflects the position of the Fascists' propertied—especially agrarian—allies. It is a far cry from the Fascist program of barely two years earlier. To the extent that both programs represent the political positions of the Fascist leaders in the respective periods, their differences reflect the extreme transformation if not rupture experienced by the movement in its first two years of existence.[3] The PNF's 1921 program is a far more elaborate document than the earlier "manifesto" (1919) drafted by the Syndicalist De Ambris and the Futurist Marinetti (both had resigned from the movement by 1921). Specifically, it relates to many issues that had not been raised in the first document (Seton Watson 1967, p. 518, n. 1).[4]

Taken from the 1921 program, the following refers only to those issues raised in both the 1919 and 1921 programs. The 1921 version contains no mention of workers' rights or of progressive taxation, let alone expropriation of wealth. Regarding the relationship between the state and private property, the Fascist Party now states clearly explicitly asserts that "the state recognizes the social function of private property which is at the same time a right and a duty....The state is to be reduced to those functions which are essential, the political and the juridical...." The only proper function of the state is, therefore, procedural, and far from the implementation of any radical alteration of property rights or class relations (Seton Watson 1967, pp. 594-5). The state's main responsibility is to protect the class of "producers" that, the Fascists now insist, includes not only the workers but also industrialists and managers. In contrast, the 1919 program includes some specific and radical demands concerning the rights of industrial workers, actions to be taken against war profiteers, as well as general political demands for the introduction of universal suffrage and the abolition of the Senate. Although the new party's program continues to call for an eight-hour workday and for social legislation guaranteeing workers' health and retirement insurance, it also states that these policies would be implemented only under the condition that "there shall be no interference with production."

Historians of Italian Fascism generally agree that the later program attempted to reconcile the divergent views lying at the heart of the debate over the establishment of the Party, that is, Mussolini's centralism and shift to the right; Grandi's insistence on the Syndicalism of D'Annunzio, and the opposition of the Fascist *ras* to any form of centralization, which they saw (probably with reason) as undermining their independence. Mussolini's pronouncements during this period confirm the character of these contradictions. He attempted to portray the new party in militant terms but, at the same time, to "prove" himself to the movement's more conservative allies. On November 1921, in the *Il Popolo d'Italia,* Mussolini describes the new PNF as a "party which very probably will resemble no other existing party: a party which is also a militia, in the most literal sense of the word" (in Seton Watson 1967, p. 595). Concurrently, in an overture to leaders who demanded the reinstitution of authoritarian government, he wrote in the second issue of his review *Gerarchia* ("Hierarchy") that "it may be that in the 19th century capitalism needed democracy; now it can do without it....Democracy in the factory had lasted only as long as a bad dream....Now it is the other democracy, the political one, which is about to end, which *must* end" (quoted in Lyttelton 1987 p. 75, emphasis in the original).[5]

While these internal debates were taking place, the Fascist organization experienced a remarkable growth in its rank and file. From a relatively small, almost negligible organization of about 65,000 members in March 1921, the Fascists had enrolled over 310,000 members by May 1921, prior to the "March on Rome." However, as we shall see, this trend, too, remained essentially a local phenomenon. Fascism was still confined to the regions taken over by the Squads, leaving the rest of the country practically untouched.

THE NEW FASCIST MEMBERS

There are several studies of the composition and scope of membership in the Fascist organization (see for example, Corner 1974; Peterson 1975; Zangarini 1978; Revelli 1987; Brustein and Markovsky 1989; Brustein 1991). Common to these studies, as discussed in Chapter 2, is their assumption that membership was voluntary and that we can therefore conceptually equate this social movement's political power with the size of its social base of support or official number of members. This equation allows scholars to employ data on both the nature and size of enrollment as measures of the movement's social and political strength. However, in the case of Italian Fascism, I argue, this assumption does not hold because the Fascists gained their political power through violence, not by the mobilization of a mass social base. Albeit, the opposite may be true: Fascist political control in a province may have led to an increase in membership.

Accordingly, PNF enrollment is important in an additional sense, one that supports the general theoretical argument made in this study: It indicates another transition in the character of the Fascist organization. Here, too, as in the altered balance of power among the Party's cadres and the change in the Fascists' political program, we can locate the effects of the Squads' strategy on the nature of Fascism. This pertains to both the general increase in membership and to its composition.[6] The question is, then, did the political strategy of *squadrismo*, the violence, punitive expeditions, and the provincial takeovers that had won the Fascists political power, also lead to the increase in the Party's enrollment?

The data on Fascist membership collected by De Felice (a portion of which was analyzed in the previous chapter) show the relative growth in membership from the onset of the Fascist punitive expeditions in March 1921 until May 1922.[7] In March 1921, 65,165 members were enrolled in the Fascist organization. The numbers rise quite steadily until May 1922, reaching 310,628 members. Table 9.1 shows two specific periods of increase. The largest increase was between April and May 1921 (91,115 additional members, a growth of about 113%); and another, smaller increase, exactly a year later, between April and May 1922. The number of Fascist members in that period grew from 202,058 to 310,628 (108,570 additional members, a growth of 54%). Between these two periods, the enrollment appears to have stagnated. At the same time, as is shown by the last column in Table 9.1, the average number of members per *fascio* declined steadily. Revelli, who examines De Felice's membership data, suggests that this indicates the failure of the new party to recruit members and translate their territorial expansion into a mass social base (1987, p. 13).

National events may explain the first increase, between April and May 1921. It was precisely at this time that Giolitti accepted the Fascist organization into the Liberal Party's National Bloc, just before the May 1921 elections. Giolitti's embrace led the Fascists not only to electoral victory, but also to a more "respectable" position among the political parties. This, we may assume, gave membership in the organization a completely different social and political significance. The Fascists were no longer defined as a brutal association of *squadristi* but as a new party blessed by the reigning powers. Although we have no additional data to support this contention, it is reasonable to interpret the growth in membership as a product of the Fascists' new legitimacy. At this stage, the strategy of violence may have won the Fascist organization political power in the provinces, but it was the retreat to an electoral strategy, even if ephemeral, that stimulated membership.

To explore this possibility further, we can examine the geographical distribution of the growth of membership in Italy's sixteen regions. Tables 9.2 and 9.3 show the regional variance in the growth of membership and the relative weight of each region in the total national increase for two periods: The initial expansion in the spring of 1921 and in the following period, April-May 1922. The rate of increase is far from homogeneous. As shown in the third column in Table 9.2, growth in membership in absolute numbers is confined to four regions in the country's north and center: Lombardy, the Veneto, Emilia, and Tuscany. Together, these regions account for 48,783 additional members, about 55% of the total national growth of 91,115. (Sharp increases were also recorded in Umbria and the southern region of Apulia; each of which accounts for an additional 13% of the total increase.) The remaining regions show no significant increase in membership.

Table 9.1
Fascist Membership: Monthly Rates of Increase (March 1921 - May 1922)

Month and Year	Number of Fasci (Chapters)	Increase in Fasci per Month	Total Number of Members	Increase in Members per Month	Increase in Members (%)	Average Number of Members per Fascio*
March 1921	283	—	65,165	—	—	230
April 1921	435	152	80,897	17,833	.22	190
May 1921	959	524	172,012	91,115	1.13	178
June 1921	1,114	155	186,812	15,290	.09	167
July 1921	1,156	42	191,691	4,879	.03	166
August 1921	1,175	19	195,225	3,534	.02	166
Sept. 1921	1,188	13	195,897	672	.00	165
Oct. 1921	1,231	43	199,338	3,441	.02	162
Nov. 1921	1,238	7	199,522	184	.00	161
Dec. 1921	1,253	15	200,719	1,197	.00	160
April 1922	1,301	48	202,058	1,339	.00	155
May 1922	2,055	754	310,628	108,570	.54	151

* This column is adapted from Revelli 1987.
Source: De Felice 1966, *Mussolini il Fascista,* Vol. I, Pt. 1, pp. 8-11.

Table 9.2
Increase in Fascist Membership by Region
(April -May 1921)

Region	Membership April 1921	Membership May 1921	Increase (N)	Increase (%)	National Increase (%)
Piedmont	2,896	7,821	4,925	170	.05
Liguria	2,959	7,332	4,373	148	.05
Lombardy	15,724	28,851	13,127	.3	.15
Veneto	11,409	24,451	13,042	114	.14
Emilia	18,337	30,456	12,119	66	.14
Tuscany	3,845	14,340	10,495	273	.12
Marche	1,093	1,984	891	81	.01
Umbria	485	4,000	3,515	724	.13
Lazio	2,132	4,163	2,031	95	.02
Abruzzi e Molise	2,393	4,217	1,824	76	.02
Campania	4,438	11,149	6,711	151	.07
Apulia	6,412	17,621	11,209	175	.13
Basilicata	500	610	110	22	.00
Calabria	1,083	2,236	1,153	106	.01
Sicily	6,091	9,951	3,860	63	.04
Sardinia	1,100	2,830	1,730	157	.02
Total	80,897	172,012	91,115	113	1.00

Table 9.3 shows the regional breakdown of this gain. Even after the Fascists' participation in the national elections and the founding of the PNF, the regional character of the party, at least in terms of membership, remained firm if not more pointed than previously. Of the national increase of 108,129 members, 89,729 (about 82%) were concentrated in only three regions: Lombardy, Emilia and Tuscany. The greatest relative increase in membership occurred in Tuscany, where enrollment rose by 32,899 (about 178%) from 18,473 to 51,372 members; in Lombardy, with 37,939 members, which saw an increase of 41,390 (about 109%) to 79,329; and in Emilia that, beginning with 36,197 members, witnessed an increase of 15,440 (43%), to 51,637 members, all in the period from April 1922 to May 1922.

These regions, as we have seen, were almost completely under Fascist control. By July 1922, three of Lombardy's eight provinces were taken over; six of Emilia's eight provinces; and all of Tuscany's eight provinces. All told, these represent seventeen of the total twenty-five takeovers in the country. Again, as in the year before, the remaining regions were almost completely excluded from this Fascist social expansion, just as they were from its territorial one.

Table 9.3
Increase in Fascist Membership by Region
(April 1922 - May 1922)

Region	Membership April 1922	Membership May 1922	Increase (N)	Increase (%)	National Increase (%)
Piedmont	9,764	14,526	4,762	49	.04
Liguria	7,440	8,841	1,401	19	.01
Lombardy	37,939	79,329	41,390	109	.38
Veneto	27,205	34,396	7,191	26	.07
Emilia	36,197	51,637	15,440	43	.14
Tuscany	18,473	51,372	32,899	178	.30
Marche	2,267	2,311	44	02	.00
Umbria	4,000	5,410	1,410	35	.01
Lazio	4,213	9,747	5,534	131	.05
Abruzzi e Molise	6,253	4,763	- 1,490	-23	-.01
Campania	13,394	13,944	550	04	.00
Apulia	18,856	20,118	1,262	07	.01
Basilicata	610	565	- 45	-07	.01
Calabria	2,406	2,066	- 340	-14	.00
Sicily	10,110	9,546	- 564	-05	.00
Sardinia	3,372	2,057	- 1,315	-39	.01
Total	202,499	310,628	108, 129	53	1.00

As was already noted, these figures, being purely descriptive, probably do not contain the answer to the question regarding the cause of the sharp increase in membership in the Fascist organization between these two periods. They are instructive, nevertheless, in at least two respects: First, it is clear here, as from the foregoing analysis, that there is little sense in discussing the Fascist organization, its ideology, strategy, leadership, financial resources, and grassroots membership on a national level of analysis. The structural, economic, and political variation among Italy's regions is clearly expressed in the Fascists' fortunes. Second, and related to the first, is the absence of Fascist members in provinces that were not penetrated by the Squads. The intransigents, then, may have had a solid reason to demand control over the PNF because it seems that only in the regions they captured could the Fascists claim to have some significant following. The remaining question relates to the identity of these new joiners and its affect on the original cadre, the *sansepolcristi*.

As could be expected, the new wave of Fascist members brought a notable change in the Party's social and ideological character. The influence of men of property on provincial leaders, and through them on the Fascist organization spurred many revolutionary Syndicalists and ex-Socialists to quit. The protest and exodus of these "leftist" radicals testify to the extent of the transformation brought about by the Squads' political ascendance.

From the initial stages of the *squadristi*'s advance in the agrarian provinces, many *sansepolcristi* voiced their disappointment at the emerging alliances with conservative elements, and protested against the transformation of Fascism into a "white guard," "the body guards of the profiteers" (Cardoza 1982, p. 303; Corner 1975, p. 123). This became clear as early as May 1920, at the second Fascist congress, held in Milan. The decline in the influence of the radical ex-Socialists, Futurists, and Syndicalists was obvious: "[O]nly ten of the nineteen members of the organization's central committee were re-elected." The congress elected eleven new members, who belonged predominantly to the right. One of the most prominent leaders to leave the Fascist organization was Filippo Marinetti, the Futurist, who resigned from the Central Committee in 1920, no longer able "to stomach...the transformation of Fascism into a reactionary and traditionalist movement" (Seton Watson 1967, pp. 572-3, p. 573, n. 1).

Objections to this transformation came from almost every major Fascist stronghold. So visible, for instance, was the shift of the Bologna *fascio* in favor of the local landowners that Umberto Pasella, a former Syndicalist and the secretary of the Fascist central committee, warned its leader, Leandro Arpinati, in a personal letter, that "precisely because it has grown so suddenly as to become obese, your *fascio* is carrying out its functions in a confused manner, and many recent converts are Fascists like I am a country priest....I know that the Fascists have been placing themselves too completely in the service of the retrograde elements in Bologna, which could be politically damaging to the *fascio*" (cited in Cardoza 1982, p. 304). Similarly, Umberto Banchelli, a veteran Fascist leader, voiced his resentment of the new members recruited into the Fascist organization on account of the Squads' alliance with men of property. They were, he declared, the "sons and hangers-on of the bigwigs" who were joining the Fascist organization "not as Fascists, but as sons of the lawyer, of the doctor, or the war profiteer" (cited in Salvemini 1973, pp. 293-4).

A similar reaction was found in Ferrara. The influx of "respectable" elements, the original core of members argued, led to a change in the character of their *fascio* because it obliged a compromise with the Agrarian Federation (Corner 1975, pp. 122-23). One member, Gaggioli, wrote a formal complaint to the Fascist Executive Committee. There are elements in the *fascio,* Gaggioli warned the Committee in Milan, that missed the "true significance" of Fascism. "The *fascio* in Ferrara is nothing more or less than the guard of the *pescecanismo* ["sharks," a term for the war profiteers] (in De Felice 1965, p. 658). In the industrial city of Turin, the head of the local *fascio,* Cesare Maria De Vecchi, likewise did not conceal his disdain for the support given the Fascists by the industrialists. For example, when an industrialist representative "showed up at Fascist headquarters soon after the [striking workers'] Occupation of the Factories with generous offers of financial aid [for the Fascists], De Vecchi had him ejected from the premises with an unceremonious kick in the behind" (Sarti 1971, p. 30). This trend intensified during the first year of Mussolini's premiership: About half of the movement's total enrollment, more than 30,000 members, resigned that year from the newly formed Fascist Party.[8]

The communist theory of fascism, John Cammett argues, "has nothing to be ashamed of in relation to the work of the bourgeois historians and theorists" (1967, p. 154). As we saw in Chapter 5, contemporary Marxist observers of fascism made the most acute and precise observations about Italian Fascism. The Communists were convinced that fascism was not reducible to issues of class or social base, or to the question of the crisis of capitalism. Rather, they claimed, it emerged and prospered in the course of a concrete political struggle against the left and within its own ranks. According to Beetham, once the Fascists took power, the Marxists anticipated the "suppression of the independence of the Fascist Party and its fusion with the existing structures of bourgeois class power." This indeed occurred because the Party carried out policies that hurt its original mass base: "Its original cadres (the 'Fascists of the First Hour') were replaced by members of the bourgeoisie or their representatives...though not without a struggle" (1983, p. 10).

The analysis of the internal transformations of Fascism—the founding of the Party, the renunciation of 1919 radicalism, the growth in membership—attests to the significance of the Fascists' strategy of violence in defining Fascism itself. It shows that Palmiro Togliatti's 1952 critique of his own view of the concept of "social base," originally formulated in 1928, was correct. An analysis of the social base, said Togliatti, must also account for the movement's "objectives, of its actions [and] of those of who dominate and lead it" (cited in Cammett 1967, p.158 n. 23).

NOTES

1. "Complete Fascism," as manifested in the corporate state (established in 1934) was, I would suggest, also a product of significant political struggles, mainly within the Fascist Party, and was not simply inherent in Fascism's origins. This continued long after the seizure of state power, especially in the early years, 1922-26, which Adler terms "liberal Fascism: "a contradictory, unstable, transitional phase characterized by selective Fascist repression" (1976, p. 194).

2. The relative independence of "agrarian Fascism" was to remain a major dilemma for Mussolini after the Fascists' seizure of national power. One method Mussolini employed to submerge *squadrismo* was to incorporate its members into the MVSN, (*Milizia Voluntaria per la Sicurezza Nazionale,* the Voluntary Militia for National Security). Established in December 1922, immediately after the seizure of power, the MVSN was under Mussolini's direct command (Rochat [1967] 1974, p. 45).

3. This discussion of the Fascists' programs does not relate to the debate about whether a "Fascist ideology," or doctrine, exists (see Zeev Sternhell 1976 and 1995). It attempts merely to establish the argument that the Fascists' external struggles affected their internal conflicts and hence the ideological character of their organization. Nevertheless, a word about the issue seems in order. In his masterly study of National Socialism, Franz Neumann (1944) argues that National Socialism had "no theory of society," and thus no coherent ideology. This thesis is part of the rationale for his characterization of Nazism as "Behemoth," the monster of chaos. I venture that this may apply to Italian Fascism as well. Theoretically, Neumann cuts through some general confusion regarding what constitutes a coherent "ideology"; a confusion that intensifies when carried into the empirical realm of Italian Fascism. If "ideology" is a debatable concept, and Fascism, to quote Sternhell, is one of the most "notoriously blurred and

imprecise in outline," we may gain little by attempting to explain one confused concept ("fascism") by drawing on another, ("ideology") (1976, p. 315).

4. For the full text of the Party's program see De Felice 1966, Appendix b.

5. This attempt to reconcile his propertied backers is further manifested in Mussolini's implicit support of the so-called revisionists who opposed the Squads. This friction was at the helm of another party crisis, in late 1922 and early 1923, which came to be known as "dissidentism." Intransigent leaders like Dino Grandi, Italo Balbo, and others, rebelled against what they saw as the "parliamentary perversion" of Fascism, and against Mussolini's overtures towards the Liberals and the King. This time however, Mussolini was already in a position to use the PNF against the dissentors (Seton Watson 1967, p. 605).

6. The following tables are based on the regional level of analysis (N=16), unlike the analyses provided in the previous chapters which are based on the provincial level. Since the information provided is purely descriptive, I use it, not as a "test" of specific hypotheses but to illustrate the trend experienced by the Fascist organization.

7. There are two sources of data on membership: the Fascist secretariat, and the Italian Ministry of the Interior. De Felice uses that latter, not because it is necessarily more reliable, but because it is more inclusive (See 1966, p. 6, n. 1). The numbers presented here, and the calculations based on De Felice's data, are different than those he reports because there are some infelicities of calculation in his tables. Also, the numbers here are smaller because I exclude two provinces, Trento and Trieste, which were not included in the previous analysis for reasons of missing data (see chapter 4). For the sake of consistency, the analysis relates only to the 69 provinces discussed in earlier chapters.

8. Edward Tannenbaum (1972, p. 44) cites this figure, taken from Rocca (1952). I have no additional references to support it. However, other evidence about the internal struggles in the organization, especially regarding Marinetti's withdrawal, suggests that this figure is not implausible.

Afterword

"To define fascism," in the historian Angelo Tasca's words, is "to surprise it during [its] development in a given country, at a given time, and to seize upon its essential differences." In "surprising" Italian Fascism as it was being made, I have sought to uncover its concrete process of determination. For, as Tasca continues, "Fascism is not a subject with definite attributes, which need merely be selected, but the product of a situation apart from which it cannot be understood" ([1938] 1966, pp. 337-38).

Contrary to the prevailing sociological theories, I have tried to show that the Fascists' seizure of power was neither pregiven nor foretold by the organization's "historical origins," nor was it determined by its "social base." Rather, it was the outcome of concrete political struggles guided by specific strategies employed by political organizations. The Italian Fascists did not take political power in an electoral campaign that won "the hearts and minds" of a broad and free "mass base," but in a violent struggle in the streets, aided and abetted by the propertied class and state authorities. In a similar vein, Moore is correct in arguing that Italy's specific postwar circumstances supplied the raw materials used in the construction of the political strategies employed by the antagonists. But these materials, in and of themselves, determined neither the existence nor the course of the contest between the Fascists and the Socialists, let alone its results. The organization of the Fascist Squads, the incorporation of the veterans' cause into their program, the maximalist revolutionary position of the Socialists, the militancy of the landlords and the industrialists, and the collusion of state authorities with the Fascists' violence all had independent effects with respect to the specific paramilitary character of Fascism. Similarly, while the *agrari*'s militant tradition depended on their alliance with the state, as Moore argues and as we have seen, this in itself was not the crucial determinant in the actual rise of Fascism. The importance of the prewar landlord-state alliance lies in the degree to which it facilitated the formation of a more crucial alliance, that between the landlords and the Fascists. This chain of events was not immanent in the "origins" of Italian Fascism. Neither was the collusion of the state authorities with the Fascists an inherent characteristic of the "bourgeois state," as Poulantzas and others have argued. On the contrary, this collusion was, in itself, a response to the respective and conflicting political strategies of the Socialist Party and of the Fascist organization.

While further research is required to ascertain whether the question about the Socialist's strategy is a legitimate counterfactual question, it raises some difficult and weighty issues concerning its role in the Fascists' advance. Although I could not address these issues in this study, I believe that an attempt to explore them would enhance our understanding of the Fascists' triumph. The specific questions to be asked include, then, to what extent did the Socialists' political strategy itself determine the Fascists' seizure of power? This question pertains to two other, discreet questions about the political power potentially available to the Socialists. First, could a different Socialist strategy have prevented the landowners' alliance with the Fascists? My reading of the historical evidence pertaining to the landowners' prewar militancy suggests that the answer would be negative. From the landowners' point of view, there was no distinction between "reformists" and "maximalists." They were as outraged by "reformist" demands (e.g., collective labor contracts) as they were, if not more, by "maximalist" revolutionary rhetoric.

The second question relates to whether the Socialists could have undermined the political power held by the landowners and thus diminished the effectiveness of their alliance with the Fascists. In other words, what was the Socialists' potential for counteracting, or even subverting, the landlords' power over the Liberal state? Both postwar premiers, Nitti and Giolitti, had offered the Socialists a position in the government and had tried to address the demands of the workers and peasants. Had the reformist leaders retained the leadership of the PSI and continued its prewar collaboration with the Liberal government, we may venture that Socialist participation in government might have countered the influence of the propertied class on state officials and hardened the government's resolve to act against the Fascists. If that had been case, the Fascists' alliance with the landowners would not have provided them with any direct political advantage over the Socialists. Moreover, a moderate, "reformist" Socialist strategy might have affected the Fascists' strategy. For example, the ascendance of the Syndicalist faction in the Fascist organization was a real historical possibility, at least in the first year of the organization's existence. In what direction might this radical ex-Socialist revolutionary faction, which vehemently opposed the alliance with the landowners even if that alliance spelled a political triumph that was otherwise unattainable, have influenced Fascists' strategy?

Another point relates to the Liberal constituency. Although it seems clear that Liberal leaders were willing to share power with the Socialists, we cannot assume that this was necessarily true of their constituency or of other state institutions, such as the Army. To examine this issue would require the study of an aspect of post World War I Italy that has been neglected here: The emergence, as a result of the war, of a militant nationalism within the Liberal state. Giolitti himself had opposed Italy's intervention in the war, and lost; he was consequently forced to leave the government. *Diccianovismo*, or the "postwar mood," involved a resurgence of the chauvinism that had led to Italy's initial intervention in the war. We may conclude, therefore, that the appearance of the

Fascist organization was an integral reflection of and, later, additional source of this nationalist upsurge. The episodes of sedition in the Army and Gabriele D'Annunzio's occupation of Fiume suggest that the incorporation of the Socialists, who had opposed Italy's intervention in the war, into the Liberal state would have taken more than the good will of Liberal Party leaders. Hence, any response to the issue of the Socialists' potential to affect the Liberal state "from within" requires analysis of the extreme nationalists' capacity to oppose a Liberal-Socialist coalition. In such a study, the pivotal relationship would not be between the Socialists and the Fascists but between the moderate Liberals and the extreme nationalists.

An analysis of the making of Italian Fascism is first and foremost an analysis of the militarization of the political struggle. The Fascists' campaign was a methodical operation, embodying a strategy having coherent tactics and identifiable targets. Their tactic of violence was first and foremost an anti-Socialist reaction. Their alliance with the propertied class determined that the Fascists' attacks would be aimed almost exclusively against the Socialist provincial strongholds that constituted the greatest threats to propertied interests. The absence of such attacks in provinces under the political dominance of the ruling Liberal Party supports this observation. Apparently, the Fascists' main advantage over their Socialist opponents lay in their ability to alter the very conditions under which the political struggle took place. Hence, Italian Fascism can best be understood not as a "social movement" or in terms of its ideological appeals to a social base but as a political organization with distinct (but not fixed) structural contours, leadership, strategy, and program. It was the directed use that the Fascists made of the historical possibilities created by the war and the postwar crisis—especially their "offensive alliances" with the propertied class and the subsequent "defensive alliances" with a Liberal state dominated by the propertied class—that determined the specifics of their seizure of state power.

The Fascists' first and perhaps most decisive success was in transforming the terrain of political struggle into, literally, a battleground. Here, their "soldiers," the *squadristi*, backed by their propertied supporters, could determine not only the odds of political success but also its very definition. *Squadrismo* rendered obsolete the operative political strategy of all the main political forces, but mainly that of the Socialists. No longer the product of a popular vote or of a mass organization of workers, political power was now defined by and consisted in the ability to employ violence and to physically destroy opponents. It was this militarization of the political struggle that became the Fascists' distinguishing characteristic. The Fascists' paramilitary strategy, their actual modus operandi, shaped the character of the political struggles in which they engaged. In the course of these struggles, the Fascists also created their own identity and determined their own unique political significance. It is in this sense that the "making of Fascism" represents a specific analytical stance and methodology.

Glossary

Affituario: Peasant leaseholder.

Agrario: Landowner. Usually refers to landowners of large estates (over 200 hectares).

Arditi (the Brave): An organization of demobilized officers of the Italian Army's elite assault unit.

Arditi del Popolo: An anti-Fascist military group formed in 1921 against the Fascist Action Squads.

Avanti!: Socialist newspaper.

Biennio rosso ("Red Biennium"): The years 1919-1920, immediately following World War I, a period noted for labor upheaval and worker achievements.

Bloccho Nazionale: Electoral coalition formed by Giovanni Giolitti in 1921. It incorporated the Fascist Party for the first time.

Bonifica: State-sponsored land reclamation projects.

Braccianti ("hands"): Day laborers.

Carabinieri (Carabinieri Arma dei Carabinieri Reali): State police force, responsible directly to the Ministry of Interior.

CGII (*Confederazione Generale dell'Industria Italiana, Confindustria*): General Confederation of Italian Industry.

CGL (*Confederazione Generale di Lavoro*): General Confederation of Labor.

CIL (*Confederazione Italiana dei Lavoratori): * Catholic Confederation of Workers.

Classe dirigente: Ruling class.

Collocamento di classe: Centralized assignment of workers by unions, designed to guarantee an equal distribution of labor among the workers.

*Fascio (*plural*: fasci):* Local chapter of the Fascist organization.

Fattore: Estate manager.

Federterra (Federazione Nazionale di Lavoratori dell Terra): National Federation of Agricultural Laborers.

FIOM (*Federazione Italiana Operai Metallurgici*): Federation of Metallurgical Workers.

Gabolletos: Estate managers.

Imponibile della Mano d'Opera: Requirement, negotiated by collective labor contracts, that landowners employ a minimum number of laborers per hectare.

Latifundists: Large landowners in the South.

Mezzadria: Sharecropping system in which the tenant and landlord are supposedly equal partners in agricultural production.

MVSN (Milizia Voluntaria per la Sicurezza Nazionale): The Voluntary Militia for National Security.

PNF *(Partito Nazionale Fascista):* National Fascist Party.

PPI (*Partito Popolare Italiano):* Italian Popular Party, also known as *popolari.*

PSI (*Partito Socialista Italiano):* Italian Socialist Party.

Questore: Provincial chiefs of police.

Ras: Leaders of provincial *fascio*; the name adopted from title given to Ethiopian chiefs.

Salariati: Fixed-salary laborers employed on large farms in the northern regions.

Sansepolcristi: Fascists who attended the 1919 founding rally of the *Fasci di combattimento* at the Piazza San Sepolcro in Milan.

Squadristi: Members of the armed Fascist Action Squads

Syndicato autonomo: Fascist labor syndicates formed to replace the Socialist workers' organizations.

Bibliography

Abrate, Mario. 1966. *La lotta sindicale nella industrializazione in Italia 1906-1926*. Milano: F. Angeli.

Abse, Tobias. 1983. "Mussolini and his Historical Context" *Historical Journal* 1:237-254.

Abse, Tobias. 1984. "Recent Works on Nineteenth and Twentieth-Century Italian History." *Historical Journal* 27:1019-1036.

Adler, Franklin H. 1976. "Italian Industrialists and Radical Fascism." *Telos* 30: 193-201.

Annuario Statistico Italiano, Anni 1919-1921. 1925. Roma: Ministero dell'Economia Nazionale, Direzione Generalle della Statistica. Provveditorato Generale dello Stato.

Arendt, Hannah. 1979. *The Origins of Totalitarianism*. San Diego: Harcourt Brace Jovanovich.

Arlacchi, Pino. 1980. *Mafia, Peasants and Great Estates: Society in Traditional Calabria*. London: Cambridge University Press.

Aymard, Maurice. 1982. "From Feudalism to Capitalism in Italy: The Case That Doesn't Fit." *Review* 6: 131-208.

Banti, Alberto Mario. 1988. "Elites Agrarie e Organizzazione degli Interessi in Prussia e in Val Padana, 1880-1914." *Annali dell'Istituto Storico Italo-Germanico in Trento* 14: 413-460.

Baran, Paul A. 1957. *The Political Economy of Growth*. New York: Monthly Review Press.

Beetham, David. 1983. "Introduction." Pp. 1-62 in *Marxists in Face of Fascism*, edited and translated by David Beetham. Manchester: Manchester University Press.

Bell, Donald Howard. 1984. "Working Class Culture and Fascism in an Italian Industrial Town 1918-22." *Social History* 9: 1-24.

Berger, Peter. 1963. *Invitation to Sociology: A Humanist Perspective*. Garden City: Doubleday.

Bertrand, C. L. 1970. *Revolutionary Syndicalism in Italy, 1912-1922*. Ph.D dissertation. University of Wisconsin.

Brustein, William. 1991. "The 'Red Menace' and the Rise of Italian Fascism." *American Sociological Review* 56:652-664.

Brustein, William and Barry Markovsky 1989. "The Rational Fascist: Interwar Fascist Party Membership in Italy and Germany." *Journal of Political and Military Sociology* 17:177-202.

Buci-Glucksmann, Christine. 1980. *Gramsci and the State.* London: Lawrence and Wishart.

Burris, Val. 1986. "The Discovery of the New Middle Class." *Theory and Society* 15: 317-349.

Cafagna, Luciano. 1976. "The Industrial Revolution in Italy: 1830-1914." Pp. 279-309 in *The Fontana Economic History of Europe: The Emergence of Industrial Societies.* England: Harvester Press.

Cafagna, Luciano. 1973. "Italy 1830-1914." *The Fontana Economic History of Europe IV:* 279-328.

Cammett, John. 1967. "Communist Theories of Fascism, 1920-1935." *Science and Society* 31:149-163.

Cannistraro, Philip V. 1982. "Dissidentism." Pp. 172-3 in *Historical Dictionary of Fascist Italy,* edited by Philip V. Cannistraro. Westport: Greenwood Press.

Cardoza, Antony. 1979. "Agrarian and Industrialists: the Evolution of an Alliance in the Po Delta, 1896-1914." Pp. 172-212 in *Gramsci and Italy's Passive Revolution,* edited by John A. Davis. New York: Barnes and Noble.

Cardoza Antony. 1982. *Agrarian Elites and Italian Fascism: The Province of Bologna, 1901-1926.* Princeton: Princeton University Press.

Cardoza, Antony. 1991. "Commercial Agriculture and the Crisis of Landed Power: Bologna 1880-1930." Pp. 181-198 in *Landownership and Power in Modern Europe* edited by Ralph Gibson and Martin Blinkhorn. London: HarperCollins Academic.

Cavandoli, Rolando. 1972. *Le origini del Fascismo e Reggio Emilia 1919-1923.* Rome: Editori Riuniti.

Censimento della Popolazione del Regno d'Italia al 1 Diciembre 1921. 1927. Vols. 1-18. Rome: Stabilimento Poligrafico.

Ciocca, Pierluigi and Gianni Toniolo. 1984. "Industry and Finance in Italy, 1918-1940." *Journal of European Economic History* 39:113-136.

Clausewitz, Carl Von. [1832] 1968. *On War.* London: Penguin Books.

Clough, Shepard B. 1964. *The Economic History of Modern Italy.* New York: Columbia University Press.

Clough, Shepard B., and Salvatore Saladino. 1968. *A History of Modern Italy: Documents, Readings, and Commentary.* New York: Columbia University Press.

Cordova, Ferdinando. 1970. "Le origini dei sindicati fascisti" in *Storia Contemporanea* I: 925-1009.

Corner, Paul. 1974. "La basse di massa del fascismo: il caso di Ferrara." *Italia Contemporanea* 26:5-31.

Corner, Paul. 1975. *Fascism in Ferrara, 1915-1925.* London: Oxford University Press.

Costanzo, Giulio. 1923. "The Principal Types of Agricultural Co-Operative Society in Italy." *International Review of Agricultural Economics* V:50-80.

Cunsolo, Ronald S. 1991. "The Great Debate on Prime Minister Giovanni Giolitti and Giolittian Italy." *Canadian Review of Studies in Nationalism* 18: 95-115.

D'Agostino, Guido. 1990. "A proposito di un 'Atlante' elettorale." *Italia Contemporanea* 180: 535-545.

Davis, John A. (ed.). 1979. *Gramsci and Italy's Passive Revolution.* New York: Barnes and Noble.

Davis, John A. 1987. "Rural Roots of Fascism in Southern Italy." *European History Quarterly* 17: 229-234.

Davis, John A. 1988. *Conflict and Control: Law and Order in Nineteenth-Century Italy.* London: Macmillan Education.

De Felice, Renzo. 1964. "Primi elementi sul finanziamento del fascismo dalle origini al 1924." *Rivista Storica del Socialismo* 22: 223-251.

De Felice, Renzo. 1965. *Mussolini il rivoluzionario, 1883-1920.* Turin: Einaudi.

De Felice, Renzo. 1966. *Mussolini il fascist.* Turin: Einaudi.

De Felice, Renzo. 1968. *Mussolini il fascista: l'organizzazione dello stato fascista,* Vol. II. Turin: Einaudi.

De Felice, Renzo. 1974. *Mussolini il duce: gli anni del consenso,* Vol. IV. Turin: Einaudi

De Felice, Renzo. 1977. *Interpretations of Fascism.* Cambridge: Harvard University Press.

DeIanni, Nicola. 1984. "Operai e Industriali a Napoli tra Grande Guerra e Crisi Mondiale: 1915-1929." *Cahiers Internationaux d'Histoire Economique et Sociale* 16:1-452; 17:1-123.

Dunnage, Jonathan. 1989. "Istituzioni e ordine pubblico nell'italia Giolittiana: le forze di polizia in provincia di bologna." *Italia Contemporanea* 177: 5-26.

Dutt, R. Palme. [1934] 1974. *Fascism and Social Revolution: A Study of the Economics and Politics of the Extreme Stages of Capitalism in Decay.* New York: International Publishers.

Duverger, M. 1954. *Political Parties.* London: Methuen.

Elazar, Dahlia Sabina. 1993. "The Making of Italian Fascism: The Seizure of Power, 1919-1922." *Political Power and Social Theory* 8:173-217.

Elazar, Dahlia Sabina. 1996. "Agrarian Relations and Class Hegemony: A Comparative Analysis of Landlord Social and Political Power, Italy 1861-1920." *British Journal of Sociology* 47: 232-254

Elster, Jon. 1978. *Logic and Society: Contradictions and Possible Worlds.* New York: Wiley.

Engels, Frederick. [1894] 1967. "Preface to Volume 3 of Capital." Pp. 1-21 in *Capital.* Vol. 3. New York: International Publishers.

Farneti, Paolo. 1978. "Social Conflict, Parliamentary Fragmentation, Institutions Shift, and the Rise of Fascism: Italy." Pp. 3-33 in *The Breakdown of Democratic Regimes,* edited by Juan J. Linz and Alfred Stepan. Baltimore: The Johns Hopkins University Press.

Faustini, Gianni. 1992. "Giornali e Movimenti Politici nel Trentino dal 1918 al 1926." *Studi Trentini di Scienze Storiche* 71:67-124.

Finley, M. I., Denis Mack Smith, and Christopher Duggan. 1986. *A History of Sicily*. London: Chatto and Windus.

Forgacs, David (ed.). 1986. *Rethinking Italian Fascism: Capitalism, Populism, and Culture*. London: Lawrence and Wishart

Fried, Robert. 1963. *The Italian Prefects: A Study in Administrative Politics*. New Haven: Yale University Press.

Gentile, Emilio. 1984. "Il Problema del Partito nel Fascismo Italiano." *Storia Contemporanea* 15:347-370.

Gentile, Emilio. 1985. "La Natura e la Storia del Partito Nazionale Fascista nelle Interpretazioni dei Contemporanei e degli Storici." *Storia Contemporanea* 16: 521-607.

Germani, Gino. "Fascism and Class." Pp. 65-96 in *The Nature of Fascism*, edited by S. J. Woolf. London: Weidenfeld and Nicolson.

Gerschenkron, Alexander. 1962. "Notes on the Rate of Industrial Growth in Italy, 1881-1913." Pp. 27-89 in Alexander Gerschenkron, *Economic Backwardness in Historical Perspective: A Book of Essays*. Cambridge: The Belknap Press.

Gill, D. 1983. "Tuscan Sharecropping in United Italy: The Myth of Class Collaboration Destroyed." *Journal of Peasant Studies*: 10:146-169.

Giolitti, Giovanni. 1923. *Memoirs of My Life*. London: Chapman and Dodd.

Giusti, U. 1922. *Le correnti politiche Italiane attraverso due riforme elettorali dal 1909 al 1921*. Florence.

Gramsci, Antonio. 1926. "Lyons Theses." Pp. 341-379 in *Selections from Political Writings*, edited and translated by Quintin Hoare. Minneapolis: University of Minnesota Press.

Gramsci, Antonio. 1971. "Notes on Italian History." Pp. 52-120 in *Selections from the Prison Notebooks of Antonio Gramsci*, edited and translated by Quintin Hoare and Geoffrey Nowell Smith. New York: International Publishers.

Gualtieri, Humbert. 1946. *The Labor Movement in Italy*. New York: S. F. Vanni.

Guerin, Daniel. 1973. *Fascism and Big Business*. New York: Monad Press.

Hamilton, Richard. 1982. *Who Voted for Hitler?* Princeton: Princeton University Press.

Hembree, Michael. 1982. "Constantino Lazzari." Pp. 300-1 in *Historical Dictionary of Fascist Italy*, edited by Philip Cannistraro. Westport: Greenwood Press.

Horowitz, Daniel. 1963. *The Italian Labor Movement*. Cambridge: Harvard University Press.

Hughes, Serge. 1967. *The Fall and Rise of Modern Italy*. New York: Minerva Press.

Hughes, Steven C. 1985. The Theory and Practice of Ozio in Italian Policing: Bologna and Beyond." *Criminal Justice History* 6: 89-103.

Jonsson, Ulf. 1992. "The Paradox of Share Tenancy Under Capitalism: A Comparative Perspective on Late Nineteenth and Twentieth-Century French and Italian Sharecropping." *Rural History* 3: 191-217.

Kelikian, Alice A. 1986. *Town and Country Under Fascism: The Transformation of Brescia, 1915-1926.* Oxford: Clarendon Press

King, Bolton and Thomas Okey. 1909. *Italy To-Day.* London: James Nisbet.

King, Gary. 1997. *A Solution to the Ecological Inference Problem: Reconstructing Individual Behavior from Aggregate Data.* Princeton: Princeton University Press.

Lanzillo, Agostino. 1922. *Le rivoluzioni del dopoguerra: critica diagnosi.* Citta di Castello.

Ledeen, Michael A. 1971. *The First Duce: D'Annunzio at Fiume.* Baltimore: Johns Hopkins University Press.

Lederer, Emil. 1940. *State of the Masses: The Threat of Classless Society.* New York: W. W. Norton.

Lenin, V. I. [1916] 1917. "The Military Programme of the Proletarian Revolution." *Jugend-Internationale* Nos. 9 and 10, September and October 1917.

Leonarduzzi, Andrea. 1989. "Storiografia e Fascismo in Friuli: Partito, Gruppi Dirigenti, Societa." *Italia Contemporanea* 177: 27-47.

Linz, Juan. 1976. "Some Notes Toward a Comparative Study of Fascism in Sociological Historical Perspective." Pp. 3-121 in *Fascism: A Reader's Guide,* edited by Walter Lacqueur. Berkeley: University of California Press.

Lipset, S. Martin. 1963. "'Fascism'—Left, Right and Center." Pp. 127-179 in *Political Man: The Social Bases of Politics.* New York: Doubleday & Company.

Lyttelton, Adrian. 1973. *Italian Fascism: From Pareto to Gentile.* New York: Harper Torchbooks.

Lyttelton, Adrian. 1976. "Italian Fascism." Pp. 125-150 in *Fascism: A Readers' Guide,* edited by Walter Lacqueur. Berkeley: University of California Press.

Lyttelton, Adrian. 1977. "Revolution and Counter-Revolution in Italy, 198-1922." Pp. 63-81 in *Revolutionary Situations in Europe 1917-1922, Germany Italy, Austria-Hungary,* edited by Charles Bertrand. Canada: Interuniversity Center for European Studies.

Lyttelton, Adrian. 1987. *The Seizure of Power: Fascism in Italy, 1919-1929.* London: Weidenfeld & Nicolson.

Mack Smith, Denis. 1959. *Italy: A Modern History.* Ann Arbor: University of Michigan Press.

Mack Smith, Denis. 1981. *Mussolini.* London: Weidenfeld and Nicolson.

Mack Smith, Denis. 1989. *Italy and its Monarchy.* New Haven: Yale University Press.

Maier, Charles. 1975. *Recasting Bourgeois Europe.* Princeton: Princeton University Press.

Maier, Charles. 1976. "Political Crisis and Partial Modernization: The Outcomes in Germany, Austria, Hungary, and Italy after World War I." Pp. 119-130 in *Revolutionary Situations in Europe 1917-1922, Germany Italy, Austria-Hungary,* edited by Charles Bertrand. Canada: Interuniversity Center for European Studies.

Marx, Karl. 1967 [1894]. *Capital: The Process of Capitalist Production as a Whole.* Vol. 3. New York: International Publishers.

Mason, Tim. 1991. "Whatever Happened to Fascism?" *Radical History Review* 49: 89-98.

Mason, Tim W. 1968. "The Primacy of Politics: Politics and Economics in National Socialist Germany." Pp. 165-195 in *The Nature of Fascism,* edited by S. J. Woolf. London: Weidenfeld and Nicolson.

Melograni, Piero. 1972. *Gli industriali e Mussolini. Rapporti tra confidustria e fascismo dal 1919 al 1929.* Milan: Longanesi.

Merton, Robert K. 1987. "Three Fragments from a Sociologist's Notebooks." *Annual Review of Sociology* 13: 1-28.

Moore, Barrington Jr. 1958. *Political Power and Social Theory.* Cambridge: Harvard University Press

Moore, Barrington Jr. 1966. *The Social Origins of Dictatorship and Democracy: Lord and Peasant in the Making of the Modern World.* Boston: Beacon Press.

Moore, Barrington Jr. 1978. *Injustice: The Social Bases of Obedience and Revolt.* New York: M. E. Sharpe.

Mussolini, Benito. 1928. *My Autobiography.* London: Hutchinson.

Natoli, Claudio. 1992. "Continuita e Fratture Nella Storia dei Comunisti Italiani Tra Le Due Guerre." *Studi Storici* 33: 393-433.

Nazzaro, Pellegrino. 1970. "Southern Italy in the Political and Programmatic Vision of Luigi Sturzo's Popular Party." *International Review of History and Political Science* 7:77-90.

Neufeld, Maurice E. 1961. *Italy: School for Awakening Countries.* New York: Cayuga Press.

Neumann, Franz. 1944. *Behemoth: The Structure and Practice of National Socialism, 1933-1944.* New York: Oxford University Press.

New Columbia Encyclopedia. 1975. "Strategy and Tactics." Pp. 2632-2633. New York and London: Columbia University Press.

Nitti, Francesco. 1927. *Bolshevism, Fascism and Democracy.* New York: MacMillan.

Nolte, Ernst. 1966. *Three Faces of Fascism: Action Francaise, Italian Fascism, National Socialism.* New York: Holt, Rinehart and Winston.

Olivetti, Gino. 1922. "Collective Agreements in Italy." *International Labor Review* 5:209-228.

Organsky, A. F. K. 1968. "Fascism and Modernization." Pp. 19-41 in *The Nature of Fascism,* edited by S. J. Woolf. London: Weidenfeld and Nicolson.

Paige, Jeffrey. 1975. *Agrarian Revolution.* New York: Free Press.

Parsons, Talcott. 1954. "Some Sociological Aspects of the Fascist Movement." Pp. 124-141 in *Essays in Sociological Theory.* Illinois: The Free Press.

Pepe, Adolfo. 1992. "Il socialismo Italiano e il Rinnovamento del Capitalismo (1900-1922)." *Studi Storici* 33: 353-365.

Petersen, Jens. 1975. "Elettorato e base sociale del fascismo negli anni venti." *Studi Stroici* 16:627-669.

Petracchi, Giorgio. 1993. "22 Ottobre 1922 e Dintorni: La Genesi des Fascismo a Pistoia (1919-1925)." *Storia Contemporanea* 24:663-685.

Piccioli, Lorenzo. 1985. "Il Ceto Politico Amministrativo Fiorentino dal 1910 al 1926." *Rassegna Storica Toscana* 31:87-119.

Ponziani, Luigi. 1986. "Dopoguerra e Fascismo in Abruzzo: Orientamenti Storiografici." *Italia Contemporanea* 164: 93-103.

Poulantzas, Nicos. 1974. *Fascism and Dictatorship: The Third International and the Problem of Fascism.* London: NLB.

Preti, Luigi. 1955. *Le lotte agrarie nella valle padana.* Turin: Einaudi.

Przeworski, Adam. 1985. *Capitalism and Social Democracy.* Cambridge: Cambridge University Press.

Pugliese, Emanuele (ed.). 1984. "L'esercito Nei Giorni della "Marcia su Roma": dalle "Memorie Storiche" della 16a Divisione di Fanteria di Stanza a Roma nel 1922." *Storia Contemporanea* 15: 1207-1210.

Revelli, Marco. 1987. "Italy." Pp. 1-39 in *The Social Basis of European Fascist Movements*, edited by Detlef Muhlberger. London: Croom Helm.

Roberts, David D. 1979. *The Syndicalist Tradition and Italian Fascism.* Chapel Hill: University of North Carolina Press.

Rochat, Giorgio. [1967] 1974. "L'esercito italiano da Vittorio Veneto a Mussolini (1919-1925)." Pp. 43-58 in *The Ax Within: Italian Fascism in Action*, edited and introduced by Roland Sarti. New York: New Viewpoints.

Rueschemeyer, Diertrich, Evelyne Huber Stephens, and John D. Stephens. 1992. *Capitalist Development and Democracy.* Cambridge: Polity Press.

Ruini, Meuccio. 1922. "The Italian Co-operative Movement." *International Labor Review* V:13-33

Saija, Marcello. 1985. "Un Prefetto Nittiano di Fronte al Fascismo: Achille de Martino a Brescia nel 1922." *Italia Contemporanea* 159: 5-43.

Salomone, William A. 1945. *Italian Democracy in the Making: The Political Scene in the Giolittian Era, 1900-1914.* Philadelphia: University of Pennsylvania Press.

Salvatorelli, L. & G. Mira. 1964. *Storia d'Italia nel periodo fascista.* Turin: Einaudi.

Salvemini, Gaetano. 1927. *The Fascist Dictatorship in Italy.* New York: Henry Holt and Company.

Salvemini, Gaetano. 1936. *Under the Ax of Fascism.* New York: Viking Press.

Salvemini, Gaetano. 1945. "Introductory Essay." Pp. vii-xviii in William A. Salomone, *Italian Democracy in the Making: The Political Scene in the Giolittian Era, 1900-1914.* Philadelphia: University of Pennsylvania Press.

Salvemini, Gaetano. 1973. *The Origins of Fascism in Italy.* New York: Harper Torchbooks.

Sarfatti, M. 1925. *The Life of Benito Mussolini.* London.

Sarti, Roland. 1970. "Fascist Modernization in Italy: Traditional or Revolutionary?" *The American Historical Review* LXXV: 1029-45.

Sarti, Roland. 1971. *Fascism and the Industrial Leadership in Italy, 1919-1940: A Study in the Expansion of Private Power under Fascism.* Berkeley: University of California Press.

Sarti, Roland. 1974. *The Ax Within: Italian Fascism in Action.* New York: New

Viewpoints.

Schmidt, Carl T. 1937. "Agricultural Property and Enterprise under Italian Fascism." *Science and Society* 3: 326-349.

Schmidt, Carl T. 1938. *The Plough and the Sword: Labor Land and Property in Fascist Italy*. New York: Columbia University Press.

Schmidt Carl T. 1939. *The Corporate State in Action: Italy Under Fascism*. New York: Oxford University Press.

Segre, Claudio. 1987. *Italo Balbo: A Fascist Life*. Berkeley: University of California Press.

Sereni Emilio. [1946] 1975. *La Questione Agraria nella Rinascita Nationale Italiana.* Turin: Piccola Biblioteca Einaudi.

Sereni, Emilio. 1968. *Il Capitalismo nelle Campagna, 1860-1900*. Turin: Piccola Biblioteca Einaudi.

Serpieri, Arrigo. 1930. *La guerra e classi rurali italiane.* Bari: Laterza & Figli.

Seton Watson, Christopher I. 1967. *Italy From Liberalism to Fascism*. London: Methuen.

Sirianni, Carmen. 1980. "Workers' Control in the Era Of World War I." *Theory and Society* 9:29-88.

Snowden, Frank M. 1972. "On the Social Origins of Agrarian Fascism in Italy." *European Journal of Sociology* 13: 268-95.

Snowden, Frank M. 1986. *Violence and the Great Estates in the South of Italy: Apulia, 1900-1922*. Cambridge: Cambridge University Press.

Snowden, Frank. 1989. *The Fascist Revolution in Tuscany, 1919-1922*. New York: Cambridge University Press.

Spencer, Henry Russell. 1932. *Government and Politics in Italy.* New York: World Book Company.

Spriano, Paolo. 1964. *The Occupation of the Factories, Italy 1920*. London: Pluto Press.

Squeri, Lawrence. 1983. "The Italian Local Elections of 1920 and the Outbreak of Fascism." *The Historian* XLV: 324-336.

Squeri, Lawrence. 1990. "Who Benefited from Italian Fascism: a Look at Parma's Landowners." *Agricultural History* 64: 18-38.

Stepan-Norris, Judith and Maurice Zeitlin. 1989. "'Who Gets the Bird?' or, How the Communists Won Power and Trust in America's Unions: The Relative Autonomy of Intraclass Political Struggles." *American Sociological Review* 54: 503-523.

Stephens, John D. 1989. "Democratic Transition and Breakdown in Western Europe, 1870-1939: A Test of the Moore Thesis." *American Journal of Sociology* 94:1019-1077.

Sternhell, Zeev. 1976. "Fascist Ideology." Pp. 315-376 in *Fascism: A Reader's Guide*, edited by Walter Lacqueur. Berkeley: University of California Press.

Sternhell, Zeev. 1995. *Neither Right Nor Left: Fascist Ideology in France*. Princeton: Princeton University Press.

Sullivan, Brian R. 1981. "*Arditi*." Pp. 34-5 in *Historical Dictionary of Fascist Italy*, edited by Philip Cannistraro. Westport: Greenwood Press.

Szymanski, Albert. 1973. "Fascism, Industrialism and Socialism: The Case of

Italy." *Comparative Studies in Society and History* 15: 395-404.

Tannenbaum, Edward R. 1972. *The Fascist Experience: Italian Society and Culture. 1922-1945.* New York: Basic Books.

Tasca, Angelo. [1938] 1966. *The Rise of Italian Fascism, 1919-1922.* New York: Howard Fertig.

Thalheimer, August. 1928. "On Fascism." Pp. 187-194 in *Marxists in Face of Fascism,* edited and translated by David Beetham. Manchester: Manchester University Press.

Tilly, Charles, Louise Tilly, and Richard Tilly. 1975. *The Rebellious Century, 1830-1930.* Cambridge: Harvard University Press.

Togliatti, Palmiro. 1928. "On the Question of Fascism." Pp. 136-148 in *Marxists in Face of Fascism,* edited and translated by David Beetham. Manchester: Manchester University Press.

Togliatti, Palmiro. [1935] 1976. *Lectures on Fascism.* New York: International Publishers

Tranfaglia, Nicola. 1989. *Labirinto Italiano: Il Fascismo, l'Antifascismo, gli Storici.* Perugia, Italy: Nuova Italia.

Valiani, Leo. 1985. "Il Fascismo: Controrivoluzione e Rivoluzione." *Rivista Storica Italiana* 97:86-101.

Vivarelli, Roberto. 1968. "Italy 1919-1921: The Current State of Research." *Journal of Contemporary History* 1:103-112.

Vivarelli, Roberto. 1991a. "Interpretations of the Origins of Fascism." *Journal of Modern History* 63:29-43

Vivarelli, Roberto. 1991b. *Storia delle Origini del Fascismo: l'Italia dalla Grande Guerra alla Marcia su Roma.* Bologna: Mulino.

Volpe, Gioacchino. n.d. *History of the Fascist Movement.* Roma: Soc. An. Poligrafica Italiana

Weber, Eugen. 1966. "The Men of the Archangel." *Journal of Contemporary History* 1: 101-126.

Webster, R.A. 1961. *Christian Democracy in Italy, 1860-1960.* London.

Young, Wayland Hilton. 1949. *The Italian Left: A Short History of Political Socialism in Italy.* London: Longmans, Green.

Zangarini, M. 1978. "La composizione sociale della classe dirigente nel regime fascista: il caso di Verona." *Italia Contemporanea* 30:27-47.

Zeitlin, Maurice. 1984. *The Civil Wars in Chile (or the Bourgeois Revolutions that Never Were).* Princeton: Princeton University Press.

Zeitlin, Maurice and Richard Earl Ratcliff. 1988. *Landlords and Capitalists: The Dominant Class of Chile.* Princeton: Princeton University Press.

Zetkin, Klara. 1923. "The Struggle against Fascism." Pp. 102-13 in *Marxists in Face of Fascism,* edited and translated by David Beetham. Manchester: Manchester University Press.

Zetterberg, Hans L. 1965. *On Theory and Verification in Sociology.* Bedminster: Bedminster Press.

Zibordi, Giovanni. 1922. "Towards a Definition of Fascism." Pp. 88-96 in *Marxists in Face of Fascism,* edited and translated by David Beetham. Manchester: Manchester University Press.

Index

About the Author

DAHLIA S. ELAZAR is Assistant Professor in the Department of Sociology and Anthropology at Tel Aviv University in Israel.